PRAISE FOR *STICK TO MY ROOTS*

'Tippa Irie is one of the greats; a legend, a teacher and a pioneer of reggae dancehall music in the the UK and worldwide.'

—Julian Marley

'A powerhouse, an icon. The OG—original groundbreaker—is instrumental in carving a foundation for young Black British youths of my generation. This heartfelt and honest window into Tippa Irie's historic rise to fame is the blueprint of a pioneer's life. Stick to my Roots shows how hardship, sheer talent and community link the founding generations of Black British culture to the vibrant, world changing artists who produce work today.'

—Courttia Newland, author of *A River Called Time*

'I remember the very first time I heard Tippa Irie's music, it was from my brother in law Handel McNeish, Tippa's cousin. I know that Tippa is a conscious artist doing the work of the most high. His lyrical content and written testimony verifies this and gives hope.

I embrace and support his work of consciousness for positive change through music. We need more artists like Tippa to write, sing, and perform. His words and work may encourage those that are going through darkness.

Tippa's written story will let them see him as the example, that if they continue with determination they too can persevere through all obstacles to obtain their goals. His written words will lend an ear to those who may be feeling despair and lost. I endorse and encourage readers to imagine.'

—Sandra Izsadore, Artist, Activist and author of *FELA and ME*

'A powerful book from one of Britain's top MCs who has blended the music genre of Jamaican roots and British identity as a fusion of the

Black lived experience covering joy, pain, resilience and identity. This book is a powerful story of sufferation and resilience as a child of the Windrush Generation.'

—Patrick Vernon

'This is a great read for our generation as it embodies, what life was like for black kids up and down the country during the 70s. I always remember, seeing him, driving through Birmingham in his VW Cabriolet convertible.

He has taken his toasting talents around the world representing his upbringing and culture, truly a pioneer for toasting about 'Roots and Culture' but from a British-Jamaican aspect rather than the other way round.

This book, is a must-read for anyone growing up in Britain in the inner cities of all cultures.'

—Dennis Seaton, Record Producer, Musical Youth

Stick to My Roots

The Life and Times of Tippa Irie

An autobiography

Tippa Irie

JACARANDA

This edition first published in Great Britain 2023
Jacaranda Books Art Music Ltd
27 Old Gloucester Street,
London WC1N 3AX
www.jacarandabooks.co.uk

Copyright © Tippa Irie 2023

A CIP catalogue record for this book is available from the British Library

ISBN: 9781913090845
eISBN: 9781913090852

Cover Illustration: Chali 2na
Cover Design: Rodney Dive
Typeset by: Kamillah Brandes

Photos courtesy of
Simon Buckland
Greensleeves Records
Maverick
Sir Lloyd
Bob Burger
Lynn Rossetto

This autobiography is dedicated to my late parents Celeste Henry, Steven Alexander Henry, Avril Elaine Henry, (AKA Miss Irie), my sister Jacqueline Henry, Uncle Hubert McNish, Uncle Clifton, Uncle Mackie, Aunty Merkel and Aunty Lou.

I would also like to dedicate this book to my children whom I am very proud of, Micah Newell, Raphael Kash Powell, Rochelle Henry Redway, and my beautiful granddaughter Jada Henry.

Foreword
by Mark Wallis

WELCOME TO THE LIFE STORY OF GRAMMY-NOMINATED
Tippa Irie, one of the founding fathers of UK dancehall music. Over
a successful career spanning 40 years, from his beginnings chatting on
King Tubby's Sound System and later in the eighties when he joined
forces with the mighty Saxon Studio International, Tippa is instrumental in embedding reggae culture across the globe. Tippa pioneered
a unique blend of south London chat fused with reggae, always cham-
pioning its proud Jamaican origins. In performance Tippa is like a
hungry, conquering lion, taking up any sound challenge put his way,
never shying away from competition. A sound clash competition, for
the uninitiated, takes place when two opposing sound systems perform
in a musical challenge against each other, resulting in a 'clash' of music
and words.

Already achieving fame as an MC in his up-and-coming teenage
years, Tippa steps on the mic as bold as brass, expressing with speed,
powerful lyrics combined with bouncing melodies, and perfect
rhythming. As British reggae ambassador carrying dancehall music to
the four corners of the Earth, Tippa has performed live worldwide
and possesses a formidable back catalogue of 50 singles and over 20
LPs. Producing innumerable tracks for various compilations, he has
worked in partnership with newcomers as well as the most established
artists in a countless flow of dubplates. Tippa is also a gifted songwriter
and producer in his own right.

Tippa has captivated smiling crowds in thousands of concerts, headlining along with his backing band at Reggae Sunsplash, Sting, Summer Jam, Reggae on the River, Boomtown, and Glastonbury, to name a few. He is motivated by bringing joy and keeping the faith with international reggae, from Jamaica to the UK, and extensively to Asia, the USA, and Africa.

The kind of fame, glitz, and glamour Tippa has enjoyed poses multiple temptations for any performer. Against the odds, he has stayed true to himself, remaining connected and sticking to his humble, working-class Brixton roots. Tippa's unique style is based on maintaining a positive mentality, promoting progression 24/7. He established himself in the eighties by putting on his own musical shoes, tying up his laces, raising his game, and reaching the national charts with the release in 1986 of his breakout hit single 'Hello Darling', catapulting his MC patterns from the streets of Brixton to live appearances on *Top of the Pops*. Tippa would go on to achieve three consecutive Number 1 hits on the UK reggae charts. It needs little explanation then that the title of this book embodies Tippa's guiding principal: that by putting in the work and keeping a positive focus and most importantly, staying true to where you come from wherever you may go, you can reap the rewards of a successful life and career.

Tippa Irie is 'Mr Versatile', and his ability and talent to excite both young and old alike has led him to have voiced a range of reggae musical styles including ska, roots reggae, dancehall, dub, lovers' rock, jungle, and drum and bass. In 1993 he featured on and co-produced 'Shouting for the Gunners'—Arsenal FC's anthem—and in 2004 he featured on 'Hey Mama' alongside The Black Eyed Peas, which reached Number 10 on the UK national pop chart; it was also nominated for a Grammy award.

Each chapter of this book contains testimonies from prominent people within the music industry and from the world of reggae in particular. UB40's Ali Campbell, Maxi Priest, and UK lovers' rock sensation Janet Kay are among the many notables. If you're a reggae or dancehall fan, or a sound system enthusiast, this book is for you. If you enjoy true-life stories or discovering more about British and Jamaican cultural history… read on. And if you're a musician, an artist, or a performer, these pages will *empower* you. Get ready to see the bigger picture as Tippa describes the ups and downs he experienced throughout his years in the music industry.

Stick To My Roots tells the story of a man who has experienced immense sufferation, but who has risen up against all adversaries and overcome personal trauma. Daddy Tippa has walked through the fire without getting burnt.

Enjoy this journey of a life.

Mark Wallis,

Author, writer. Music producer, manager, long-time fan, and family friend

Mi, na water down and mi, na dilute
Done, tell you say. Tippa, speak up the truth
Mr Irie, mi don radical, from me a youth
and that's why the DJ have fi stick to my roots
'Cause sometimes it's better to stick to what
you know
You build a foundation and make it grow
Remember say you reap, well what you sow
and that's why mi Roots, Tippa not let it go.

Tippa Irie and the Far East Band,
'Stick to My Roots'
from the LP *Stick to My Roots*
(Lockdown Productions, 2010)

Chapter One
Mi Roots and Culture

I AM TIPPA IRIE, AND I WOULD LIKE TO INVITE YOU ON my journey. I truly hope you enjoy the ride.

Let us start from the beginning. To know me is to know my culture, and where my roots originate. I was born Anthony Henry on June 7, 1965. My parents are of Jamaican heritage, both Mum and Dad hailing from the rural parish of Trelawny in the county of Cornwall, situated in the northwest of the island, a region known for its sugar mills and plantations. Falmouth, the capital of Trelawny, is surrounded by beautiful beaches and littered with deep caves. It is famous for its rich limestone, phosphate, and other natural resources.

Most of Jamaica was named by colonial British authorities. These white settlers named the places after their hometowns. 'Trelawny', for instance, is a Cornish name from the parish of Pelynt meaning 'open/clear town'/'Trelawne, a tree homestead'. My parents' birthplace was named in 1770 after Sir William Trelawny, the governor of the island at that time, whose family came from the manor of Trelawny in Cornwall, England. Trelawny, Jamaica, is a deep green area, home to some of the island's most famous yam produce. Parts of Trelawny are so dense, in fact, that they are uninhabitable, but they are full and deep, covered with beautiful vegetation.

Allow me to describe my Jamaican heritage, the culture and roots of my parents' birthplace on this small Caribbean island that lights the musical fire in me and continues to warm my heart to this very day. It's the birthplace of reggae music, the power of which has reached people's hearts, homes, and dance floors across the globe. To truly understand reggae and its lyrical content, its origins and its movements, from Toots and the Maytals to the anthems of Dennis Brown, Daddy U-Roy, Bob Marley and the Wailers, to know *true roots* music, you must first understand the journey of the Jamaican people. The elders taught us that in order to know where you are going, you must first know where you're coming from.

Jamaica is the third-largest country in the Caribbean. Its original inhabitants were the native Arawaks, whose cultural roots on the island span back to 600 BC. The Arawak people were savagely eradicated at the hands of the Spanish after Spain's colonial invasion in 1509 (Columbus had first landed there in 1494). England overthrew Spain on the island in 1655, claiming another brutal hold on it. This second wave of foreign invaders was aggressive; fleets of English trading ships carried cargoes of rum and refined sugar molasses from Jamaica to sell in Europe.

In 1662, the Euro-American slave trade became the new currency of the day. Captured, sold, snatched from their families and tortured, African men, women, and children were shipped to Jamaica and across the Americas. The majority of the enslaved people came from Ghana's Gold Coast and elsewhere in West Africa.

Across the length and breadth of the island, English-owned (and, from 1707, British-owned) plantations became the sites of enforced labour as the arrival of enslaved Africans increased. True to Jamaicans' defiant nature, a number of rebellions and uprisings—led by the likes of Queen Nanny and Cudjoe of the Maroons to Tacky, Paul Bogle, and Sam Sharpe—loosened British rule. The colonial invaders could no longer flourish on the island in safety, oppressing its inhabitants with brutality. Jamaican rebels prevented the smooth operation of

Well to-deh down a yard it's a lesson, even though this place yah a blessing
Got to be streetwise, got to realize, how hard it is to survive
'Cause mi say people under pressure find it hard to do better
Well, we must stick together like sister and brother and love one another
in a sweet, sweet Jamaica, cause it bound fi mek we stronger.

Tippa Irie, 'Jamaica Way'
from the LP *Living the Dream*
(Lockdown Productions, 2016)

colonial business, putting a spanner in Britain's profitable works and making life dangerous for the oppressive settlers.

Jamaica became an official Crown Colony in 1866, and nearly one hundred years later—after three hundred and seven years in total of England and Britain benefiting financially from Jamaican soil and its people—the island declared its independence to the sound of large, joyful crowds dancing with jubilation. Here, the red, white, and blue Union Jack was lowered, and the new national Jamaican flag, the yellow saltire (a reference to the colonialist presence of Scotland) on a green-and-black background, was hoisted above the head of Prime Minister Alexander Bustamante.

Under British colonial rule, it has been estimated that the City of London made over £3 trillion in profit from Jamaica and the West African slave trade. No compensation or reparations has ever been offered to the people of Jamaica in recognition of the multi-generational trauma and economic devastation experienced as a result. To add salt to the wound, when slavery was abolished, it was the *slave traders* and *plantation owners* who were richly compensated for their personal and financial loss—and this compensation ended only in 2015. Unbelievable. You can't make it up, can you?

Despite their best efforts Jamaica's people have always had to struggle with poverty. The number one lesson learned as a Jamaican is how to survive living on the breadline. Like many other Caribbean people of the era, and many people across the world today, my parents were forced to leave behind their country, their families and friends, in search of employment and financial empowerment. For them this came when Britain, in an effort to rebuild after the Second World War, came to the Caribbean and offered people the possibility of careers in nursing, the building trades, catering, and jobs with British Rail and London Transport.

The Windrush generation, as they became known, and their predecessors, left their beautiful, lush lands, taking up the offers of job opportunities and full citizenship overseas. These Caribbean folk were transported by several ships, the most known being the HMT Empire Windrush, and many by commercial planes, to the grey, cold, unwelcoming streets of Britain. They settled in the country of the very same colonial power that had governed Jamaica during the slave trade. Linking the timeline of slavery to my personal history, my grandpa's father would have been an enslaved African, uprooted from his homeland and transported by force to Jamaica where his name was changed and his culture denied. This is my heritage… a Caribbean heritage.

My father, Mr Stephen Alexander Henry, known by fellow Jamaican locals as 'Bredda Manny', was a traditional, humble, country man. Daddy had a dislike for the fast pace and hustle and bustle of Kingston city life. He was a yam farmer by trade. The root vegetable, one of the most ancient African foods, travelled to Jamaica with West Africans and was planted by them as escaped, free, former slaves. He would wheel and deal with other local farmers and drive for up to three hours to take his produce to the marketplace in Ocho Rios, sleeping outside the market gates to get the best start in the early morning.

In 1963, Dad left his beloved birthplace community of Troy in Trelawny, with its rich, fertile soil that he had farmed for so long. He travelled to London in search of a better life and greater economic stability. He was not alone. Between 1958 and 1970 half a million Caribbean people were attracted by the Crown's invitation of citizenship and employment. Britain required fresh labour in the fallout of the Second World War. And today you can see many local landmarks commemorating this exodus and arrival, such as Windrush Square (the HMT *Empire Windrush* docked in Essex on June 22, 1948, with some 500 Jamaican immigrants aboard, though these were far from the first arrivals to Britain from the island) in Brixton, south London.

My mother, Celeste Mae McNish, joined Dad later. It was quite commonplace, back in Jamaica, for a young man to marry his

Tippa Irie, I'm Blackman, I'm an African
And mi parents are Jamaican, an' I grew up
inna London
So, you know I know, where I am coming
from
'Cause mi parents were captured
taken to Jamaica by the Spanish and British
colonial masters
In 1962, they get dem independence. And
them fly go-ah Britain for some pounds and
pence
I am coming from London, place of Cockney,
place of the lovers' rock, rhyme and junglist
Place of Romans, Queen deh a Buckingham
Fish and chips and egg and bacon
Nuff taxation, rainy, cloudy, House of
Commons
Nuff politicians and a lot of institutional
racism.

Tippa Irie and O.B.F.,
'I'm An African' from the LP *I'm an African*
(Dubquake Records, 2022)

childhood sweetheart. Often, these marriages would span decades. Bonds of love, loyal and strong, these relationships that endured through life's ups and downs, were a joint commitment to be admired; we hardly ever see this type of unconditional love nowadays. If one party reached Britain first, be it husband or wife, they would work hard, day and night, steadfastly saving their pennies to 'send for' their other half. My father concentrated all his energies towards sending for Mum, like a king preparing for his queen to join him. They resided first in a small house in East Dulwich, opposite the local hospital.

My dad did eventually find his feet on UK soil by continuing in what he knew best, the food trade. He opened a family grocery specialising in West Indian products, meeting the needs of the Caribbean residents in our neighbourhood.

But life wasn't easy for Black people in the UK at the time. Let me set a scene. One night in August 1958, in Notting Hill, West London—in which a very large population of West Indians lived—a group of racist Teddy Boys (young white youths characterised by their fashions inspired by the styles of the Edwardian era, hence the moniker), attempted to intervene in a dispute between a white woman and her Black husband. By the following evening, white mobs were rioting violently through the neighbourhood, bike chains and flick knives their weapons of choice. In response, Black men were called from across London, and pitched battles took place on the streets as they defended their brothers and sisters who were physically under siege from the white racist mobs.

But in other ways, things were changing. In 1958, the Guyanese-born actor Cy Grant became the first Black person to feature regularly on UK television; Nat King Cole appeared on our screens a few years later. Also in 1958, the movie *The Defiant Ones* featuring the legendary Sidney Poitier was released. As I grew older and was able to see his films, I so admired him and wondered what his recipe for life was—I wanted some of that.

But as they say, the more things change… Saturday-night TV entertainment included the degrading *Black and White Minstrel Show*, featuring white men performing in thick blackface. British families loved it. Minstrelsy originated in the 1800s in the US, but this show aired in the UK right into the seventies. Cartoons featuring similar racist images were also prevalent.

In 1965, the year I was born, the first Race Relations Act was passed in Parliament, declaring it illegal to discriminate against anyone on grounds of colour, race, or creed. This was needed, despite the fact that, remember, West Indians had been *invited* to British shores. Nevertheless, the government had not prepared for our arrival, while the British public was often downright hostile, displaying unwelcoming signs: 'No Irish, No Blacks, No dogs'. Working-class Black families in search of places to stay were told by racist landlords to move on: for our black faces there was no room at the inn. Black people were blamed for housing shortages, the rise in unemployment, and the taking of white jobs. Anything that did not work in British society was pinned on us.

On April 20, 1968, Conservative MP Enoch Powell's infamous 'Rivers of Blood' speech was publicly broadcast. Powell voiced racist objections to immigration from the Commonwealth, and his words became a rallying cry for white racists. Powell declared that foreigners were invading British soil, that Blacks planned to take over and flood once-white communities. He firmly and sternly warned that if immigration continued, Black people would one day have—using the words of a constituent—the 'whip hand over the white man.' Powell prophesied race riots in the streets if Britain continued with its immigration policies. Ironically, it was Enoch Powell as Health Minister in the early 60s, who directly invited Caribbean nurses to come to England to work for the NHS.

It still baffles me today how, after they took us from Africa by force, shipped us from our motherland and abused us in Jamaica, took our labour for free under threats of violence and death, then invited us to

Britain where we died in wars, and where those who survived, along with the new arrivants, built up the country—we were then told we were not at all welcome. Once again, my people, you could not make this up!

Isolated within our own communities and locked out of the mainstream economic banking system in the UK, the new immigrants had to rely on tried and trusted methods from back home. In order to survive we had to master existence outside the mainstream. Pardners helped save the day. The pardner system is a Caribbean method of joint savings, planned between a group of people whereby an agreed amount of money is collected monthly, then distributed to one participant at a time. It's a pot into which everyone pays until it's your turn to receive the 'draw' from that pot. That's how our families' struggles first began, and this, too, is part of my cultural history.

Beginning in 1969, a campaign of systematic harassment against the growing West Indian community was undertaken by the London Metropolitan Police, targeting the Mangrove, a small café/restaurant owned by Frank Crichlow, a man who would become an important community activist and civil rights campaigner. The Mangrove was situated in All Saints Road in Notting Hill—by then home to the annual Carnival—and was frequented by locals as well as by famous faces. It was an important meeting space for artists, intellectuals, and activists such as Bob Marley, Jimi Hendrix, Nina Simone, and the leadership of the Black Panthers, to name a few.

The police raided the Mangrove persistently, day and night, on a weekly basis, without cause. On August 9, 1970, during a peaceful protest against the sudden withdrawal by the local council of the Mangrove's licence to operate, nine West Indian individuals were arrested for inciting riots after fighting broke out later that day. Black people had gathered and marched in their hundreds, showing united opposition to local police brutality exercised on Black families. Some Notting Hill police officers known as 'the Heavy Mob' held that

Black people were guilty until they could prove themselves innocent. Prejudice and discrimination reigned, based purely on differences of skin colour and cultural traditions.

The case of The Mangrove Nine became famous. I knew Darcus Howe, one of the Nine, personally; I had met him on several occasions in Brixton, where he lived at the time. Across the water in the US, support for The Mangrove Nine was further raised through the efforts of Muhammad Ali, Malcolm X, and Martin Luther King, Jr.

A jury would eventually conclude that all suspects were *not* guilty, and the Nine were acquitted. The Mangrove Nine court victory had exposed racism in Britain and led to the first judicial acknowledge- ment that the behaviour of the Metropolitan Police was motivated by racial hatred. That quaint little restaurant thus played a central role in the history of Black British culture and community.

The seventies also saw the rise of Britain's first openly racist polit- ical party, the National Front (NF), and the birth of hooligans with shaved scalps appearing on football terraces, selling racist newspapers, and organising public street rallies. The usual themes and slogans applied. 'Wogs out!' we were told; go back home to the jungles of Africa, and so on.

These boneheads were very different from original skinheads, whose origins were rooted firmly in Jamaican sixties culture and ska music, and who formed part of what was then the newly created Anti- Nazi League. Musicians united across the length and breadth of the UK, including punks and Rastas; from the Clash to Misty in Roots and the Reggae Regulars, it was protest music with conscious lyrics. Rock Against Racism was formed, its banners proudly portraying the words BLACK AND WHITE—UNITE AND FIGHT—SMASH THE NATIONAL FRONT!

In south London in the mid-seventies there were many incidents of racist profiling within the Black community culminating in dawn raids on several Black families' homes. These actions led to tensions building up between areas connecting New Cross and Lewisham, leading to the formation by local community members of the Lewisham Defence Committee. On August 13, 1977, 500 NF supporters and members made a grave mistake and became too bold for their own good; the racist movement decided to march through the multicultural streets of Lewisham, south-east London. Well, the NF *attempted* to march. Until they faced over four thousand anti-racists. That day they received a pasting along with the boys in blue that would go down in the history books as the people's victory. As we would say, *'A wa dem tek man for?'* Being born in south London, whenever this trope of 'go back to your own country' came up I would ask myself: *Go back? Home? Where, exactly?* Mum and Dad had been given legally stamped documents notifying one and all of their British citizenship. Yet Black people in the UK were labelled criminals and society dropouts who did not belong—this did not quite make sense to me. The facts did not add up. How could we be called lazy while at the same time be accused of stealing white people's jobs!

The very first time I faced racism was at age five. Mum and I were travelling on a bus through East Dulwich when a tall, large, white lady got on. As soon as she set eyes on our black faces, she began disrespecting us, racially abusing both of us in the presence of all onlooking passengers. Mum, who was only a short woman, out of nowhere pulled out some live Bruce Lee moves and struck the racist lady. The incident came in like David and Goliath. Then Mum turned and spoke to me, calmly: 'Tony, let's get off the bus and get the next one coming.' In the seventies, those good old days, it would have taken a good few hours for the police to arrive. So, by the time Old Bill got there, me and Mum were at home having tea with bun and cheese, or whatever was on the menu that day.

Mum was a creative entrepreneur, with a double-edged career. She was a hairdresser, and later started her independent catering business, cooking and serving meals for the students and staff of

Brixton College. In typical raw Jamaican style, she had no need for chatting behind your back. If good old Mummy didn't like you or something you did, then she was going to *tell* you, live and direct: in ya face. No mistaking, no hiding. Mum was kind and caring, but wise, and a good judge of character. She told me not to marry my now ex-wife; I ignored her, but I wish I had bloody listened. It would have saved me a few bob.

Mum was an independent spirit—one of the first Black women locally to drive a car. After her seventh and first successful attempt at passing her driving test, she proudly drove up and down in her VW Beetle. She would never take *no* for an answer, always pushing on with persevering might, just hard-working and moving through the obstacles until she reached her goal. She possessed the energy and the strength of a lioness.

Dad, on the other hand, was a strict disciplinarian, sharp as a pound note. He was never one to suffer fools gladly, nor did he have time for any acts of stupidity, especially when you should have known better. Dad was a silent man, and serious about life. On balance, though, his character was sprinkled with a certain amount of joviality, and a wonderful sense of humour. Family was central to his very being, and *teamwork*, togetherness within the family, was what made his heart tick. He lived and worked every moment for the upliftment of our family unit, the Henrys.

The day would start at 5 AM with Dad driving the milk van. The next task: stocking, opening, and serving in the grocery store from dusk to dawn. I watched him graft all the hours God sent. He had no time to waste, and so he waited for no one. To truly understand Dad's behaviour, you would need to have been raised in a Jamaican household. He laid down rules and firm boundaries; this strict conservative culture was brought down through the struggles and hardships of previous generations. My dad's father back in Jamaica would have also been ultra-firm with him and so it was passed on to us.

Back in the day, if you disrespected your Jamaican elders and guardians, you would end up the worse for wear—guaranteed. The same moral code applied here as back in Jamaica, the same parental discipline. *If you don't hear, you shall feel* (Who nah hear will feel!) was the household motto. My parents would even grant permission to other elders to discipline me as a child. Central to our culture's golden rules was respect for elders, and this was an essential part of my heritage, too. As the Bible states: 'Honour thy father and thy mother, that thy days may be long.'

I understood where this strictness originated, and in fact, for me, it came from a place of love, care, and protection, not anger or abuse. Even when the belt was wrapped around my stinging backside, 9 times out of 10 I knew that it was I who had stepped out of line and had been caught out. In my community children learned their place very quickly, but along with that came lessons of patience and self-discipline, of respecting yourself and others.

I was born in Dulwich Hospital, as were most of my Black school pals. Our little family home was situated opposite the hospital, in fact. We were south London children, loud and proud. I was in the middle, Madge's only son, between my elder sister Jackie and my baby sister Avril. In the beginning, life was treble tight. We all slept in the one room: me in between my sisters in one bed, and on the other side of the bedroom, Mum and Dad. But we never went without essentials. My dad's rented grocery shop in East Dulwich brought in a stable income.

Food was always on the table, and we all gave thanks. Dad blessed our family with the shop, from which he served and fed the community. At school, I became extremely popular. I often possessed an array of penny sweets; Kola Bottles, liquorice sherbet and remember those giant gobstoppers that took hours to suck down. In these times, people might describe my upbringing as poor, but in truth, I never knew anything else. For me and for thousands of other local Lambeth working-class families, young and old, Black and white living in over-crowded environments, privately rented homes or high-rise council housing estates, this was the norm.

Our Jamaican community had a stronghold within Brixton, where from our elders' hard work and ingenuity they had made the grey, dimly lit streets of London come alive. The community was infamous for the energizing sounds of reggae music, playing alongside the sweet aroma of Caribbean food, in particular jerk chicken, and the scent of food frying in the streets. In my community were an array of vinyl record shops, butchers, bookies, clothing boutiques, pubs, domino clubs and the renowned Brixton market. The neighbourhood was close, every-body knew everybody, having lived next door to the same families for decades. We shared good times and hard times together, taking the rough with the smooth. Money was hard to come by but still, in ways I was better off than many back in Jamaica, the other Caribbean islands or Africa. We may have lived in housing like sardines in a can, but we were united; we had no other choice. It was about collective strength and family bond, and it was a place of security. Our parents' aim was to protect us, to shelter us from the stresses our elders had faced. In conversations with and around us, we were shielded from the negative. We were never exposed, as children, to the obstacles of adult life.

Education is key in Jamaican families, and ours was no different. My parents did not want me to have to struggle to get through as they had. Instead, they viewed education as the road offering a brighter future within British society. I was instructed to keep my head down and study. But I had a rebel spirit within me and I did not follow their guidance. I left secondary school without sitting one single GCSE examination. Despite this I left school on a Friday and by Monday I had a paid job. To me, the central emphasis in life was on personal development, staying wise, and sharpening the iron. It was not about how many certificates one had to their name. I wanted to rise above all forms of poverty, both mentally and physically.

But I digress. We moved to Brixton when I was six and I attended Brockwell Primary School, opposite the Tulse Hill Estate. My father had expanded his grocery business, and it was now also a newsagent. Our family's business progression allowed us to upgrade our accommodation. Our first family home was situated at 87 Helix Road, SW2. We relocated to 52 Eastlake Road, SE5, between Loughborough Junction and Camberwell Green. As kids, we could not believe our luck, moving out of a cramped one-bed home and into a six-room property. I loved the size and spaciousness of the new family environment: four rooms upstairs and two rooms downstairs, with a large, empty basement. It was like a mansion to us, the biggest housing upgrade we could have ever dreamed about. With a bigger home, came longer and more numerous family chores, although these new additional daily duties were delegated and shared evenly. We operated as one productive team.

I moved again and attended Loughborough Primary School. My PE teacher Mr Sing—my favourite—was the first adult to instil in me a keen interest in sports. He was a very fair, kind, role model, but he would put you straight immediately if you dared to step out of line. I loved school: it offered a freedom that could not be expressed within my strict Caribbean family home.

That said, I got into a few scraps with some other feisty pupils. In primary school, I recall an embarrassing incident that forced me into retreat: a girl had got the best of me and had left me winded on the ground. *Win some, lose some.* My school uniform was always kept neat and tidy, though; any mark or tear would earn a beating, so I had to dust myself down and fix up myself sharpish, or a worse hiding would follow from my dad. Mum was also strict: if I was found rude or in a lie, she would take no time in slapping them lies back down my throat. But as a young boy, I was thankful that Mum was the family referee, as she was the more liberal of my parents. Dad could get a bit carried away with his trouser-belt beatings, but Mum would have mercy and thankfully throw in the towel, often instead stepping in to protect me or my sisters.

At home, everything had a time and a place. After school it was my duty to be ready and motivated for my homework and do the evening household chores as well. The expectation from Jamaican parents was that your school friends would stay at school, not find themselves arriving home with you, so if the school closed its gates at 3:30 PM, you would be expected home soon thereafter. My journey was thirty minutes door-to-door and in military style, at 4 PM on the dot, I would arrive at the family doorstep.

Dad's communication was skilful; he possessed the ability to ask and answer a question at the very same time:

'Do you have schoolfriends?'

'Well, yes.'

'That's good; best make your schoolfriends, stay at school.'

Values were instilled in us little ones, as an assortment of life wisdom and moral codes. *Always be sure to provide fairness to your fellowman. Do unto others as you would like done unto you. Do good, live long. Good ways, long days. Show me the company you keep, and I'll tell you who you are.*

From my early morning rise, I would await scrambled eggs and plantain, or thick, seasoned-up porridge, spiced with nutmeg, cinnamon, Nestlé milk, and a pinch of salt. As a growing young lad with his belly rumbling, I would lick my fingers at dinnertime: the aromas in the kitchen of rice and peas, fried dumplings, mutton, curry goat, brown stew chicken with stuffing, red peas soup, oxtail and butterbeans, bammy, escovitch fried fish, snapper, small sprats… Any of these foods could be cooking on the stove. Mum's home baking would be in the steaming oven, and all types of hot, sweet bread would be served to us. Scotch bonnets, hot pepper sauces, and pickles… like back in Jamaica, everything was seasoned and spiced—even the bread.

I am the rebel, on da roots corner
Cause, I am African and proud of dat
Well as a little youth, as a little youngster
Mi grew up in the ghetto with mi two sister
My mother, mi father dem did under pressure
One little room the whole a we sleep inna
We struggle every day, just to make things
better
Just to make tings better, mi say for the
future
Nuff times mi hear mi mother ask mi father
I don't know why we left Jamaica
just come a England and work in a freezer
Fe mek a white guy cuss me and call we nigga
But its milk and honey, dem did a look for
that is the only reason they did a come ya
True the white man think dem superior
and they look pon we as the inferior
Well day after day, they try keep we under
but we know we gotta fight, cause it in our
nature.

Tippa Irie, 'Rebel on the Roots Corner'
from the LP *Rebel on the Roots Corner*
(Ariwa Records, 1994)

As a young boy, I never loved my vegetables, but with Dad a former farmer and Mum, a versatile cook who could turn her skills to creating any dish, Jamaican or European—there was no escaping it for me. 'Eat your veg, it's good for you,' was the instruction. We were truly blessed, our table laden with all types of mouth-watering meals. My father, the recognised head of the household, would be seated securely at the head of the table. We were all ordered to gather round, no excuses. First came prayers: blessing the food, giving thanks in the name of the Almighty Creator for what we were about to receive. Dad was so firmly in control, I remember one of his own famous sayings: 'Don't leave it to God, leave it to me.'

Come morning, me and my two sisters would again have our chores delegated to us. At 5 AM we received the bread and milk deliveries. Then came scrubbing the house clean from top to bottom, making sure the skirting boards shined. There were no washing machines back in the day for us ordinary, working-class folk. We washed clothes by hand with a good bar of Jamaican red soap, our backs aching from working over the bathtub.

Being the middle child with two sisters was fun. We were cared for and shared for, 24/7, so intertwined that our love could be tested at times. Naturally, there were sibling disagreements, but nothing ever caused us to truly fall out. The three of us played together on the street outside the house. A little knock-down ginger, skipping, hide-and-seek, all wonderful innocent childhood memories. Small and nimble, I was the family hopscotch champion. We never needed to go out for much, having everything around us in the family shop, busy and occupied with family tasks, all mucking in together as 'more hands make lighter work.' We all jelled well together, never one above another. Thankfully, we functioned with care and consideration; lots of love and thoughtfulness abounded (The Henrys never visited family members or friends without bringing something). *All for one, and one for all*: we possessed a community spirit built on integrity.

We were raised with excellent life and teamwork skills. One of my weekly routines was going to the local newsagent to buy *Sporting Life* magazine for my dad. My father, like so many West Indians, was drawn to the local betting shops, putting in betting slips and praying for a win. I remember Dad would take me to Wimbledon, our local greyhound dog track for a little gamble on the greyhounds, or maybe the horses. Back in the day, every man gathered at Ladbrokes—and for the big racing events even children were permitted to put in bets for their parents. For us the Grand National was a family affair: I put my few pennies on Red Rum, my favourite horse. I cheered as he faithfully passed the finish line. Dad would not be so lucky, backing a losing horse. Once again: *win some, lose some.*

Me and my neighbourhood mate Neil would accompany Dad in our white VW van to buy groceries and shop in the cash-and-carry stores, purchasing stock for our family corner shop. I'd watch Dad measuring, smelling, and examining the produce, hustling and bartering to save money on the goods. My two sisters, most of the time, would stay indoors with Mum while I was free to roam as Dad's little helper. We'd sit in the front seat of the van as he took us all over, moving from A to B. The van hardly ever broke down; if it did, it was easy to fix and get back on the road. From seeing my dad on his run with the van, never taking a break, just going from one stop to the next, a strong work ethic was instilled in me, hand in hand with an understanding of the the need for reliability, responsibility, and good organisational skills. Thing was, that's how we lived our lives in my family; seeing the work and hearing the edicts: 'By the sweat of your brow, you shall eat bread.' And 'If you want good, you nose have fi run.'

Describing the Eastlake Road family corner shop/grocery/newsagent as a place merely to get food would not convey the true essence of the place. 'Henry's store' was a buzzing hive in the local Black community for two reasons: good, fresh food by day, and a central spot for Brixton parties at night, when Henry's would be transformed.

From the fifties to the early seventies, West Indian gatherings were called *shebeens* and were commonly held in family homes as these were the only spaces where people could gather safely and freely. 'House parties' and 'blues dances' were other terms used.

My dad was an original sound system man from Jamaica. His sharp DJ selection featured tunes from big bands to bluebeat and ska. At home, Dad would play a vast selection of music on the gramophone, including country and western singers such as Kenny Rogers and Jim Reeves ('It Is No Secret (What God Can Do)'). Our elders from the Caribbean loved their country and western music; they had been raised on it. Although they were Black from a Black country, British colonial authorities were still in charge of the radio. This is also why our elders on the island made reggae cover songs of classic Motown tunes and popular music from Europe and America. That is where John Holt's influences come in—you just have to listen to the traditional cover songs on *1000 Volts of Holt*. This is also where Bob Marley's 'Kinky Reggae' comes from. As the years passed my dad's selection would then move from country and pop songs on to reggae, with songs such as 'Two Sevens Clash' by the mighty Culture, with frontman Joseph Hill, alongside the Abyssinians' classic tune 'Satta Massagana'.

Dad would build his speaker boxes with his own hands (one thing about the people of the Caribbean: they can turn their hands to anything!). He used old-time valve amps and Dad had to be careful with these, as occasionally they would overheat. He turned his musical vibes into a second business, downstairs in the family shop's basement. His own sound system was called 'Musical Messiah'. Dad was the top selector, spinning and rewinding the latest vinyl reggae hits imported from Jamaica. Playing 45s on his turntable, he had a firm, rooted collection of tunes with artists such as Ken Boothe, John Holt, Burning Spear, the Heptones, Gregory Isaacs, the 'Cool Ruler' and Dennis Brown, the 'Crown Prince of Reggae' (Dennis was my favourite: to me he was the '*King* of Reggae').

The basement of house was where we kept the family shebeen. You would walk through the front door to the left of our shop and walk down a flight of stairs. As you hit the bottom there was two rooms. The first was the music room, in which there were a few chairs and tables where people would dance and listen to the sound system. This was also where the turntable was situated and the amp and preamp were set up. Those present who were seated around the table were ready for dominos and card games. If my mum was in the mood sometimes food would be available that she would have prepared. And a variety of hard and soft drinks for sure was on sale. The second room was where my dad set up the speakers and empty except for that, where people would dance the night away.

Those nights you had people from all walks of life; hard working people that just needed to let their hair down after a hard-working week. A few people that come there may have been able to sell a draw of weed but definitely no hard drugs, my dad would not stand for that. So it was, all shapes and sizes and backgrounds dancing, drinking, eating, playing together. People with money, people that were poor, they all would come and shake a leg all through the night until sun rise. Some people would dress up and others were dressed simple, my parents never minded. We did not mind as long as your behaviour and dress were both decent.

The party would begin around 10 PM in the basement, proceeding until 5 or 6 AM. A crowd of 40 or so would gather—the men smart casual, smelling fresh, dressed to entice the beautiful ladies. As a child, I witnessed reggae music offering those present an escape from their long, hard week. When work finished, they would party hard. Reggae music was their reward. Some people would party Friday and Saturday, but would still manage to wake up in time for church on Sunday; or some brothers would rise fresh to play Sunday football down at the local parks. I could be up all night, but still manage to muster up the energy to score a few goals the next day.

The locals coming to the basement paid a small entrance fee. There was hot food for sale, and strong punch and a mixture of alcoholic drinks—all sold by my family, serving from a makeshift bar with a table wedged in the kitchen doorway. Money changed hands with the punters, and all those present and enjoying themselves would be served.

My family served Special Brew, Tennent's, Skol, Red Stripe, and Foster's, plus brandy or rum and Coke; the women had Babycham, Canei, and Pink Lady. The adjacent room in the basement was reserved purely for playing of Ludo and dominoes, the winner passionately slapping down his hand on the table to let everyone know he won the game. It would be sweeter if his opponent got six love (6-0). The sound system area would be divided for games, separate from the dance floor: as it was a Jamaican social event, our elders could safely gather together, so playing cards, dominoes, Ludo, etc, would have to be available. As a small boy, I learnt to play well just by observing the elders' skilful moves.

The early-morning hours provided the only opportunity for us children to sneak down and take in the vibes as we would be waking up just as things were ending. I was taken in by the tunes playing on the turntable. The dance hall was the only place you could hear newly released reggae music, so sound systems would play the role of radio stations for us; our music did not feature on the mainstream station playlists, just like back in Jamaica, where our own music was not promoted. The sound system vibes echoed through me, grabbed me; as did the dancing, the joy and togetherness centred around the music. I was spellbound.

My dad also rented out our basement to musicians as a rehearsal space. The international smash-hit soul and funk band The Real Thing, amongst other artists, would practise downstairs, rehearsing their chart-topping song 'You to Me Are Everything'. They were awarded silver-record sales status, making them the most successful UK soul band of the seventies, as one of the earliest Black bands to feature on the live BBC talent show *Opportunity Knocks*. The Real Thing were mesmerising. As a little boy, sitting silently watching them perform, and the smooth way they rolled through their numbers, this was my first taste of real live music, performed by real, successful artists.

In the seventies, the major local sound systems playing across London and the surrounding counties were Duke Reid, King Tubby and Coxsone. The whole of SW9 postcode had talent pouring from it. These sound systems were pillars of the community, and very much necessary: they were the only exposure we had to *our* genre of music. I was born into south London sound system culture. Music was never far away; it featured on our own family premises, from both Mum's and Dad's Jamaican roots and culture. It developed and influenced the entire family, musically. Tony Murrey, my old schoolfriend from south London, describes one of my junior school experiences:

> Our junior school was Beaufoy, and I can recall exactly—
> the year was 1976. We little kids were all gathered round
> in assembly. The head teacher had asked all the children
> to bring a favourite poem or performance. The aim was to
> recite in front of the other pupils, and we patiently awaited
> the teachers as they all lined up. When it was Tony's turn,
> he performed his own unique version of a tune by the
> reggae MC U-Roy. I'll never forget that day, and no one
> else present would either. Looking back, it was history is
> the making: the launch of what was to become Mr Tippa
> Irie.

My big sister Jackie is a gifted, powerful soul singer in her own right, with perfect pitch and timing. She describes the early influences on her own journey as well:

I was influenced by my mum, playing vinyl records on the gramophone. I was drawn like a magnet to the American soul sounds of Black women. Singing out their hearts, their journeys, their stories. Dreams. Joy. Heartbreak. The sounds of Patsy Moore, Tia Maria, Gladys Knight, and Millie Jackson. Black American female performers, from West Indian origins. You must remember, these tunes were our music, because you would never hear Black women singing on the radio shows; it was our Caribbean parents who brought forth the vibes and the music that we listened to as children.

I went on to become a soul performer, following in the footsteps of my early musical influences. I performed as a lead soul vocalist with my live band, Metropolis, at Ronnie Scott's and various other jazz and soul venues. I was also part of the IRIE! Dance Theatre, an independent Black musical and theatrical experience, the first of its kind in London.

My greatest memories of our family dances back in the day would be witnessing my dad in his element, rocking away by himself, grooving to the sounds of Bob Marley with his eyes closed, drifting. In truth, Dad was always missing his birthplace, his sunny home of Jamaica. I believe the roots songs would transport him there, while his feet were in London.

My little sister Avril was more of a run-around, a tomboy, rough-and-tumble, unruly and hyperactive. From a young age, she developed her own independent spirit. As the youngest of us, she was the apple of my father's eye. Avril and I were raised on a strict diet of reggae. We were drawn to lively raw DJ vibes. Avril and I rolled together, like bench an' batty.

My old friend from the neighbourhood, Neil Sarisom, paints a picture of the Henrys and our childhood:

> I was raised in Brixton, and I was a neighbour of Tony's, living across the road from the Henry family. I have known Tony, aka Tippa Irie, from the age of eight. We became as thick as thieves, spending all the spare time we had together. I first got to know the family from visiting their grocery store, called Henry's. It was a sparse shop, with not that much on display, but Mr Henry would sell local families larger portions than they could afford. This customer service also helped me and my own family.
>
> I had a brother and a sister, all living with our single mum. My dad had died early on, when I was just seven. We were 'latchkey kids', that's what they would call us back in the day. Basically, Mum worked all the hours God sent and we would come from school as little ones with no parents at home, fending for ourselves. The Henry family took me in, treated me as one of their own. Mr Henry would take me and Tony to the cash-and-carry, purchasing bulk items for the family store. We would drive up and down, and it was like a proper adventure for us kids.
>
> Tony's elder sister Jackie was always helping her mum with household chores. His little sister Avril was a cheeky, feisty girl, very confident and in your face. She was the first girl I ever witnessed routinely kissing her teeth at people. Avril being the last daughter, the youngest, she was not allowed out so much. Me, Tony, and Avril would spend long periods of time sitting together, chatting on the stairs of my house or their shop's doorway.
>
> What connected me and Tony was our love of street games, marbles and penny-up-the-wall. Every waking

hour we were on it, competing, circling the marbles in a straight line. Up and down, back and front… we played night and day. On the streets under the council lighting, it was always marbles, marbles and more marbles. We were mad for it; it was our childhood sport. I would even get into local, derelict houses, take the doors off their hinges with my screwdriver and remove the large steel ball bearings from the closing mechanisms. These were great for our games.

We had worked out together that if we walked to school, we could save our bus fare and spend it on ourselves, and this would also give us more time to play penny-up-the-wall. One day, as we were out competing, from the side I spotted the family's white VW. It pulled up slowly, and Mr Henry chased Tony down the road with his trouser belt in his hand. He caught him down the bottom of the road and gave his son a good hiding in full public view. Mr Henry was the sweetest man and so was Tony's mum Madge, but they were old-school Jamaicans—so not the people to get caught up with. The Henrys were very loving, but doubly strict.

The night would take on a different role, I suppose you would call them, now, illegal raves. Mr Henry would put on dances in the basement of Henry's grocery. Me and my brother would slide down the drainpipe from our bedroom windows and sneak out in the night. We would marvel at all the adults going in, wearing their posh clothes; we could hear the pumping dancehall reggae beat, and as white kids, this was the first time we heard reggae music. We loved taking in all the energy and excitement from across the road. Me and my brother would hide and watch carefully. We just dreamed about what it must have been like downstairs in the basement.

Me and Tony would sadly part as school buddies. I hated school; in Year 4, I had only attended school for two days, and in Year 5, one day. So, I would be hopping the wag. This rebellious nature of mine, plus having a little bovver from Brixton's Old Bill, led to me being taken from my family home by Lambeth Social Services and put under council care. So, I lost touch with my best mate Tony and the Henry family. I missed his cheeky grin and his distinctive, high-pitched voice. Sadly, it was to be the end of our marble challenges, and he would not like me to say it, but I am sure I left with the winning title.

The schools we went to grouped us. As a Black kid, I witnessed many Black children being labelled educationally subnormal by the British school system. The career advisors visiting secondary schools would also stereotype us. Girls' employment prospects: cooks and cleaners. Boys': labourers or sportsmen. These two avenues were the only futures put before us. They had low expectations. The first time I experienced *class* division, though, was not in secondary school, because we all dressed in the collective trousers, shirt, tie, and blazer uniform (for me, at that time, social division was not based on race. Neil, my good mate across the way, was from a working-class white family, and they experienced the same overcrowded housing conditions and other material difficulties that affected us, too: we were eating out of the very same pot). However, it was the clothing *outside* school that was the giveaway, those kids wearing designer clothes, neatly pressed name brands such as the well-fitting Farah trousers and the latest Adidas Gazelle or Samba trainers.

Yet sports were a distraction, my first real true love. In fact, back then I was deeply motivated to develop a successful sports career. I was thin and small enough to cross over in any sport, and I loved it all, from football and cricket to basketball. May 8, 1971, was the day that

27

hooked me on football for life. That day I watched the FA Cup final and Charlie George's triumphant goal for Arsenal, leading to a 2–1 victory over Liverpool. I became a certified sports addict in general, watching *Match of the Day, Grandstand, World of Sport,* and *Sports Night* and I possessed a fanatical passion for football, wearing the Gunners red and white or yellow and blue away kit. I will forever be a 100 percent Arsenal fan. My favourite sportsmen of the day included Laurie Cunningham and Viv Anderson. Paul Davis, who played for the Gunners, was a football coach at Beaufoy, my secondary school in Kennington. Having professional footballers from my own school was an indication of how close to home getting a professional football signing could be—a reality within my reach. I would play for my school team, left side, while Thomas Nicholls played on the right. Another schoolmate, Tony Grant, would have been signed by Coventry FC had it not been for a troubling knee injury. Kenny Sansom was another pupil who turned professional.

I remember, clear as day, attending football trials for my school team. I did not own a pair of football boots, so I played in my school shoes—Toppers, which had quite a high sole. Football boots and sports equipment would have been a luxury in our house: sports attire did not fall into the category of 'life essentials' in the Henry family. No shame, no frowning, I just carried on smiling. I would think to myself that life could have been a lot worse. Nor did the experience hold me back: I was still picked to play for the team.

As a young teenage boy coming to terms with disappointments, I would think, no matter how fortunate another might be, my skills would still stand out. I knew my talents spoke for themselves. Putting hardship on the back burner, family values firmly imprinted, I continued to push on through with a positive mindset, my self-respect intact. My teachers could see clearly that I had what it took, on and off the pitch.

Still, I was sports-bonkers, and loved watching Black sportspeople I admired on TV. They represented our country, champions of England in their own right. I was also a fan of cricket and supported Viv Richards, Michael Holding, Gordon Greenidge and many others. Winston Roberts and Michael Edwards were both my schoolmates. The three of us had trials for London. Winston and Michael got through, but I did not make it onto the squad.

My school was near the Oval cricket ground home of the legendary Surrey County Cricket Club. My best schoolmate, Derek Bryan, *aka* MC General Slater, Ras Triumphant, was an expert cricketer. At times, the Surrey cricket team would come to my school to teach and train us. Slater had a unique style and bowling action; I can recall when he bowled out the legendary England captain and batsman Graham Gooch. I looked at Derek, smiled and said, 'A dis, a de England captain?'

I also loved basketball, and my stars of the day were many, including Michael Jordan, Scottie Pippen, and Magic Johnson.

My early musical influences drew me with the same passion as sport. I would take any opportunity I could find to express my creativity, such as joining the choir at secondary school and attending singing practices. My great music teacher, Zach Herbert, opened a new cultural door for me, playing the steel pans. I became proficient at the pans, putting in the practice that always makes perfect, and even performed live at the Dorchester Hotel. The greatest gift the school's steel band received was an invitation to participate in the annual Notting Hill Carnival during summer holidays. Our wonderful Mr Herbert organised a minibus, and we, excited, hungry, kids arrived on location in early morning and set up our pans in the allocated space. We were called The Paddington Youth Steel Band. The energy was electric.

At Carnival I witnessed the sound systems busting out max volume and the heaviest bass lines which rolled and echoed across the streets of west London. I saw grown-ups having a whale of a time… it was truly glorious to see. All colours, races, and nations partying and dancing in harmony. I remember going around on the floats filled with the sounds of reggae and soca. The smell of chicken, curry goat, rice and peas drifted past our nostrils, alongside the familiar aroma of sensi wafting through the air. While travelling back to Brixton after our show, I thought to myself that one day, I would *love* to come back. Little did I know then that I would be returning to the Notting Hill Carnival later, and this time as a famous reggae MC. I had experienced getting very close to a professional sporting career, I could feel it in my bones that music was calling me and putting forth its hand. I had seen how discrimination can affect the lives of young Black people. Knowing how to duck and dive, living and surviving the streets of London. My family and my Jamaican heritage gave me lessons in keeping your head up high and your shoulder to the wheel. So that is what I was made of, pushing on forward. Growing up in Brixton, I had seen around me many examples of what it can be like to lose but by any means necessary, I just wanted to win.

When I think 'bout what used to happen
when police used to beat us with them batten
Life use to stressful, life use to rotten,
like when my parents used to pick cotton
Mr Irie, I have not forgotten
this is plain English, this is not Latin
Pon our bedsheets, there was no satin,
same old sheets with the same old pattern
Me and my family inna one room,
nothing but doom and nothing but gloom
I could not wait until the seventh of June
because I know better must come soon
We used to watch Jackson Five cartoon
and jump up and down to the Bob Marley
tune
Although times were hard, we feel no way
always used to rock to the reggae.

Tippa Irie, 'Looking Out My Window'
(2008 Yeti Beats Records)

From me eye deh a me knee,
from mi a little pickney,
I feel the beat and harmony
From the great Sly and Robbie, Lee Perry,
King Jammies, Joe Gibbs and Mr King Tubby
Make me dance, make me free,
like a bird up in the tree
Channel One, Scientist,
make the music, sounds so crisp
Backing band, Roots Radics
Music that you can't resist.

Tippa Irie and the Far East Band,
'Stick to My Roots' from the LP *Stick to My
Roots* (Lockdown Productions, 2010)

Chapter Two
Born in the Dancehall

'NEWSREADER', 'TOASTER', 'CHANTER', 'DJ', AND 'Master of Ceremonies (MC)'... these were the dancehall titles that became a part of me. 'Rewind selector and come again', '"lick-wood"mean "rewind" and "gunshot" mean "forward"'... These were the terms used for MCs in dancehall. The strong influences of reggae playing from within the doors of my family home, the vibrant tunes coming like my very best-seasoned Caribbean dishes, just like Mum's cooking, the tunes from my dad's sound system (the Musical Messiah)—the rhythms and vibrations of the music were built into my bones. The structure of reggae, the way it's put together, made me feel good, and the music flowed constantly through my blood. The words of the songs ran around in my mind and the beat shook the inner parts of my soul.

I was hypnotically drawn to the energy of reggae music—played by our parents, on vinyl on the gramophone by day, and through the sound system experience by nightfall, as if an invisible friend had physically gripped me. Reggae enabled me to get a better understanding of where my mum and dad came from; we were being culturally schooled without even knowing it! Through the songs and messages conveyed by the artists, I was transported to the roots of reggae music, and it was being recorded subconsciously in the memory bank of my mind.

But reggae music belonged to *us*; it was our own pulsating heart-beat. It was our world. It taught us our history, delivered our very being to us from the essence of the songs, woven through hit after hit, tune after tune, in fine rhythms and the sweetest melodies.

Some of my favourite teachers included the Abyssinians, telling us to look towards Africa, the motherland, 'a land far, far away'; Dennis Brown journeyed us to 'The Promised Land'; Burning Spear boldly declared, 'Christopher Columbus is a damn, blasted liar'—a very different story from what was taught to us in the history schoolbooks. Sadly, even today, our kids are still not taught about their culture. Mutabaruka chanted, 'It nuh good fi stay inna white man country too long'; Pablo Gad warned us of 'Hard Times'. Back in the UK, Reggae Regular asked us to travel on 'The Black Star Liner'; Aswad affirmed that we were 'African children living in a concrete situation'; and Matumbi presented 'The Man in Me'.

Dancehall music sprang from the sound systems of Jamaica, tracing back to 1940s Kingston town. The first known clash occurred between the legendary, pioneering selector/DJ, the Chinese-Jamaican Tom Wong and his Great Sebastian sound system, against Jamaican police inspector-turned-DJ Duke Reid. The clash famously featured Duke Reid pulling a gun from each side of his waist and squeezing the triggers. He then shouted the war cry, 'forward, forward!' going into clash-battle mode.

The early producers and pioneers were Count Matchuki and the world-famous Clement 'Coxsone' Dodd. The Jamaican film classic *The Harder They Come*, featuring Jimmy Cliff, provides raw insight into the trials and tribulations of the early Jamaican dancehall sound system days. Our original MC dancehall forefathers were the top-ranking Daddy U-Roy and Big Youth.

Jamaica's sound system culture later led to the formation of rap and hip-hop across the US. The rap nation just consisted of reggae

MCs' younger siblings. This emergence originated with Kingston-born DJ Kool Herc, stringing up speaker boxes in the Bronx back in the seventies and adapting his Jamaican selector and MC styles to his new home in America. He mixed a unique scratching sound and added a new creation called 'breakbeat'. DJ Kool Herc perfected this sound, isolating the tunes and the drumbeat, and finally adding synchronised vocals. DJ Kool Herc brought the potency of his island's reggae vibes into the streets of America, evolving and inspiring future generations and bringing forth the careers of great foundation rappers such as The Sugar Hill Gang, Grandmaster Flash, Grandmaster Melle Mel, Afrika Bambaataa and—my all-time favourites—KRS-One, DJ Premier, and Guru from Gang Starr.

It is obvious to me that Jamaica's sound system culture is wholly responsible for giving birth to the combined sounds of hip-hop, techno, drum and bass, junglist music, and warehouse raves. That is the power of dancehall and reggae, moving infectiously through generations.

The literal building of a Jamaican sound system is another layer of my musical culture. This required skills such as carpentry and welding, fitting the grids, wrapping and backing the speaker sealed with rubber and lined with cloth. There were four columns with eight boxes per column, providing a sound wall of sixteen boxes. Traditionally, these were painted black, with 12- and 15-inch speaker sizes; the speaker walls were up to seven speaker stacks. The system would pump out up to 30,000 watts. The speakers were divided into high, low, midrange, bass, horns, and tweeters. This building process produced an impressive and towering five-way crossover system. The sound system setup enabled the selector to mix live aby dropping out the treble and bass, while spinning his 45s.

Once the sound was strung up, the power it produced shook the very ground you stood on, rattling your bones with palpitating vibrations right through your heart. I used to find it amazing how some guys could stand so close to the pounding speaker and not worry about their hearing. I used to run from it! I was lucky, because I would be stood up around the sound on the mic, not in front of the speakers. This powerful energy would shake the windowpanes of the house parties and the clubs. No one could ignore our reggae music when the mighty sound systems came to town. I certainly couldn't. At the ripe age of sixteen I would often wait on the street corner, just in time to catch the sound system van coming. I would then try to befriend the soundman and volunteer to carry some speaker boxes into the venue— this, I knew, would guarantee me a free pass into the dance. Sound system sessions took place at venues such as 4 Aces in north London, Moon-shot in south-east London, Lewisham Boys Club, St Mary's in Ladywell, Colosseum in Harlesden, Uppercut Stadium Forest Gate, Hackney Downs school, 4 Aces club in Brixton, Lambeth Town Hall, St Matthews in Brixton, Galaxy in east London and the After Dark club in Reading.

Dubplates were an essential part of any event, providing you with a competitive edge in a clash with an opposing sound. The small reggae labels and independent pressing plants would produce and master our white-label vinyl dubplates, and each sound system would invite a variety of different artists to sing over the dubplates. The selector always carried his record box inside, which would contain 7- and 12-inch dubplates amongst his exclusive collection of vinyl. The sound system possessing the freshest dubplates would rule the night, and the session.

Sound system culture is not merely a musical experience. Sound systems are like a religion, and dancehall is the church. The mixing desk is the pulpit, and MCs, mic in hand, replace the pastor. Educating the people with knowledge, passing the spoken word on to the congregation, reggae, just like bluebeat, rocksteady, and ska had in my parents' time, became the religion of my generation.

Yet it was like I lived in two worlds, which made me laugh. Around the house I would speak in Jamaican patois with my parents, but when my mate Neil knocked and stood there, I reverted naturally to being the cheeky cockney chappie that the outside world knew.

At the age of thirteen on the way to school I would be chatting words, the lyrics buzzing around my mind in the playground; I was forever reciting. At times, my schoolfriends would look at me and wonder if I was right in the head. They would take a double check to make sure that it was just me rehearsing my lyrics again. In fact, I found myself mumbling words wherever I was. In my bedroom I would pose with my afro comb in my right hand, pretending it was a microphone. I was already famous in the mirror reflection, imitating my reggae idols, drawn from the word go by the influence of the original Jamaican MCs. They could take the mic and confidently ride the rhythm on version after version. It was poetry—lyrics that told a life story. Dennis Alcapone did it. Daddy U-Roy did it too with his tune 'Wake the Town and Tell the People'. And Josey Wales with 'Na Lef' Jamaica'. And Tappa Zukie and Horace Andy with 'Natty Dread Ah Weh She Want'. And Brigadier Jerry 'The General' expressing his pride for 'Jamaica, Jamaica': he did it too. These tunes motivated *me* to take up the microphone.

I began to immerse myself, practising. And the more I rehearsed, the better I got. I also started to develop my own identity. On the mic, I initiated a unique musical fusion: a London accent in a Jamaican DJ style. My family supported and encouraged me. My cousins started to comment, saying 'Tony, you are getting good at this.' My musical desire was so powerful, no one around me could deny my inner passion. Strict as my dad was, he still allowed me to perform on his sound system, Musical Messiah. Down in the shop basement, I would get in a sneaky practice when no elders were around. Eastlake Road is where my very first performing experience began.

Apart from home, the second-best place for me to express my creativity was alongside my brethren at the Crawford Youth Club, the

Flaxman Sports Centre, the Cowley Community Centre, the Ferndale Community Sports Centre, the Dick Sheppard Youth Centre and the Abeng Youth and Community Centre. The closest to me was the Marcus Lipton Youth Club and adventure playground, situated off Loughborough Junction. These places were like homes to us. My friends and I would spend as much time there as possible, chatting about what girls we did and didn't like, enjoying each other's company. In those early days, I had three main motivations in life. My first love was sports. Second dancehall music, and finally young women. Well, what more could I possibly want? This was all I needed to keep me happy. And it was within this local youth-club environment that I met my eldest son's mother.

The youth clubs were full of excitement, featuring activities such as pool, cricket, five-a-side football, boxing, weightlifting, and martial arts. The girls usually played netball and rounders. The adventure playgrounds were also great fun and were free spaces. In the evenings, dances were held at the youth clubs. These were good times. We moved tight, me and my little crew—General Slater, Raymond Roberts, Patrick Kenton, Patrick Binns, Raymond Harris, Eustace Bee, Trevor Johnson, Winston Johnson, Kirk Douglas, Denver Douglas, and Arnold Catlin.

I will always give thanks to our youth and community clubs. The majority of the time they were safe and secure places where arguments and conflicts were resolved peacefully, with the occasional fight over losing a game of pool or whose turn it was to play next at the table; it was very rare that something more sinister would occur in the environment. Of course, it was not just youth who attended these clubs; at times 'big men' would come along and cause a disturbance. Sometimes even local gangsters would turn up. I will now describe one such sinister incident.

I would routinely attend Marcus Lipton my local youth club, and on one occasion I was playing pool and it was hard to get me off the table as it was one of my skills. I glanced behind me, and I saw a friend of mine, he had a worried look on his face. I asked him if he was cool? He replied he was and I knew this was not true. He had gotten into a fight with the brother of a local bad man and my friend had cut the bad man's brother with his ratchet knife. My friend had a gut feeling that the bad man's brother was going to come for him and he was someone you just don't want to mess with, a real nasty piece of work.

Anyway, I don't know why he was at the club because if that was me, I would be safely inside my home. So, I told my friend, 'Yo Bro you should be at home, not here.' No sooner had I said that, guess who walked into the youth club? The guy's brother. My friend tried to make a hasty exit and just as he made it outside, he got caught. They brought him back into the club. My friend was dragged into a side room called the 'quiet room', but this time the quiet room became a very noisy room. All we could hear was screaming, the guy's brother was in there with a baseball bat and beat him over and over again. There was a few of us present outside the room but there was nothing we could do to help him, apart from call the police, which, to be honest, back in our day in Brixton was waste of time. After the screaming stopped, there was a period of silence. Even the so-called youth workers were frightened of the man, they did nothing apart from call the ambulance. My friend was taken out in a wheelchair, he was covered head to toe in blood. Still, I was thankful he was ok and, as they say, he lived to tell the tale.

My next story is about the two brethrens, both called Tony. One was about six foot six and one was about five foot eleven. The taller Tony was okay and friendly but because of his size you just could not mess with him, plus he had three brothers the same size as him. Now the other Tony simply was just not a nice person, bit of a bully. That Tony would do all kind of crazy shit, like he would boldly go to night clubs and stick up the owner and extort them of their nights cash takings.

Even kidnap women and bribe their partners to give them money. A real nasty piece of work, 100% a dickhead to be honest. These two Tonys would come to the youth club to play table tennis and pool.

On one particular day the two Tonys got into a heated argument over a game of pool. From where I was watching I could see trouble brewing up and I could sense what was going to happen. I stepped back and let them get on with it. It was getting more heated and, out of nowhere, smaller Tony threw the pool stick at big Tony. Then all hell broke loose. Once again, the youth workers did not even help diffuse the situation. The youth worker's only words were, 'look take it outside and don't mash up the club.' Little Tony knew he could not handle big Tony, but nonetheless he was not backing down. It was fist to fist at first, little Tony immediately coming off the worst. Next thing we know he's pulled out a knife and in response big Tony pulled out an even bigger knife. It was like a scene for a comedy movie, but in truth looking back it was not funny. They went for each other, ducking and avoiding contact with little quick moves, yet still managing to break the skin of the other a few times. Both Tonys refused to back down, but in the end smaller Tony, he could not even get close to big Tony. Thankfully by then, the staff and everybody present sensing the stale-mate, joined in and managed to break it up before someone got killed.

Youth workers became like mentors and teachers, empowering us to seize positive opportunities and encouraging us to develop our creative skills. Most of the time our clubs were places where we could keep out of the way from the fussing and fighting of local badmen. Thankfully, I always stayed out of trouble. I still have close brethren and sistren that I met some 40 years ago at our local centres. As young boys, we had each other's backs; we moved unified, and in one accord.

Great youth workers such as Clovis Reid MBE helped to develop a community spirit amongst us. These centres showed us a new, positive way by opening doors in a society that was closing them. We were taught *we can* instead of *we can't*. Our youth clubs were an extension of our family homes, except we had more freedom there: in the youth clubs, you could be your own person. These environments offered me a place where my talents could grow and provided a little release from the discipline at home.

I remember one time my dad arriving at a youth club. He caught me playing pool when I should have been at home doing my chores. Not a good look. Time to 'have it on my toes', as they say in England, which means, *time to run!* Unfortunately, I had nowhere to hide. I knew then that I had another warm backside coming.

These were also the places in which I truly began to learn my craft, MCing at the weekly dances in the youth clubs and chatting lyrics to the young audiences. I started to save all the pocket money so I could to buy my own sound system, which I would call 'Tippa Graff'. This nickname combined a play on the word 'tipp', which was used to describe the end of a spliff, and 'graff', which was commonly used back then around sound systems, as in 'stereograph'. Soon, in partnership with my childhood brethren, Commander B and our friend Andrew Chung, I purchased a small system. Tippa Graff our Brixton sound system was formed in Commander B's flat in Kennington. Me and B grew up together, attended the same primary school, and later became neighbours in Helix Road. We both shared a love of reggae (in fact, all my friends shared the same feeling).

The MC's vocal skill challenge was to engage on the spot, with off-the-cuff creativity. Our sound competition was to perform without warning to any different beat, tune or rhythm that the selector would choose. So as an MC, I had to be original and spontaneous. I would make up lyrics and vibes as I went along, without pen or paper. I first learnt lyrically from Daddy U-Roy, leading me to develop my own original writing. I would perform by chatting my lyrics on the flip side of vinyl 45s. Prior to the days of CDs, vinyl records would feature the A side as a vocal mix and the B side as the instrumental. The instrumental side would be called 'the version'.

Know say reggae music have the African drum
and the heartbeat is the bass,
well the piano it a chop and the guitar it a rock
and the Congo drum na stop knock
Well, it comes from Jamaica
fresh from Yard and Toots and the Maytals bring go abroad
Mr Irie, a no fraud, mi na draw no card
Reggae music you know
it comes straight from the Lord
Well, the father a the one who create everything
He created the instrument born of the wind
and nothing but love reggae music a bring.
So Mr Horns Man keep on blowing.

Tippa Irie and the Far East Band, 'Horns Man Blow' from the LP *Stick to My Roots* (Lockdown Productions, 2010)

I would step up to the sound eagerly, seeking every opportunity to take the microphone in my hand. In my earliest performances I would move with the foundation sound systems like King Tubby's and Coxsone's. The local sound systems at the time who were bigging up the place were Sledgehammer, Small Axe, Jamdown Rockers, Taurus, I Spy, Mombasa, Saxon Sound, and Nasty Rockers. People would pour into the streets to attend dances featuring Tubby's and Coxsone, often creating a roadblock. Sir Lloyd's dances were also guaranteed to be packed-out house parties. Back in the day I was close with Mikey Dread, who was the brother of Cecil Rennie, the originator of the Brixton-based King Tubby's Hometown Hi-Fi. Mikey was one of the first to invite and welcome me into the sound system community. My cousins, the Whitley family, were also linked to Cecil. I began as a sound boy for Tubby's, stringing up the sound and giant speaker boxes.

Tubby's was also one of the first systems upon which I was invited to chat, expressing my new-born talent on the microphone. This offered me another training ground on yet another community platform. Tubby's were experts at cutting white-label dubs and versions to perform on. I took up the mic alongside selector Mikey Dread on his sound system Channel One Sound; Big Jiggs and Baby Jiggs were the selectors on King Tubby's. Some dances took place at the Cowley Community Centre. Cecil has been a resident of the Cowley Estate for many years. The experience of working alongside Tubby's enabled me to stretch my MC skills and I knew, one night soon, I would confidently take control of the mic. Tubby's became a well-established UK sound, starting London-wide and branching out across the country. Currently, every August, Tubby's has an annual place at the Notting Hill Carnival.

The origin of King Tubby's goes back to the early sound system history of Jamaica. Its founder was Osbourne Ruddock, who started performing in downtown Kingston. Ruddock was one of the original selectors on the island, playing ska, bluebeat, and rocksteady, and also experimenting later with early dub and roots reggae mixes and collaborating with the likes of studio mixing legends Lee Scratch Perry, Bunny Lee, and Prince Jammy. He later worked with famous labels such as Trojan Records.

The sound system family near and far was devasted to hear of Osbourne Ruddock's death in 1989. He was brutally gunned down just minutes from his home after a regular daily studio mixing session at Waterhouse Studios in Kingston. Father Tubby was only 48.

Cecil Rennie named his King Tubby's Hometown Hi-Fi out of admiration and respect for Osbourne Ruddock's original Tubby Sound System (Kingston Jamaica). Cecil has spent a life in the sound system culture. Here is his account of how it started:

> My name is Cecil Rennie, aka King Tubby. I was born in the parish of St Thomas, Jamaica, and raised by my elderly grandmother. As a youth I always had a love for music. As early as the age of 10, I would sneak out of my grandparents' house and listen to a local sound system, Lady Pat. This was one of the earliest on the island—a fusion of Jamaican and Chinese migrants. As well as other competing sound systems—Duke Reid, Count Shelly, and Fatman—I would listen to my favourite artists of the day, Prince Buster and Derrick Morgan. I loved versions and instrumentals that took me musically to a different space, with artists such as Johnny Moore.
>
> In 1968 I left Jamaica and arrived in Brixton, south London where I am still a resident today. At the age of 19 I was the youngest to build my own sound system, King Tubby's Hometown Hi-Fi. This title was out of respect for, and honouring, the original Tubby—Osbourne Ruddock. I appreciated Tubby's unique sound so much. This was part of our culture: a sound system from back home would

be remembered in this way by fans in the UK. That is why you have 'Coxsone' in Jamaica, and also in Brixton. Taurus, V Rocket, Duke Reid in the UK are all established as tributes to foundation sound systems from the island. My own King Tubby's has lasted 50 years—even longer than the founding sound—and I have worked with many famous producers such as Joe Gibbs.

I returned to Jamaica in 1974 and was moving with I-Roy and Bunny Lee. I went to see them perform at the National Stadium. Later, Bunny Lee introduced me to the legendary Osbourne Ruddock at King Tubby's studio. He was always pleasant and respectful towards me and invited me to watch him produce dubplates (back in the day we called dubplates 'soft wah').

Back home in Jamaica, my cousins lived at the bottom of Bull Bay in Kingston, 10 miles near the Bobo Shanti Rasta camp at a place called Windsor Lodge. Bob Marley was on the corner just across the way from my family. Bob was a humble man, loving his football; my own family would kick ball with the great legend. This was the early seventies.

Back in the early days I invited Dennis Brown, U-Roy, I-Roy, Sir Harry and Delroy Wilson to come on the mic. I also worked with Cornell Campbell and Clancy Eccles, who had a hit reggae song, 'Fattie, Fattie'. Most of the top reggae performers lived local to me, around south London, like Gregory Isaacs and Dennis Brown, and it was good-quality British reggae music that drew them to move here, because we created the greatest roots reggae. We opened the doors within the music industry from the UK; we promoted so many different styles from lovers' rock to roots reggae, from dancehall to dub. In the seventies in

London there were several good reggae sound systems: Sir Lloyd, Count Shelly, Neville the Musical Enchanter, Sir Fonso.

At my King Tubby's dances, I established party-blues vibes. The girls would come to our shows because they felt safe and protected. I had lots of female cousins that would come support my sound, so I had a duty to keep a lookout for them. My part was to play music that made people happy and dance. The most important part for a DJ and selector is to entertain the people to get up on their feet, good vibes and good, clean behaviour. Back in the day I managed a pub called The White Swan in Stockwell, opposite the Tube. It was a joy to see people leaving my dances after King Tubby's played at about 11 PM. I would see and hear the crowd singing the choruses of the reggae songs on the way home, in the streets. Such a great feeling. You don't have songs or dances anymore like that; you don't see that community connection nowadays. Things have changed.

The year 1982 was the first time I got to meet my little soldier, Tippa Irie. My junior brother Mikey Dread, who had his own sound system, introduced Tippa to me alongside his mates, fellow south London MCs General Slater and Daddy Rusty. I invited them to chat and took them on King Tubby's, giving them their first real exposure. I took them all under my wing and guided them. They were talented young guys who had good manners and principles.

At first, Tippa was following more of a Jamaican MC style, but I advised him to use his British vocal style to sing about things locally, that people could relate to. Sing and chat, write lyrics about what you know and where you come from, create a unique, authentic British MC style, be yourself. Don't follow anybody else, be true to yourself. At the time, most British reggae artists were singing, writing lyrics, and performing in a Jamaican style—but they were not from Jamaica, so it was copy music. Tippa Irie changed that. He brought British MC to the platform for the first time, and it was a hit with the crowd. I continued to make it my business to support good up-and-coming London reggae talent, offering my King Tubby's as their platform.

One August bank holiday, I took Tippa Irie and Slater to meet David Rodigan, who was playing at a south London club called Cat's Whiskers. I asked Rodigan to give them a turn on the mic. He asked me if they were good, and I replied, 'Of course they are good, otherwise I would not have brought them to you.' They were both given the opportunity, and they simply tore down the place. Rodigan gave them the thumbs-up. I could clearly see their talent, so I supported them, giving them a platform to become part of reggae's future.

One of my greatest and earliest memories of Tippa Irie is being King Tubby's leading MC in sound clashes with Jamdown Rockers. Tippa really done his training and his homework against Jamdown Rockers, leading MC champions. The battles were fierce and required plenty lyrical talent. King Tubby's on a Friday night at Vassal Road in Brixton was serious roadblock dancehall sessions. Tippa leading as an MC would be like a rottweiler glued lyrically to the mic; when he became hot with his delivery and lyrical talent, it would vex competing MCs.

Tippa Irie has had longevity because he makes good music, and he has a great presence and ability to entertain. His style is original, and he has a belief in himself as an artist. We are still good friends today, like family. He has a very humble spirit, not into any hype business. Tippa will never pass any man in the street. He has, from the beginning, had a deep belief in his own music, and strong faith where nothing and nobody can distract him from his destined musical path. This is why he is still holding his ground today.

And here, my good friend, old Brixton mate, pioneering drum and bass DJ, producer, and one of the greatest jungle DJs of all time, Jumpin' Jack Frost, provides his testimony about the UK dancehall clash times:

I was born and raised in Brixton. My parents are from the West Indies and Guyana. Back at home in our family house, music was always on the turntable: James Brown, Bunny Wailer, Bob Marley, Dennis Brown. Reggae, ska, funk, soul.

I was tall and big-framed for my age, so from 10 years old I would moody my way in to shebeens and blues parties. My uncle would carry me as a young boy to Bali Hai nightclub in Streatham. Jah Shaka was my first love as a sound system: booming bass and dubplates. I would break in through the back door, getting in free without a soul noticing, instead of trying to blag in front. I followed Shaka, Earth Rocker, all over. Loved it.

I lived in Vassal Road, Brixton. My neighbour was King Tubby's, the great selector Cecil. This was the first time I would set eyes on Tippa Irie, a local youth like me, a Brixtonite. King Tubby's held their dances at the Cowley Estate community centre. This was where Tippa Irie first grafted and manifested his MC chatting craft. Working as an MC or selector with your very first sound system was like your musical apprenticeship. Tippa first began by being a sound boy, carrying the boxes for Tubby's. It was a process. In the early sessions, our Brixton-sound King Tubby's was clashing another local sound champion. Tippa was the frontman MC for Tubby's on the night. To cut a long story short, the champion murdered King Tubby's that night. It was a big ting. People had travelled from all over. The dance was being recorded for a tape cassette, to later release the live clash. Well, as they say, you live and learn. It was a good lesson, as I witnessed Tippa returning to the drawing board. He practises his MC craft double hard, returning to the mic with a polished perfection. Tippa Irie had birthed, he had come of his time. All who had ears could hear. Tippa had become the mic controller: fast chat, storytelling, and humour. Sharp dancehall, reggae vibes. Tippa had delivered his style. He was smashing up the dances.

I found Tippa a great brother. Always willing to give people time. Judging no one. Happy to give you advice and always willing to reason on his best love… Music. We developed a long-lasting, tight friendship. I was part of the Irie family, always welcomed at the house, sleeping, eating, and chilling there. The family always gave love, and were accommodating. Great vibes from Mum and sister Jackie. I was really good friends with Avril, Tippa's younger sister, another top MC: Miss Irie.

The highlight of the dances was finding a woman to dance *with*— simply put, where the ladies were, the man dem would follow. At our blues parties, we would groove away till the early hours of the morning.

The female MCs of the dancehall breaking through at the time were New York's Lady English and Shelly Thunder. The Jamaica ladies were Lady Saw, Lady Mackerel, and Patra. From the UK you had Cinderella, Mumma Alle, Sister C, Lorna G, and my own little sister, Avril, who was following in my footsteps. I would be her ghost-writer as we bounced lyrics off one another. I knew from her beginnings that MC Miss Irie would become a force to be reckoned with.

One of the first real big people's dances that offered me a regular weekly platform was with south London's Sir Lloyd Sound System. As a teenager, it provided one of my first public exposures. This was the era of the bustling, private house parties that had good vibes—old and young, man and woman, all moving as one, on the dancefloor.

Along with the music, the fashion of the night was an essential part of the event. The guys wearing middle-pressed Farah slacks or heavy, thick corduroy trousers with a handkerchief folded and hanging out the pocket, rude boy style. Styling a Gabicci jumper featuring the *G* logo with diamond socks and matching tank tops. Leather bomber jackets, Kangol caps, wearing beavers (the tall, furry hats popularised by Rastas). I became famous for wearing my black leather, peaked cavalry hat with the two crossed-swords badge on front. Clarks shoes and desert boots worn proud on our feet, while Adidas sportswear started popping about on the street. Rest assured, we were dressed smart, but casual. Men finished off their style with a splash of Brut 33, as advertised by the old British boxing legend Henry Cooper.

You had to also have the right jewellery to complement your outfit. Reggae fans at dances would sport gold sovereign rings and thick gold Belcher chains. The ladies, smelling of Charlie perfume, wore modest below-the-knee dresses, silk blouses, long tartan kilts. The women had natural hairstyles: neatly maintained afros were cutting it back in the day. For the guys, either natty dreads, a regular shave down the local barbershop or the odd wet-look Jheri curl perm. This latter greased-down style never attracted me; I could never work out why a man would want it. My favourite barbershop was Ozzie's, in Ferndale Road, Brixton. Ozzie was always friendly, and we shared a love of cricket.

I would prepare my vocals prior to my shows by practising nightly, perfecting my lyrical skills to ensure I was on point. As an MC, you were required to be sharp; Afro-Caribbean crowds are famous for not being easy to please. So, you only had two choices: prepare to succeed, or prepare to fail. There being so much hot talent within the community, the competition was fierce. If you did not cut it as a dancehall artist, your performance would be quickly followed by boos and cussing from the audience. On failing to deliver, you would face public humiliation. As harsh as it may seem, this was how it was, and you best hastily hand over the microphone. I would confidently step on the mic like a soldier on the battlefield, bold as brass. In truth, your reputation would depend on it. After all, it was a dancehall *competition*. As I picked up the microphone, I always felt the anticipation of the audience, wondering what I was going to come with next. People in the audience would root for me, but people also wanted me to fail.

I would perform about four to six hours straight, on the mic from dusk till dawn, reaching the dancehall maybe at 11 PM and leaving at 6 AM with the birds in the trees whistling. This is how I lived. To be an MC you had to have lyrical stamina. The sound system decks were crowded, line after line of all shapes and sizes, shoulder to shoulder, side by side. To be serious about music, it must become part of your lifestyle; it is a day-and-night thing. Boxers use physical might to win their battles, but as MCs, we use words to clash on our battlefield. My job was to be versatile and entertaining, providing a lyrical challenge. Adding a sprinkle of ridicule, humour, wit, and sarcasm, taunting the next DJ: it was all part of the process of defeating the opposing sound system.

The working-class community in which I lived had its hard roads, with tough streets and gangs, but as youthful Brixtonites we were the new kids on the scene, the second generation classed as 'Black British'. We MCs saw it as our duty to share the joy and spread the love, so we made it our business that cussing and dissing competing performers would be in pure fun, merely for entertainment. The battle would still get red hot; but nothing serious was meant. To us young ones coming up, it was all in the name of dancehall.

Some of the long-standing foundation sounds would be vexed, as they could not take a loss of pride and reputation alongside the shame of losing; in some instances competing sounds would even get physical. Fortunately, we had people who would look after us. My sole purpose as MC was to generate positive vibes and togetherness, letting the good times flow.

Our MC style of cussing and raw talk on the mic originated from Jamaican street culture and humour. Back in Jamaica, for instance, if you looked slim, you were called 'maga dog'. People of the island use direct humour, ridiculing and joking at you, in ya face—that's just how it is. So, if you are fat, they call you that, and if you are skinny, they let you know also. Jamaicans are infamous for having a dialect of plain, straight-talking, with a bit of humour thrown in.

Being Brixton frontline youths, black, brown, yellow or white, from secondary school days we all smoked the 'green'. If you knew the right Rasta herbsman, three single pounds could purchase you some top-grade sensi. We would all gather around in our little group, having fun, chilling with lighter and Rizla in hand, smoking the finest Jamaican marijuana. In the reggae community, everyone was puffin' on a spliff. In my early dances, I would promote the use of herbs like I promoted reggae music, big bold and blatant. As Peter Tosh sang, 'legalise it!' This would be my chant in the eighties.

Many of our parents were blessed with large families and lots of sons, so there were plenty of men on the road, and all of us guys were drawn to sound system vibes. We were celebrating and continuing our parents' Jamaican traditions, playing and performing reggae. The sound system events provided us with a platform, independent of main-stream society. These same British who had rejected our abilities also rejected our music; therefore, ours was a DIY culture. Establishing our own music industry, our own studios, recording labels, distribution and marketing outlets, our reggae family was self-reliant and self-sponsored. We had to create our own network, 'cause no one else was going to do it for us. This lifestyle provided my bread and butter. Our sound system movement was, in reality, one of the first working-class Black businesses.

My childhood brethren and partner MC from King Tubby's Sound System General Slater talks of our times together performing in Brixton at the beginning of my exposure as an entertainer.

My name is General Slater I was born in Dulwich hospital, south London in 1966, the year England won the World Cup. I was brought up in a strict Christian Seventh Day Adventist household and at the age of three my mother took me to live in Jamaica, where I lived in the parish of Clarendon in an area called Rock River where I was brought up my aunt who was also a strong Christian. She attended Sunday church where I went along with her.

My first musical influences were Gospel music. In Jamaica church music is well lively and vibrant and I saw how music had the ability to move people. The first time I was exposed to any form of reggae music was when I witnessed my older sister skanking to the Horace Andy hit, 'Skylarking', I thought to myself this is great.

July 16th, 1975 at the age of nine, my family brought me back to Brixton to live. This is where I first met Tippa Irie. We immediately became close brethren and we shared our love for sports. Even though I was coming back to me place of birth, it was a total culture shock for me. I was speaking straight up Jamaican patois. Everyone around me found it strange, so I had to reintegrate myself.

We went to Loughborough primary school together

alongside Daddy Rusty, who later also became a Saxon MC. Tippa was top class and excelled at all sports, even getting picked for UK trials. Football, cricket, basketball and even he was a table tennis champion. I was ahead of my game in cricket, I even bowled out Graham Roope who at the time was opening batsman for Surrey and in fact the number fourth best batsman in the country. I had previously broken my arm back in Jamaica, it kind of became double jointed so I had developed a unique skill of high-speed bowling. As young boys growing up together me, Tippa and Rusty all we dreamed about was being professional sports men representing our country.

The first time I presented publicly my skill in performing on the mic was at our school assembly. After our fellow school pupils, the Harvey brothers sang the first opening song, as the new Jamaican kid on the block I readily jumped up and sang in my natural patois a rendition of a festival song, 'Play the music, Uncle Benji', to a roar of applause. I was aged nine.

From that point my musical interest grew and Tippa Irie, Commander B, Swify, Babby Face, Spunky, Rusty and Andrew Chong all local teenagers from Brixton formed our own sound system entitled, 'Tippa Graff'. I fell in love with the music. I developed my own name as General Slater which I had taken from the captain's name of the ship in an old black-and-white naval movie.

We practised and kept our sound in the basement at Tippa's family grocery store at East Lake Road. Tippa's Dad had his own sound system and his parents used the basement to put on shebeens parties. I recall one night I was asked by my mum to go at buy some paraffin from the shop and I crept in to listen to the big people's reggae music. Taking in the vibes, I must have forgot how long I was there, the next thing I knew my Mum appeared and licked me across the back with an umbrella. Our Caribbean parents were not easy back in the day, they required of us kids' strictness and niceness, nothing else was acceptable.

In our little sound system, we would play with Tippa's cousin's Gary Whitley's Sound from Acre Lane Brixton Sound. Mikey Dred 2, the name was in tribute to Cecil (King Tubby's') brother's own sound system Mikey Dred. We would play at Brixton Town Hall, the Abeng centre and Dick Shepherd Youth Club.

One thing many people would not know is that Tippa's first exposure to being an entertainer, was as a dancer, the don of the dancefloor. We would all create a circle and he would bust his moves inside the circle. Tippa was a chief skanker. They were great days with great memories.

We would attend local dances with sounds like Nasty Rockers, witnessing top 80s MC from the streets of Brixton like Fluxy Welton and Ricky Rankin. It was Beaver hats, Clarks shoes and tailored trousers with a rolled-up rag in your back pocket, dancehall style.

I would lead in encouraging us as MCs to rehearse on a weekly basis at Babby Giggs's (Choice FM) flat in Dog Kennel, Camberwell SE5. We would organize ourselves, practising verse and chorus, when and who should come in on what line of lyrics. As a team we were sharpening our vocal craft to perfection. I could not get a real angle on the cockney London chatting style so I used my Jamaican natural yard flow to complement our MC team.

Our teenage sound system Tippa Graff was visited by Cecil Renae who run King Tubby's Sound. Cecil was impressed by our vocal talents on the mic and asked, 'who are these two bad men on the mic?' That was me and Tippa. So, Cecil gave Tippa and I our first real break to play out in front of large audiences. We played out Vassal Road Brixton. Wessex House, Clapham Junction and the Abeng SW9. As MCs on the front line on King Tubby's Sound, we clashed local Sounds like Dred Diamonds, Jamdown Rockers and Stereograph. Together as teenage MCs Cecil and Tubbys took us up and down, all over travelling in the back of the removal van, in traditional sound system transportation.

The most significant memory I have of those days was when King Tubby's clashed Jamdown Rockers. There was tension in the place as the Jamdown MC led a lyrical violation, directly dissing Tippa and his family, parents and all. Tippa took it on the chin and replied back with lyrical retaliation and I drew mi ratchet, reminding the MC on the opposing Sound to mek sure they don't call my name in any disrespect. We went on to release our well-received live LP DSYC featuring me and Tippa on King Tubby's Sound, live at Dick Shepherds Youth Club released on Sir Lloyds record label.

The year 1983 and I was at the top of my MC game and also, I had an offer of a signing for England cricket team when my parents informed me that they were retiring and had built a family house in Jamaica. I was absolutely gutted and as I left on the plane to go, it felt like my dreams were shattered and my world had caved in around me. Both my musical and sports career ended. Our Jamaican parents were strict disciplinaries and they would have the final word. I was the youngest of the family out of my six sisters and two brothers. They did respect us doing music or sports, to their expectations, we should learn a trade.

When I reached Jamaica all around me were reggae Sound Systems and I was red hot and eager to get involved, I even got interest from Jamaican top producer but guess what my parents forbid me to partake in the sound system culture on the island, even my Jamaican cousins kept reminding me, General Slater who heard your LP you could be big out there. I returned back to England but I my talent on the mic as an MC felt frozen as I had not performed for two years. In 1984 Cecil once again thankfully approached me and I re-joined King Tubby's as an MC alongside Jubby Roye.

Tippa and Daddy Rusty, had joined Saxon and was big alongside the likes of Maxi Priest, Asha Senator, Papa Levi and Smiley Culture. I remember watching Papa Levi one night performing at a BBC event with David Rodigan as the selector when Papa Levi started spitting lyrics dissing the then PM Maggie Thatcher, Rodigan pulled the plugged, censoring him and preventing him from continuing to perform.

Saxon was an excellent team back in the 80s and the management was 100 percent behind all their artists, that is who gave all the artists their first taste of true professional careers. My experience with as an MC over the years, learning both from UK and Jamaica is that there is no true, real reggae industry that I have ever found, with no real investment in reggae artists and the creation of internet has changed everything. My advice is to set your own standards and don't look up to anybody apart from yourself. Seize the time, cause life is short. Be your own general and utilize all your skills and all outlets available. As reggae artist we always have too battle, cause to be recognised for what we deserve it's a constant struggle and fight.

* * *

In South Africa during the eighties the racist apartheid system ruled the nation. On my TV screen I witnessed images of Black people segregated, mixed marriages banned by law, whites-only cafés, homes, schools, and even toilets separated by race. I followed the struggle of African National Congress freedom fighters, their leader Nelson Mandela serving life imprisonment on Robben Island. We were also threatened with nuclear war, in opposition to which we had the Campaign for Nuclear Disarmament. In the United States, one-time Hollywood cowboy Ronald Reagan was the new President, always warning us of Soviet communism. Back home in Britain, Prime Minister Margaret Thatcher reigned from the beginning of the eighties, the start of the longest period of Conservative rule in the country's history. The 'Iron Lady' presented herself like the headmistress from Hell. In front of my eyes, the divide between rich and poor widened. At the start of the eighties, working-class people began to unite and protest as tensions went up and down inner-city streets. Stiff-upper-lip, British-bulldog institutionalized racism went hand in hand with poverty and high unemployment. It was not a great mix. As Black people we felt rejected, harassed, and marginalised within British society. Like petrol added to fire, the flames ignited between local communities and the police force.

Maggie Thatcher then introduced the 'sus' ('suspected person') law, a stop-and-search version of the Vagrancy Act of 1824. It gave the boys in blue greater powers of authority to stop people in the streets who were deemed to be loitering with intent. We were perfect targets, and the guinea pigs in the new inner-city policing experiment. Subsequent tensions led to riots after hundreds of young Black people were repeatedly stopped and searched by police across the UK. Those of us in the Black community who already felt isolated became further estranged after being singled out by racist police officers patrolling our

streets, searching us forced up against cars and walls and using bully-
ing and intimidation techniques, alongside the ridicule and racist jokes
directed towards us. The authorities began flexing their new powers,
collecting and profiling Brixton residents. This discrimination provided
regular evidence of racism to my mates and me. This was the culture
of police harassment that Smiley Culture wrote about in his song
'Police Officer', with the lyrics, 'Police officer, no give me producer.'

On January 18, 1981, the whole Black community was unified
in mourning after a racist arson attack that killed 13 Black people—
all under the age of 25. Now known in history as the 'New Cross
Fire', the tragic crime was followed by a mass public rally attended by
25,000 people from across London, marching together from Deptford
to Parliament Square. Placards were carried by people of all ages and
races, calling for the police to find the criminals responsible for the
deaths. The background to all this being high unemployment and a rise
in street crime, yet police continued to systematically target our Black
communities; an increase in racist attacks ensued. We were reminded
daily that our families were foreigners, not welcome even after having
been invited. It left a sour taste in our mouths, like being dressed to the
nines and then told in front of all your mates by a nightclub doorman
that you can't come in—simply because of your black face.

I was truly shocked *again* by the events of April 10, 1981. On
this Friday evening, police officers stopped and searched a cab driver
outside a local café under the sus laws; local men surrounded them,
and their anger spilled over until mobs of Black youths went to war,
engaging in pitched battles with the Met. Police wagons were turned
over and set ablaze in the streets surrounding my family home. Local
shops and businesses stood empty after they were looted and burnt out.
Even the Brixton Police Station was boldly attacked by angry mobs.

As a young boy, I was not part of these raging street battles that
swept across south-west London, but I could hear and see with my own
eyes the scenes left by the rioting. 'It's your time now!' was the echoing

chant rising from the vengeful rioters, directed towards the police. I remember the crackling flames and the smell of burnt-out derelict buildings as the Brixton uprising raged for three days. One morning I got out of bed and looked at all the debris littering the streets, the shops completely gutted, all from the frustration of a people pushed too far. It was reminiscent of the pictures of World War II I had seen in my secondary school history books. Overnight, *this* had become my own world. I thought to myself that, maybe, winds of change were blowing. Well, it could not get any worse, that's for sure.

The year 1981 brought a fierce catalogue of uprisings. Black people rose up in their numbers in St Pauls (Bristol), Chapeltown (Leeds), Handsworth (Birmingham), Moss Side (Manchester), and Toxteth (Liverpool). Closer to home, uprisings took place in Southall and Tottenham, too. These areas were home to working-class communities and, once again, the root cause was a combination of bad housing, high unemployment, and daily police oppression, racism, and prejudice.

My beloved Brixton became globally infamous. On TV, all I saw were newsflashes featuring my local streets. We now had the respect of the world. I was even told of a Black British prisoner, in a Jamaican prison for herb smuggling, who found he had a sort of 'prison protection passport' after he informed the hardened Kingston inmates that he was from Brixton, south London. The name 'Brixton' and our televised victories against Babylon made us renowned. All this was taking place on our very own turf.

As dancehall MCs we had a responsibility to convey messages on the mic about these current affairs, sharing what we were living and seeing daily with our very own eyes. *We* were the broadcasters talking to the crowd, spreading the word via our own 'independent news'.

* * *

In 1983, at age 17, my next big platform as an MC came when I was blessed by a phone call from Sir Lloyd, who invited me to record my first single as *Tippa Irie*. 'The Opposite' featured on his own label, LGR Records. I was over the moon, of course, but the invitation was as daunting as it was exciting. Icing the cake was the fact that Aswad was performing the instrumental track. The night before, I had been at a dance and hadn't slept much, so while in the studio's waiting area, I fell stone-cold asleep, snoring like a baby—only to be awakened by none other than members of Aswad, of 'Warrior Charge', 'African Children' and chart-smashing 'Shine' and 'Don't Turn Around' fame. Yeah, the mighty Aswad, live and direct! As a roots reggae band, they were the sharpest at the time in the UK, at the top of their game. I was humbled to have the best as my early mentors (if you want to catch the energy and vibe of this time, check out the 1980 film *Babylon*, featuring Aswad's lead singer Brinsley Forde). My first single as Tippa Irie was co-produced by Tony 'Gad' Robinson and the late Drummie Zeb. 'The Opposite' was the B-side; the A-side was a lovers' rock hit titled 'My Valentine', performed by Toakes.

On that evening in the studio I recorded 'The Opposite' on a 2-inch tape—analogue, not digital, recorded on a sound craft desk. I listened to the song a few times, adapting the lyrics to the rhythm, letting it flow spontaneously as it was woven into the tune. It was my time now, and I was taking my MC talents to another level.

Alongside my first release being played by the sound system family, I was thankful that radio DJ Tony Williams chose to play 'The Opposite' on his BBC show, *Reggae Rockers*, which aired on Sunday afternoons. In the early eighties, we British reggae performers were almost entirely ignored by mainstream radio and corporate stations. It was as if the voices of UK Black performers were silent, as if we did not exist. Our talent was forced underground. This gave rise to British pirate stations; we needed our own outlets.

In fact, British disc jockeys share a long history with pirate radio

This is the opposite, the opposite
Tippa Irie, a just a talk it, a talk it
Make mi tell you about the opposite, the
opposite
I just a talk it a talk it
The opposite to man is woman
the opposite to George is the dragon
Opposite to right must be wrong
The opposite to weak, it must be strong
The opposite to Tony Williams was David
Rodigan
In case you never know, I am the lyric Banton
You ask what me a chat, it's just chat style
and fashion
The lyrics out my mind like a computer
I don't sit down and write no lyrics on no
damn paper
If you do that, you're the pupil, not the
teacher.

Tippa Irie,
'The Opposite'/Toakes, 'My Valentine' from
the 12' single (LGR Records, 1983)

stations, which originated in 1964 with the activities of Radio Caroline. Like buccaneers, dedicated vinyl selectors such as Tony Blackburn formed illegal floating radio stations in offshore ships that sailed the cold, grey North Sea. In 1967, the government passed the Piracy Act, forbidding the use of underground, independent radio music transmissions. The enforcing body, the Radio Investigation Service, conducted dawn raids with plainclothes inspectors charging people with playing unlicenced music on British airwaves.

Back on land, large aerial antennas were erected in loft conversions on council estates and on high-rise blocks of flats, transmitting illegal radio waves on the FM frequency. DJs up and down the country established their own signals, blocking transmission pathways. These pirate stations were the only outlets I could tune into at night to catch the latest reggae tunes—as well as my own music. Pirate radio was established for the people, by the people. Pirate DJs and selectors risked having their equipment confiscated, hefty penalties, and imprisonment. The Department of Trade and Industry (DTI) worked in partnership with British Telecom to enforce the ban. The DTI received a mention in the lyrics of the classic reggae song 'Pirate's Anthem' performed by Shabba Ranks, Cocoa Tea, and Home T.

Very few prominent radio DJs offered weekly reggae slots: at the BBC, Tony Williams, John Peel, and Ranking Miss P's show *Culture Rock*; there was David Rodigan on Capital Radio and later, Kiss FM. The entire UK reggae community tuned into Rodigan's show, an international sound clash firing dancehall dubplates and competing against Jamaican selector Barry G.

Pirate radio became so powerful, reaching and attracting listeners in their thousands. Pirate stations, including our underground reggae stations, were eventually offered licences. The result: Choice FM, Vibes FM, Kiss FM, JBC, Lightning Radio, Powerjam, Solar Radio, Dream FM, Sunshine Radio, Horizon Radio, LWR. Many of the stations we tune into today had their origins in illegal pirate radio. I supported

RJR London, Powerjam, Rock 2 Rock, Vibes FM, Lightning Radio, and PCRL from Birmingham. Back in the day, I did a radio show on RJR, as well as lots of interviews as an artist on pirate stations. I also presented my own show on Vibes FM on Mondays, promoting UK artists. To function within the pirate radio community, you had to keep it on the downlow, due to the risk of getting caught by the authorities and stuck with a criminal record. So many people have had to make sacrifices, fighting for our right to party.

Here, DJ and producer Sir Lloyd talks of his house parties and dancehall experience, and how he went about changing the fact that there were very few outlets for Black British artists in the day:

I was brought up in a Jamaican household. My parents would hold house parties. Mr Wilson, Mr Henry, and Mr So-and-So would arrive, in freshly pressed shirts and trousers with a bottle of strong drink in their hands, ready to party. They worked hard all week, and now weekend come—ready to boogie. I started to spin vinyl as a DJ-come-selector from the age of six, no joke—I had an ear for music and a love and passion for reggae in all its forms and styles.

In later life, I was influenced by Tappa Zukie, Augustus Pablo, and was mad in love with roots rockers and other musical flavours. In 1976, I went on to form live bands with schoolmates, which led to the formation of my first Brixton-based sound system, Raiders, going back to my talent and love of being a selector and getting the party vibes blazing—that was my culture. Finally, after several name changes, I settled on 'Sir Lloyd', an SW9 original sound system, 1978. We rocked it alongside the best sounds around town, I Spy, Stereograph, DY…

I started in three-room house parties. The crowds would

come from far and wide to catch the good vibes of Sir Lloyd, party and spread love around. Positive love is what I wanted to happen at my dances. What you have to realize is that, from early on, within music—radio, record stores, even grassroots sound systems—we would not be featured as Black British talent. Trust me, there was enough of it everywhere holding us back, with no one willing to establish an outlet for the artists.

I had a little personal money saved, so, I put my money where my mouth was and decided to be that platform, creating a live platform where the Brixton talent could flow. Sir Lloyd's dances would be the first. The first of the local talent included Commander B, General Slater, and Tippa Irie. This was back in 1982. These slim young teenagers arrived, like schoolboys. Nothing of 'em, tiny youths, but when they stepped onto the mic, they created a whirlwind, a unique creative storm at my parties.

I could not believe my ears: the speed, the lyrical talent, flow and self-confidence. They had a unique, Black British MC style, and they nailed it. The next platform I offered was an eight-inch reel-to-reel tape system to record the live dances. What drove us was the creative individual talent, the energy, the sheer love of the music vibes. Not the fame or the money: the pure love of reggae music. Sir Lloyd, yes, I mixed all types of music—soul, funk, reggae, and early hip-hop. Females were also drawn to the sound.

This process went on to land one of my live recordings from Dick Sheppard School, featuring Number 2 on the UK reggae charts in 1983. That same year, the Number 1 slot was Bob Marley's 'Buffalo Soldier', and no one could beat that. I thought to myself, 'I can settle for a Number 2 place when the King of Reggae was my only competition!'

NME included these Dick Sheppard recordings in its 'Top 100 Reggae LPs of the 80s'.

I developed my own independent reggae labels, Raiders and LGR—this next level of exposure would cement Black British talent in the minds of the public. I liken this part of the journey to our parents' struggle when they came to this country: they were refused housing, rented or mortgaged, so the elders used the pardner system. The music industry was the same back in the day; we as Black people would have to build our own music labels and create our own dances. For all our hard-working talent, we were not recognised by the regular music industry. That door was firmly closed. I took many artists into the studio for their very first time: Lorna Gee, DJ Suga B. I went on to put out MC Horseman's 'The Horse Move', and worked with Peter Hunnigale, Dee-Roy, and Peter King.

Networking in those days was not so easy, like today; back in our day we had word of mouth, or phoning a musician from a 2p London red public phone box. The person on the other end would have to have a house phone. Our love for the vibes required patience, dedication, and commitment for the pure love of it, not for ego, fame, and fortune. Music was our life, day in, day out.

I witnessed local, young, talented MC Tippa Irie mash up a Dick Sheppard dance. He had a powerful ability to get the crowd fired up, everyone shouting 'Gwaan, gwaan, gwaan!', stamping and chanting before Mr Irie, who would take up the mic and drop his unique style and pattern. In 1983, I offered Tippa his first recording opportunity on LGR, featuring his tune 'The Opposite' on the flip side of a double vinyl. At the time I was working with Aswad; the guys would perform the live backing tracks to the artists on my label. It was a pure house of Black British up-and-coming talent.

UK dancehall culture started in the house parties, formerly called 'blues parties'. Next, the audiences and events moved to our youth and community centres, south London venues—Norwood Hall, Knight's Hill, Battersea, The Providence—along with various town halls. Then we started performing in larger halls and bigger venues, such as outside summer vibes. Sir Lloyd was smashing the Notting Hill Carnival.

Tippa Irie had such a humble, kind, welcoming, sociable, and friendly character. To be around him, he oozed good vibes. On the mic as an MC, people were drawn to his bubbly, fun-loving spirit, 100 percent. Possessing the gift of the gab, Tippa had the power to draw and mash up a crowd. From 1984, I was overjoyed to see south London Black British talent killing it, all over the globe. I will always be thankful for being a part of that movement which was never to be seen again. Levi Roots bust it, Tippa Rankin, Daddy Colonel, and Tippa Irie. Maxi Priest, Aswad, and Peter Hunnigale. Acts and performers no one would turn a blind eye to now, having signings and distribution with the major labels. Everyone started to eat, for a change.

Let us not forget it was Tippa Irie and his London style of MCing that would pave the way for the likes of UK hip-hop, junglist, and grime. Yes, UK Black history, running tings. Today, I am still working on music projects, working in London and Jamaica, on the radio, promoting new performers, working with the likes of foundation reggae artists Sly and Robbie.

* * *

Time to back it up a bit. To set the record straight, the conclusion to my schooling came when I left without taking a single examination. I was offered a cash-in-hand, full-time labouring job as an apprentice, and I was off out the gates without any academic qualification to my name. At the ripe age of 16, I was grafting, doing a man's work on London building sites, knocking up three-in-one cement as a young labourer. It was hard work, filling up buckets, carrying heavy bags of cement all day long. My day would begin at 6 AM. In winter during the early eighties you would have to do battle with snow. We would all huddle around the fire at the worksite, warming our freezing cold overalls against the flames.

I was offered my first apprenticeship as a plasterer by an elder, Mr Joseph Folks. In fact, Mr Folks was having a relationship with my mum at the time, after my dad had gone back home to Jamaica, to Trelawny. I was earning a £26 weekly wage.

Within the first month I was entrusted with my very first private job. I finished it, locked up, and whistled along the street after a hard day's work well done. The problem occurred in the early hours of the next morning, when Mr Folks informed me that I had been sacked; he said I was a good, hard-working lad, but that he had, 'no choice but to fire me.'

Here's what happened: while labouring, I took every opportunity to play reggae on my cassette recorder, chatting and toasting along. I found it quite relaxing and therapeutic, but I would be slightly distracted by lyrics flowing through my head. Hence, I failed to turn the upstairs bath taps off after plastering, and the entire house flooded from the upstairs. The ceiling had soaked through to the electrics, mashing up the carpets and the lino. Mr Folks had to fit the bill to repair the damage. So, my relationship with the building trade ended abruptly, and my wage packets ceased.

My mum was not happy at all—she had convinced Mr Folks to give me the opportunity. She was also concerned that I was going to sit down loafing. Maybe some would call it destiny, but now it was music that would become my new trade. Reggae would make me the income with which I would eat and pay rent. I was determined, focused on making music my career. I soon put my building career behind me and my faith in front. It was always a struggle against the odds for us working class Black youth, a background of riots and gang conflicts. They said that we was to come nothing, I am very thankful against the odds that I managed to become something against the backdrop of discrimination I faced.

Honour pon top of honour, goes out to Mamma
Mamma make the DJ rise up the ladder
She said don't worship vanity, don't worship glamour
Put your shoulder to the wheel, be tough like a hammer
If you're a plumber or you use a spanner, no matter what you do
you have to strive to do better, learn about your art
and learn it to the letter and I know things will be better
If you are wondering why I wrote this tune 'Badda, Badda'
because Mamma would always 'badda badda' Daddy Tippa
Mum would say, 'Why you want fi sit down and write dem lyrics for?'
'Why don't you be a lawyer or doctor?'
But I know that was not what I was cut out for
when I heard, Daddy U-Roy and Dillinger
I knew straight away Tippa wanna be an entertainer
make it worse when the Tippa heard Lone Ranger.

Tippa Irie, 'Badda Badda' from the LP *Talk the Truth!* (Lockdown Productions, 2007)

Chapter Three

Saxon-International

IT ALL BEGAN ONE NIGHT IN 1983. I WAS 18 AT THE
time. After I won an MC youth talent competition at Ferndale
Community Sports Centre, I was approached by Dennis Rowe and Lloyd
Francis *aka* Musclehead, who had witnessed my performance. They
invited me straight out to join their sound. I enquired as to the name
and its location. 'Saxon Sound System,' they both replied. 'Lewisham.'

At first I was hesitant. Back in those days, sound system allegiance
was like postcode gangs—you were glued to them as a form of local
loyalty. If you were born and bred in Brixton, then naturally you would
support Brixton sound systems. At this time, I was getting paid as an MC
by King Tubby's—a fee of about £3 per dance. Saxon Sound System
offered me £10 per night, and that was a good amount back in the eighties. So, I crossed over into south-east London, not-so-familiar territory.

Off I went, leaving the safety of Brixton. Even though you're only
talking a 30-minute bus ride, I would still be viewed as 'crossing over the
border'. As a young boy, I always had faith in my own abilities, trusting
wholeheartedly that my music and talent would speak for themselves.
The public would be the judges of that. As an up-and-coming MC, I
was always ready, letting my lyrics lead me.

The mighty Saxon Sound System's roots went back to 1974. The
sound possessed a formidable array of local reggae performers, MCs,
rappers, and singers all sharing the same platform. The selector played
a versatile, hot selection of handpicked vinyl and an array of specials,

which came in the shape of unique, tailor-made Saxon dubplates. Saxon played tunes ranging from early hip-hop, soul, lovers' rock, roots rock, and dub, moving on to dancehall and bashment. It offered me countless opportunities. For me as a young entertainer, Saxon was to south London what Motown was to Detroit. It was our own movement; and we as one team shared parts in it. Saxon was an independent, successful Black UK enterprise, promoting and marketing British reggae talent, and our sound was one of a kind. The requirements to join the sound as an artist were original skill, hard work, and teamwork. And at the end of the day, we all played our equal parts.

The founding members of Saxon Sound System were Dennis and Owen Rowe. Lloyd, Bill Nathan, Curtis Henry, and Michael Rennie. These pioneering soundmen, prior to Saxon days, were influenced by an earlier London sound system called Imperial Rockers. Dennis developed his craft as a sound boy for the Rastafarian dub champion Jah Shaka. Dennis still proclaims that there was no UK sound like the legendary Jah Shaka.

The Saxon crew included the likes of 'Mini Muscle', Musclehead's brother. Bung Belly Bailey and Jackson were our security. Our van driver, taking us around the country, was Mickey *aka* Wurzel. Mikey Boops used to mix us down while we were performing, and the great Trevor Sax—one of the finest selectors to ever live—could hold his own on the mic with any opposing sound.

Henry Prento was the operator; he would EQ the preamp to make sure the sound was right, and even out and sharpen the sound by balancing the speakers. His brother Chuckie was another member of our crew, along with Paul Rowe, and Owen and Junior, Dennis's two brothers, and his cheeky older sister Faye (I had a crush on Faye, but she never knew). They all played essential parts in the Saxon movement. Nor can I leave out the Saxon box boys, even though we all chipped in as box boys, really. We had a wonderful crew, moving our speakers and equipment, travelling to all manner of destinations to assist the setting up of Saxon, week in week out till the early hours: Junior Speng, Dopson, Eric Wishbone, Glen, Devon *aka* Negus Warrior, Yellow, Reidy, Sleepy, Bird Face, Bullet, Mackie, Maxine, Squidly, GGW, Oliver, Fari, Fidler, PT, Stephen, Derek, Big Ian, Skelly, and Yardie. This is how deep Saxon ran as a collective unit, from the founders to the artists or the box boys—everyone was equally valued and respected. As you can see by the list of names, we had an army of soundmen around us. People are drawn by success, and because they could see we were on the rise, they wanted to be part of it, so they supported Saxon and had our backs in every situation, good or bad. A lot of the work the men put in was voluntary; they were not paid, they just wanted to be part of something that was blowing up.

One of the first gigs that I had took me up to the north of England. I had already been up north back in the day with King Tubby's, why I would never forget that day. It was also the first time I had ever came home from a gig and emptied my stomach, due to a bit too much weed and alcohol, on returning from Wolverhampton. There was a sound system from Wolverhampton called Skippy and Lippy that booked me and Papa Levi for a gig, came to pick us up and drove us both all the way to the Midlands. At that time I lived in Streatham south London. I looked out of my bedroom window and I saw a transit van pulling up. I was buzzing, I ran down the stairs to greet them, about three people in total, and all I could see was a cloud of smoke coming out of the van. Levi was on board and they had already started burning weed from the moment he got into the van.

I sat down next to Levi and heard about was what happening later. On the way they decided I needed a name. Dipstick was the nickname Levi gave me, as I used to have a girl for every day of the week. Everybody in the van was blazing, so as they say, can't beat them join them. By the time I got to the Midlands I was smashed and stoned arriving in the dance. I don't know how I remembered my lyrics but somehow, I did. The whole show was a blur and the guys were party animals, they continued filling me up with drink and the spliffs just kept flowing in. The budget was not so big, so in turn for performing in those days, keeping you fed, watered and boarded was equal compensation. Plus, I was having the time of my life and was happy to be in front of the crowds, money or no money. Once we finished performing, they drove us back down to London and yes, you guessed it, they had us on a roll again. I myself, had two big ones on the way back, chilling in the back of the van. When the van pulled up at my house, I thought I was okay. I got out a little shaky but still, I thought I could walk up the stairs, which I did manage to do, but as soon as I tried to put the key in the front door, I could feel this wave of nausea, coming stronger and heavier. My instinct was to panic, and I turned this way and that, looking around for what I did not know. Then I just vomited everywhere, on my best clothes, in public, on my front door, all, over the landing of the flats. I felt humiliated. I tried to get back down the stairs, but it was too late. I said to myself I'm never smoking and drinking again but that was a lie. So next week same again, back on the herb and liquor. One thing, it taught me to realise my limit and know when it's best for me to stop.

I began as a box boy for King Tubby's sound system. The job of a sound system box boy was to rig up the system, first transferring the equipment to the van, then taking it to the location several hours before the dance, setting up and unloading the equipment at the venue, lifting the speaker boxes and moving the wiring connections, amps, and endless vinyl record collections. Then, once the dance finished in the early hours of the morning, the same process would repeat back to the starting point; then the sound guys could return home to catch a few hours' kip.

Those were really fun times, pure jokes, vibes, and banter. You had to be sharp or else everybody would be laughing at you. I would arrive at the lock up and load the boxes from out of the garage into the sound van. We would pack them all in the back of the van then we would climb into the back with them, as many of us that could fit, and try to find ourselves a comfortable spot where we could jam, for in some cases many hours as the van drove down the motorways, highways and byways until we reached our destination. Packed tight it wasn't so much of a worry about anything falling on you, but good luck if you needed to go toilet once we were on the road. You would bang the side of the van and hope that the management and driver would or could stop somewhere. There were not many service stations in those days, so it was best before you got in the van, to make sure you had gone to the toilet. When we finally arrived at the venue, driven solely on collective and focused team work and especially if it was a long journey travelling up north to Leeds or Manchester, most of the time it was a mixture of relief and excitement. Relief to arrive there safe, in one piece and excitement for the show we knew we were going to be seeing or performing..

We would take time loading the sound into the venue. Typically, it was community centres and town halls we would play in the early days. Once the sound was in the space, we would find the appropriate corner to place and set up the speaker boxes, then we would have to run the speaker wires to every individual speaker. Each one would know the job description and what they individually had to do. Once the boxes were in and the wires were run then it would be handed over to the engineers to set up the sound. In those days we had valve amplifiers to drive the base mid-range and tweeters, the top section, driven by a preamp and using the EQ for the finishing touches of putting up the sound system. Once it was all set up the first record would go onto the turntable. Finally, we would walk round the dance to see and inspect how it sounded, we would monitor each box to make sure all of the speakers were playing and everything was rolling and sounded nice then the box boy job is done, hard work ended and now it's was time to party.

I am Daddy Tippa, I am a lyric maker from England, not Jamaica

I am a lyric Banton, lyric computer, can nice up any area

Gonna change to the counteraction, bring a different fashion

On the mic I am an MC, you know I am not a singer

I am a headmaster; you know I am not a teacher

I come to take over. Any MC mess with Tippa, you know their days are over

I do not check for loafers, cause loafers they are jokers

So, people get together, no matter your colour.

My name is Daddy Tippa and Colonel is my brother

Levi is my companion. The three of us, wise men and we all chat for Saxon.

We never gonna look back, the top is our destination

We are in a high position we control the whole of England

When we ride the version, people, get satisfaction

We entertain dancehall fans, in the country and the whole of London

Saxon is from Lewisham, Tippa, rest in Streatham,

Colonel rest in Clapham, Rusty rest in Brixton

We chat to perfection and a lot of education

Yeah, I am a lyric maker from England, not Jamaica.

Tippa Irie, 'Lyric Maker' from the LP *Is It Really Happening to Me* (UK Bubblers (Greensleeves Records), 1986)

* * *

The most important person in our crew was Mrs Rowe, Dennis's mother, who lived in Overcliffe Road in Lewisham. Mrs Rowe welcomed us all into her family home. She reminded me of my own mother: hard-working, God-fearing, caring, positive. A disciplined Jamaican woman. She was an absolute gem and put up with all of us congregating and making noise, chatting lyrics upstairs and downstairs in her house. I think she really enjoyed the buzz of it all. In fact, Saxon Sound System would not have been a success without her support. What a wonderful woman: may she rest in peace.

I have so many stories and memories with Saxon that three books wouldn't hold the details of all our good times on the road. I am very thankful for those days we all shared. In the beginning of my journey with Saxon, I would bring along my best friend from back in my school days, MC Daddy Rusty. Daddy Colonel was from Clapham, and one of Dennis's cousins. Daddy Sandy at the time was living in Lewisham, deejaying with a sound system called Sledgehammer. I was also joined by Papa Levi and Colonel—we were like the Three Musketeers (the crowds nicknamed us the 'Three Wise Men'). We were inseparable. Of the two Saxon female MCs one was sister C, my little girlfriend (we had some fun, me and that girl, I will just leave that to the imagination). The other was MC Miss Irie. I was so proud to see my sister Avril—it was great to witness my own flesh and blood performing alongside me. MC Miss Irie brought a different, female energy to the Saxon crew, breaking through a dancehall environment that was traditionally male-dominated; even back in the eighties MC Miss Irie was questioning female stereotypes.

In my song 'Lyric Maker' I highlight how, in the Saxon days, we operated as one unit, one creative family.

Saxon was another extension of the wider family of my own

community, playing the same role in my life that my youth-club mentors had once done. It was a home away from home. The Saxon movement shared the same principles I was raised with. The founders knew how to survive, how to hustle on the streets, just like my dad hustled in the marketplace. The Saxon entrepreneurs used music to make their income, among other things.

The sound system provided a level of employment, and I was offered a free creative platform for which I was truly grateful. I recall my first meeting with the Saxon family at the Lewisham Boys' Club. I immediately took in the crew's vibes. It was a unique atmosphere, and the talent and competition were fierce—dancehall talent, full to the brim with strictly British energy. As performers we took to the mic like a pack of hungry wolves. The original artist at this time was MC Peter King, the originator of fast chat, UK-style. There was Papa Levi, famous for his hit tune 'Mi God, Mi King', and Smiley Culture with 'Cockney Translation'. Asher Senator would join us (but not so regularly), as would Deadly Ranks, Simeon, Dezey Kojak, Dirty Dessie and Roger Robin, Mickey Mclean, Waterhouse, Sugar Merchant, Stout, and DJ Reuben *aka* Pinky Lou, all complemented by the melodic vocal talent of Maxi Priest. Colonel, Rusty, Sandy and me. We all brought something different to the table.

Ideas would flow between us. One would come with the cockney banter, or Peter King would do his double-time, original fast style. Others would develop vocal, rolling melodic hook lines. Apart from competition, versatility was the name of the game. Together as Saxon, always eager to widen our abilities, we learnt different styles from one another and mixed and blended them. I would chat on the mic, hour upon hour, flowing nonstop so I would always have something different ready and up my sleeve in competition. As MC, my role was introducing and gluing the artists together, keeping the vibes flowing, passing one mic to another.

I developed a unique tone and pitch and had a natural ability to

Lord have mercy, mercy, mercy
It's Tippa Irie in the party, party, party
Every posse, come follow me, follow me,
follow me
If you are Saxon fan, lick shot for mi, you
betta lick shot for mi
[Here the crowd would repeat:] Lick shot for
mi, you betta lick shot for mi

If you have reggae music in your mind and
soul, then: lick shot for mi.

'Lick Shot for Me'
(12' B-side, GT's Records, 1988)

keep the melody while maintaining a clear focus and direction. I had experience MCing over all types of reggae and had a love of all good music—so I kept an open mind and open ears, staying versatile. I had already gained a reputation on the streets for orchestrating dancehall crowds into a frenzy, and was motivated to interact with the audience and get a reaction. Call and repeat, using a chorus or a hook line as the crowd responded, repeating after me in turn. Below, for example, are lyrics from my song 'Lick Shot for Mi':

> *If you are Saxon fan, lick shot for mi, you betta lick shot for mi*
> [Here the crowd would repeat:] *Lick shot for mi, you betta lick shot for mi*

'Beverley' is another example of call-and-repeat, drawing on the crowd's participation:

> *Beverley—Beverley—Beverley* [Here the crowd would repeat after me]
> *Mi tek a little trip go a St Mary*
> *I buck up pon a gal by the name of Beverley.*

At the beginning of my musical career, I was on a journey parallel to the British reggae band UB40. Below, my long-time mate Ali Campbell of UB40 talks about his experience of Saxon:

> Coming from Birmingham, I would take in the local sounds: Quaker City, Duke Alloy, Jungleman, and Studio One alongside the great Jah Shaka, and great local clubs like the Lime Grove. I first came across the dancehall talent of Tippa Irie through the Saxon Sound System. Tippa, Smiley Culture, Maxi Priest, and a whole collection

Beverley—Beverley—Beverley [Here the crowd would repeat after me]
Mi tek a little trip go a St Mary
I buck up pon a gal by the name of Beverley.
She said, 'Hi, dear darling, hi, dear honey,
I hear say you name is Tippa Irie
an inna England you have a bag of money'
She hear say mi name was Anthony
She say what year me born? Nineteen sixty-three
I was surprised, what she knew about mi
All the questions she answered about mi
She know say mi daddy live a-Trelawny
She know say the Tippa had one pickney
She know say mi sister name Miss Irie
She know say a-five inna mi family
Beverley, she want mi 'cause mi a VIP
She asked, where's mi jewellery
I told her I don't deal with vanity
But one thing, Beverley, she never knew about mi
Mi na like girls who come eggs-up pon mi
an beggy-beggy grabby-grabby yammy-yammy licky-licky
Beverley—Beverley—yes, Beverley [Here the crowd would repeat after me].

(from the LP *A-Me-Dis* (IRS Records, 1989)

of deejays—Saxon was coming like the school of reggae talent, representing London.

Tippa Irie and Smiley were so welcoming and warm, such friendly guys, and the way Saxon represented themselves was inviting and non-threatening. We would go to see them and they would travel up to us, supporting each other within the British reggae family. These times were unique. I was so proud of UK artists for what they had achieved, with their national chart success, Smiley Culture with 'Police Officer' and Maxi Priest with 'Close to Me', Tippa Irie on Top of the Pops with 'Hello Darling' and Aswad with their Number 1 chart hit 'Don't Turn Around'.

In the early days, none of us were searching for fame and glory; we just loved that sweet reggae music. Entertaining the crowd was my joy, such a natural buzz. At a time when reggae artists were holding tightly to their own personal style, we as Saxon MCs prided ourselves on establishing something very different: we operated as a collective, with an each-one-can-teach-one mentality. Staying united, sharing our musical abilities amongst us, we reflected our British experience, our own culture and I would convey that to the crowd.

We coined our own catchphrases. 'Lickwood' meant 'rewind', and 'gunshot' meant 'forward'. They were our creation, direct from the Saxon camp. We had so much lyric in a song as MCs, we kept on going. As British entertainers, we made reference to our youthful influences around us, especially drawing on the British television fodder that also reflected the wider world. We had tunes weaving in the theme of the American TV western *Bonanza*, and we also had a rap about good old *Rupert the Bear* from the very British children's television show based on the original comic strip. We had grown up with these things, so we talked about them in our music, about anything we saw on the news, about daily life or what we had experienced.

* * *

There was no internet or social media back in my youthful days; I would play my part taking to the streets, handing out Saxon flyers, inviting one and all to our dances and sound clashes. Flyers delivered by hand to barbershops, bookies, pubs, and clubs: from this legwork we all reaped the benefit as Saxon dances become fatter and fuller. We would play out five nights a week at the height of Saxon's eighties reign. Our popularity was centrally built, through the distribution and sale on the streets of live TDK C60 and C90 cassettes, tape recordings of sound clashes—old school. In terms of marketing, Saxon's success was made up of a combination of activities: the flyers, the live dance-hall tape recordings, and having our dances advertised on pirate radio stations.

If Lloyd and Dennis had been more 'in the know', they would have kept closer control on the Saxon cassettes and their distribution; from a copyright/business point of view, if the cassettes had been recorded after the sessions and immediately and securely distributed through our own Saxon outlets and networks, we could have made a fortune. Hindsight is a wonderful thing, but we were all young and still learning as we went along, and we were working-class people who did not go to posh universities to learn about how to make and keep money. At the end of the day, the overriding factor was that having those sessions on cassette, bootlegged up and down the country, still gave us the expo-sure that created the name and recognition.

I have likened Saxon to Motown. Dennis and Musclehead ran a tight show, always encouraging you as a new artist to step up, proudly and confidently, and develop your own British style. They supported me and encouraged me to work nonstop, sharpening my dancehall talent. They protected us, like our elders in the game. Money upfront, paying cash

Hail up mi brethren—Peter King
Him the one who started
the double time up the ting
Speed up the talking, speed up the rhythm
and everybody just follow behind
That how we did it in the Eighties.

Mungo's Hi-Fi, feat. Marina P, Tippa Irie, and Dennis Alcapone 'And the Beat goes SKA!' from the LP *Soul Radio* by Mungo's Hi-Fi and Marina P (Scotch Bonnet Records, 2020) in hand, always on time. After a dance, Musclehead would famously open your hand and scrunch a bunch of notes into your palm. These two guys made Saxon an organised business, not a street hustle. The management invested in the sound progression. Musclehead produced first-class, high-quality dubplates. Then Saxon moved onto a different level, forming its own record label, Saxon Studio International, and releasing hits by artists such as Dennis Brown, Lloyd Brown, and Peter Hunnigale.

There were a lot of well-known people associated with Saxon. Maxi Priest was one. I first met him as part of the Saxon family and we have been brethren ever since. Below, Maxi speaks of the sounds system's beginnings, and of his own connection:

> I moved and grew with Saxon Sound System back from school days in Lewisham; I went to school with Saxon. All of us together, brethren, true bona fide family. In those times, Black people were tight. We walked everywhere in groups of fives: protection in numbers. The streets were rough... racism was rough. It was on another level. White people would drive their cars up on the pavement to clip you.
>
> The police? Stop and search. Lewisham uprisings. This was our history as young Black boys on the road. Black people moved in oneness.
>
> Dennis, me, Musclehead—schoolfriends, classes, schoolwork, that was us. Me, Musclehead, all up in the football ting, five-a-side. Spar. Saxon and me, it began as a Lewisham family affair. Saxon was a sound system coming like a school, a training ground with serious apprentices. On Saxon we all brought a new flavour, something new. I brought some original synergy; I would sing over the

versions spinning on the turntable. The crowd hooked in and boom, boom, bam.

Yes, Saxon was one family that grew up from the same root. We shared good times and hardships together. Musclehead and me, juggling, selling a bit of weed to sponsor the growth of the sound. Pure commitment to Saxon's growth and nurturing.

My brethren Smiley Culture and I started putting out the sound. Man, have fi get paid for our works. At the time we were juggling on the building sites, grafting hard. Alongside performing with Saxon. I had pickney to feed and girl, all bout the place. Dem times. So, money had to run, a living reality. I wanted to take performers and the sound to proper rewarded for all-out talent. At the time, man would say they were strictly sound MC performers.

Smiley was on the very same mission, business-wise, and intuitive. We were both driven by progression and positivity. Tippa Irie also, we had a common objective: we wanted to get somewhere. We would do live PA performances at smaller venues from the Hilltop to the All-Nations club. Maybe back in the day for fees up to £1,000 cash, per show.

Back in the eighties, I formed my own independent label, Level Vibes Records, a joint venture with my spar Barry Boom. I was responsible for putting out 'Mi God, Mi King' as a vinyl release. I can recall going to Papa Levi flat. I believe he was residing in Woolwich at the time. I actually woke him up, out of his bed on the day of the studio session. Island Records became interested, a made a deal with us.

The original Saxon MC, Peter King, was again part of our family. Peter grew up inna mi hand. Tight, close brethrens, all of we.

My vision was to take Saxon to a recording level, as one, unified unit. We all commanded very special talent. Saxon became big 'bout town. Everybody who was a performer, a player, was drawn to Saxon Studio. From Jamaica, Billy Boyo, Yellowman, a whole heap of performers. We all had trod a similar path, a similar road of cultural circumstances. As Black people in London, we were radical and opposed to injustice. And we were all students of dancehall—our first love.

The buzzing sales of the Saxon cassettes capturing the energy of our live recordings successfully transferred to studio vinyl. Dennis was skilful networking as an entrepreneur, going on to create one of the first live sound system events produced on vinyl in the world. Bringing the raw, lively, authentic sound of dancehall, marketed as a UK reggae LP, was yet another unique Saxon move for the times. Sir Lloyd was another of the original soundmen who put live sound system events onto vinyl.

As MCs on the night, the five of us would gather together, lined up around the turntable, each taking control of the mic. It was a whirlwind reaction from the awaiting audience, cheering, clapping, and giving us full respect. 'The Famous Five', that was us: Tippa Irie, Colonel, Daddy Rusty, and Daddy Sandy, alongside squadron leader Papa Levi. It was pure niceness all round. We maintained the art of surprise: the crowd never know what to expect from the Saxon MCs.

Musclehead invested a lot of money into dubplates because he wanted to be a step ahead of other sound systems, always maintaining a fresh excitement, with the latest tunes. We would chat over new instrumental versions, and he would build his own rhythms and instrumentals in the studio. Together as MCs we would then add the required amount of spice to the tunes, providing original lyrics with an explosive energy. Saxon promoted a modern sound culture, always alive and brand-new, the opposite of old-school reggae sounds that routinely played the same faithful, safe, crowd-pleasing songs. Saxon took the risk, experimenting and creating the original foundations of British reggae.

In 1984, a live-recorded Saxon dance, held in south-west London at the Factory, was released on Greensleeves Records, under the UK Bubblers sub-label. The LP was titled *Coughing Up Fire*. This legendary live LP reached the top of the British reggae charts, and we were the talk of the town. Within the same year, I also put out 45 and 12' releases on Greensleeves that featured none other than myself and Colonel, titled 'Tippa and the Colonel, Once Again'. This second release took the reggae industry by storm and sold a staggering 20,000 records.

Greensleeves Records was formed in 1975 and situated in West Acton, London. It was established by business partners Chris Cracknell and Chris Sedgwick, blossoming first as a reggae record shop and then progressing to a reggae record label two years later. The releases were distributed by Jet Star Records, owned by the famous Palmer Brothers. Greensleeves proudly displayed its red, gold, and green logo and became renowned for promoting reggae across the world. It released songs from artists such as Dr Alimantado, Reggae Regular, The Wailing Souls, Clint Eastwood & General State, and Shaggy.

Greensleeves had a load of other big-time Jamaican artists on its books, too: Barrington Levy, Augustus Pablo, Dennis Brown, Freddie McGregor and Gregory Isaacs, Mr Vegas, Vybz Kartel, Shabba Ranks, and Wayne Wonder. Being signed as a reggae artist and having my songs produced and released on Greensleeves was a personal landmark. I had stepped into another class and taken my first step on the industry ladder. It was like obtaining your first medal.

As Saxon MCs we together took on any challenge defiantly, anyplace, anytime. We would pack the sound in the van, and off we would travel, never turning down an opportunity to battle, week after week, dubplate after dubplate, lyric after lyric. On most occasions, nine times out of ten, the clash was won by our collective. We refused to surrender. We had sound clashes with the likes of Volcano and Gemi Magic; from the US, Third World and King Addies; from Jamaica, Bodyguard, Stone Love Movement, Metromedia, and Kilimanjaro. From the UK, Channel One, Mackabee, Frontline International, Fatman Hi-Fi, Young Lion, David Rodigan, Sovereign, Unity Sound, Jamdown Rockers, Downbeat, Coxsone, King Tubby's, V Rocket, Kebra Negus, Taurus, Master Blaster, Quaker City, Nasty Love, Iration Steppas, and Luv Injection just to mention a few!

Here's DJ and record producer Jumpin Jack Frost again, this time bearing witness to the unfolding Saxon explosion:

> I would like to explain the background of Tippa Irie and Saxon's early history, for I was there to bear witness. Back in the day, loyalty was a big ting, like Tippa and I was from Brixton, SW9. You were expected to stay loyal, connected to the local youth clubs, community centres, and Brixton sound systems. Tippa had committed the cardinal sin, crossing over to Lewisham's Saxon Sound. We, even as youths, could not tell our Brixton mates we were going to see Saxon: they would have disowned us. For real; it was a pride and postcode thing. Seriously territorial, sound system business. No joke.
>
> The foundation Brixton/Jamaican elders at the time, Coxsone, Blacker Dread, and the man dem kept tight control on local music. But in front of the elders, the new UK-born Black youth and MCs were on top of their game. At one dance held at People's Club, Blacker Dread, the selector for Coxsone—a rival to Saxon—was on the mic

and publicly cussed Tippa, declaring him a Brixton traitor, stepping over the invisible Brixton boundary to join Saxon.

Saxon and the local youth crew were breaking every dance, winning every sound clash. I describe this time as 'the changing of the guard'. The elders had to step aside begrudgingly, forced to let the new soldiers come guard the sound system culture. Breathing new life into dancehall culture, Saxon were all round champions. The youths had now taken over. Saxon were an explosive sound system. It was serious talent on the mic, the Famous Five. Tippa, Colonel, Rusty, Sandy and Levi, these young guys, no one could trouble them. New in town, the five Saxon MCs were well-rehearsed, extremely tight in their delivery, mashing up the crowd. Everyone was proud to be part of Saxon Studio. These guys put UK Black reggae music firmly on the map.

No one had ever witnessed anything like the standard of the Famous Five's performances. I was at the sound clash recorded live and later released as *Coughing Up Fire* on Greensleeves. This recording captured them at their best. Mission accomplished! Everyone run for cover, because Saxon and the Famous Five had landed.

August 1977 saw the death of the 'King of Rock 'n' Roll', Elvis— and almost a year into the next decade came the cold-blooded murder of John Lennon. The eighties saw AIDS sweep the globe as crack swept the inner cities; the Iran hostage crisis; the Falklands War and Thatcher's war against striking miners; IRA bombings; Live Aid; the boycott of Apartheid in South Africa; the fall of the Berlin Wall and the Tiananmen Square massacre… I was a south London MC, a newsreader speaking against downpression and politricks, advocating on behalf of everyday people, chanting for their rights and for justice. I was a UK original in chatting 'reality lyrics', perfecting my word to call out things I believed were wrong, like a dart straight to the target. I had always possessed a faithful love for my own working-class people, Black and white: we are in it together. I have always known in my heart that unity is the key to harmony. As a UK dancehall artist dealing with reality, I was drawn to the rejection of all forms of racism—direct, subtle or institutional. I set my words against the prejudice of the extremist British National Party (BNP) and the wicked South African regime. In sport, we were sick of monkey chants on British football terraces, Black players receiving verbal abuse from racist hooligans. I decided to make a stand, to speak out.

I was the first UK reggae artist to record a single opposing racist, white supremacist parties, as featured in my tune 'Rebel on the Roots Corner', released on Ariwa Records and produced by Mad Professor, south London's dub master.

As a born rebel, I did not feel the need to hide what I felt was natural. On my earliest journeys on the mic, I would promote the use and legalisation of the ganja plant. A natural healing substance made for the well-being of humankind, we have been using it for nearly two centuries in Jamaica and the rest of the Caribbean. In the eighties, when I was singing the promotion of ganja, it was still frowned upon—but today it is becoming legal across the globe. I have always sung about the free use of the green: the truth must be revealed. Let us not forget how many Jamaicans suffered at the hands of the authorities just for a little herb. Imagine how much Jamaica would benefit as a nation if it woke up to the fact that it's a natural resource we have in abundance. But there is a time and a place for everything. In my experience, some people mix business with pleasure—age also plays an important role. In my early days I would smoke herb for lyrical inspiration, but as I got

We know Botha middle name is Satan
This is Tippa Irie, I have no respect for Botha
Freedom against apartheid
Calling all artist across Jamaica,
in England, America and all over
Show the world we are all freedom fighters
All of we need to join together
Let us, show the oppressor
Show we care for one another
Keep up pressure on Botha
and make him free up Mandela
The white oppressor in South Africa
are the true mass murderer
Show him we are superior
So, the people in Soweto don't suffer
under the rule of Botha
Everywhere I play worldwide, all I want to
see
is an end to apartheid
but Botha still wants to keep apartheid alive.

Tippa Irie, sound clash,
Saxon Sound System v. Stone Love,
1988 (live)

older, it has taken a back seat: if you want to be sharp and at the top of your game, you cannot be stoned.

I was just a young reggae performer from Brixton at the time, but it was all about to explode. My dreams and positive thinking had started to manifest. Saxon began selling out all kinds of venues. Our British audiences went from hundreds to thousands, evolving from community centres and town halls to dances held in places such as Lewisham Boys' Cub or St Mary's in Ladywell, the Coliseum in Harlesden, Hackney Downs School, the Moonshot Centre in Deptford, and the Four Aces in Dalston. We even performed for Dennis Alcapone in Stratford.

We filled up mainstream venues such as the Podium in Vauxhall and Brixton Academy to capacity, as well as the Marcus Garvey Centre in Nottingham, the Hummingbird and the Oakland Sports and Social Centre in Birmingham, Chapeltown Community Centre, Venn Street in Huddersfield, Central Club in Reading, and established in 1968 the St Pauls Carnival in Bristol. One of the best stories from this time that I can recall is when I headed to Birmingham in my car. The sound had been booked to play the Oakland. On arrival, I had difficulty trying to find a parking space (nowadays promoters allocate them, but in those days, I had to make my own way). I started to walk to the venue, and the closer I got, all I could see were people *everywhere*. We did not have mobile phones in the eighties: I was unable to contact the promoter to inform him that I had arrived for the show and was waiting outside to get in. So, I had to become a fan and queue, as if to see myself to play. I was crushed and squeezed in with the people—nobody was queue-ing in a straight line; it was a free-for-all. I remember a beautiful girl looked at me and started to scream, 'It's you, Tippa Irie! What the hell are you doing outside queueing up with us? We are paying to see you!' I actually experienced this same situation on more than one occasion.

From 1984, as Saxon dances grew to major venues across the country, it was sometimes difficult to realize that our humble blues dances had come to this. The feeling was amazing, and I was thankful.

Word of mouth, flyers, and the cassettes alongside our reputation for having the best MCs, no expense spared on dubplates and an all-round, good-quality sound, all this came together and we started to reap the benefits. Saxon was creating Black musical history, responsible for providing a totally new blend of UK sound.

Back in my youthful days, playing in the steel-pan band at the Notting Hill Carnival, I told myself that, one day, I would be back to Carnival. Well, year after year, I did perform on those August holidays, entertaining the crowds in West London's streets. The difference playing at Carnival was that hundreds of thousands of people attended (today that figure is over two million), from every race and culture. We always had our regular Saxon fans around us year after year, so it was good to perform out in the streets like that, to have a different experience from the normal dancehall vibes. Other cities also held their own carnivals—Leeds, Nottingham, Derby, Bristol, Liverpool—and over time I played them all.

One hot summer day I travelled up to perform with Saxon at the Liverpool Carnival with my cousin Jeff who was a Saxon supporter. In the crowd two men got into a fight. My cousin, being the peaceful guy that he was, jumped in between them in an effort to part them, and they both turned on Jeff and stabbed him. I got off the Saxon stage, and a brethren called me over to let me know what happened. I left immediately to the local hospital where Jeff had been taken and went to his bedside. It was a shock to see him lying in the hospital like that, but I tried to not show how I was feeling. When he saw me Jeff immediately looked me in the eyes saying, 'Yo, Tip, I don't feel good.' I reassured him that everything would be okay. Later, hospital staff called me and informed me that Jeff had died from his wounds. My cousin died in his mid-20s, with his life ahead of him. That disturbing memory lasted so long within me that I did not venture back to Liverpool for many years; Toxteth was a rough place, and full of mixed-race people, so they knew straight away from appearance whether you were not from there.

But see ya, a wey dem grey people dem take me for
they must think slavery still de ye
But a long time it done, a long time it over
and dem deh kind of bullshit, mi na check for
Just like Malcolm X and Martin Luther,
well, Tippa na joke and mi na jester
Cause the National Front mi no afraid of
The Ku Klux Klan, mi no afraid of
You see the ugly Nazi dem, mi na afraid of
You see the BNP, mi na afraid of
If they wanna diss we will pull the trigger
we will pull the trigger in their jaw corner
Cause I man Mr Irie I am a warrior
with the Mad Professor
Through the colour of my skin, mi find it harder
for I man to survive in mi area
I don't have no chip on my shoulder
Cause mi I know one day I must proposer
and reach to the top up as an entertainer
but nuff obstacle they put in front of Tippa
Sometime they won't play your tune
on the radio, won't review your tune
in their newspapers
You don't get no help from the distributors
It's only fi dem tune dem they look after
Well, Tippa, never give up, no never
Cause I am a rebel on the street corner.

Tippa Irie, 'Rebel on the Roots Corner'
from the LP *Rebel on the Roots Corner*
(Ariwa Records, 1994)

I featured on mainstream radio thanks to weekly plays by disc jockeys such as Capital's David Rodigan and RJR London's Tony Williams. Later, Ranking Miss P played my music on BBC Radio. These were the only three stations that gave me radio exposure. In reality, though, Saxon Sound System, with all its artists combined, was impossible to ignore. In the eighties, if you did not recognise Saxon as the Number 1 sound, you really could not have been listening. Tony was the first radio DJ to play my first single, 'The Opposite'. I was so excited to hear myself for the first time. I could see success coming somewhere in the horizon. My family and friends gave me so much support. I was thankful for the airplay. I was only 17 then, and proud of what I had achieved.

Saxon was now firmly on the map, with sold-out shows and top-selling vinyl releases. An array of international invitations now came to our table, from UK dancehall competitions to events with international exposure. I even penned and released a track with the title 'Saxon Studio International'. I was thankful for every day that I could live and breathe reggae 24/7. Buzzing every day from the moment daylight burst through my bedroom window, I was ready for life.

Saxon's next move was a tour of Europe, this European tour began with France. We were booked by a promoter called 'Pussy'. I laughed and laughed when I first heard her name, though from what I can remember she was a lovely woman who looked after us (I asked if this was her real name, and she smiled and replied that it was). I also remember a sound system called 'Pum Pum'. I can't remember where they were from, but I knew they must be European: let's just say that it must have got killed every night (my advice: better do your research when picking a name for a sound; for sure no Black man would be naming his sound after pum pum. Next thing, they would be calling their sound 'Bloodclaat').

All our European Saxon events were successes, and we left our mark wherever we played.

Then we toured America and Jamaica.

Dennis was responsible for organising our visas and passports, looking out for us every step of the way. Our first international booking was in the US. I had never as much as seen a passport, let alone entertained the dream of flying out on one. The closest we had got to the Stars and Stripes was watching *The Wild West* movies on Saturday afternoons, or *Kojak* and *Starsky and Hutch*, or John Wayne films and cop movies. To me, coming from where I did, the US was like a different planet. Sound system culture just kept opening doors and moving mountains beyond my wildest imagination. We south London teenagers were just about to find out that, in fact, we were as green as the grass we were puffing.

It was 1983. First Avenue, New York. We felt on top of the world. We were rising stars and taking in the bustling city all around us, bright lights, tall buildings, wide cars. We had been picked up at the airport in a hired vehicle. On reaching our destination, a luxury rented house, we began unwinding in the comfort of our surroundings. This was really special treatment for a group of humble kids. Then we met the US promoters for the first time, and these guys were some seriously shady-looking dudes. Things had begun to smell a little fishy when Rusty and I were chilling together and Rusty peered through a keyhole into a larger communal lounge adjacent to our bedrooms. The door was slightly open, so he peeked further. Then he summoned me, slowly whispering while waving his hands, motioning me to take a look.

So, I did, and to my horror, I saw giant piles of snow-white cocaine—kilos and kilos of the stuff, bagged up on the kitchen table by our promoters. This was beginning to look like a nightmare. We were way out of our depth—it was not exactly turning out to be the American Dream we had hoped for, but still, we had to ride, to roll with it, front it and step up. I wanted to get out of there—but something made me stay. When you are young, you're more fearless (just like when I was performing in Kingston, Jamaica, I had no problem walking around—but my dad was wary of the danger).

The Saxon crew was destined to travel together in the States for one month, living amongst these drug dealers. But we were built robust, and our survival was a must. I was kind of trained to brush myself off and move on when faced with challenges and tough situations. Growing up in Brixton, I knew full well the road code of south London: if you were from the manor I came from, naturally you grew up knowing gangsters and rubbing shoulders with badmen. It was par for the course in the UK's inner cities. But these New York drug dealers were on a totally different level. The 'promoters' polished their machine guns in our very presence! I was just a teenager and had never witnessed anything like this in my life. This had gone from *Starsky and Hutch* to *Miami Vice*—and it was risky on so many levels.

The first gig of the tour was in Brooklyn. In typical sound system style, they loaded up the van with the equipment for the event. The big difference, of course, were the weapons. I counted about nine different ones inside the van, from machine guns to handguns. Once again, I wondered, 'What I am doing here? If the van is stopped by the police, how would I explain that none of the guns were mine?' By the grace of God I arrived at the venue safe and sound. It had just turned midnight. Trying to fit the script, to make sense of it, I talked myself into believing that these drug dealers must be our personal minders. We kept our heads down and looked straight ahead. As MCs, we were expected to step into the arena and take on any challenge. As I entered the dance in New York, I came face to face with the local sound system Saxon was clashing against. This opposing sound was up in our faces, threatening and warning us not to diss their reputation. They were vexed and wanted to slay Saxon—but they had not reckoned on Tippa Irie representing UK dancehall, and I knew an opening when I saw one. Confidently, I took the lead on the mic, ready to take on New York.

In truth, we teenagers were *way* out of our comfort zone, alone in the Big Apple. But risky as our actions were, being kept under manners was not part of our character; succumbing to defeat was definitely not on the agenda. My job was to make my presence felt in this dance, and although I was fearful of the challenge, I dared not show it. All sound system clashes, wherever they may be, are each a challenge. I was prepared to face it. We were young men and the opposing New York sound were big men and they did not want to be shown up by the new kids on the block. As we took the mic the atmosphere began to change, both the sound and the audience could not believe our charisma, style and lyrical delivery. They had heard about Saxon through our cassettes but now they were feeling our presence live and direct. As the words go in the Jamaican reggae song, 'we gonna lick them one by one and we gonna beat them two by two.' That night we put them in their place, Saxon Sound now truly International had risen to the challenge and beyond it once again.

After Brooklyn, the Bronx was next on the map. We clashed alongside Papa Toyan, Johnny Ringo, Louie Lepkie, Sister Carol, Early B 'The Doctor'. It was so crazy to see New York at that age. To me, these places were simply all full of fellow Jamaicans, people from yard who had settled in the States. Brooklyn in particular was coming just like another Brixton, a cultural hive for the Black community. I simply loved it; the vibes were cool, like home from home. The only clear difference was the segregation: you could walk blocks and blocks, never seeing a white face.

After the Saxon mini-tour of the United States, I flew back to Gatwick. We had been taken care of every step of the way and would continue to be protected from any sign of trouble abroad, the gun men promoters that were around us just slipped away into the night without any attention. I felt at home within the international dancehall communities; we shared the same food and style, and a cultural identity. Most importantly, we were unified through our love of reggae. We were all young, a new generation proudly representing our Jamaican heritage in our own ways. I was always promoting the fact that Jamaica was in my blood.

As Saxon grew internationally and took on eagle's wings, we were knocking out opposing sound systems like skittles in a bowling alley. We jet-setted to Europe, America, Jamaica… all over. Saxon played to dancehall fans from Lewisham to Zimbabwe. All things were possible; we even went to Bermuda for an international sound clash. Who would ever have believed it?

In my song 'Is It Really Happening to Me' I captured my feelings in the Saxon glory days, of raising my game:

> *The whole of us we live together, like one family*
> *Anything, we have, we share it out, fairly*
> *We live in love and unity,*
> *that why we are the best sound in the country*
> *Is it really happening to me*
> *I am taking aeroplane, like it a taxi.*

Saxon was hot all across the world during the eighties and early nineties; everyone was aware of our raw talent and vocal craft, our unique style. Even the country that invented and established the music admired our own brand of reggae, studying it and even copying our cockney flow. Yes, Jamaican foundation MCs such as Peter Metro, Tanto Metro, King Yellowman, Papa San, and Sound Creation would give respect to our British style, using our terminology ('lickwood', etc). In fact, Peter Metro performed Tippa and the Colonel 'Just a Speak' with Tanto Metro. King Yellowman chanted my song 'Good to Have the Feeling You're the Best' and also sang 'Jah Me Fear', originally

Is it really happening to me
I am taking aeroplane like it a taxi
Them say, 'Tippa Irie, you full of energy
and you have a nice personality'
Colonel got a spliff and passed it to me
We looked at each other, 'cause the spliff
was not ready
Inna England, we used to the sensi
Well, the next day I was on TV
but when I left France was very happy
'Cause to me, there is nowhere like, London
city
Home of the Saxon posse
The whole of us we live together, like one
family
Anything, we have, we share it out, fairly
We live in love and unity,
that why we are the best sound in the country
Is it really happening to me
I am taking aeroplane, like it a taxi.

Tippa Irie, 'Is It Really Happening to Me'
from the LP *Is It Really Happening to Me* (UK
Bubblers (Greensleeves Records), 1986)

recorded by Papa Levi. The yard MCs were impressed by our original, fast-chat style. We proudly wore the crown and flew the flag as Black UK artists, the stars of the show, and people started to follow what we were doing in the UK. We shook up the dancehall world, filling up tunes and complementing songs with sharp lyrics. Apart from Papa San, we had the skill to fill any tune with lyrics right until the song stopped, and we could keep going without music. In the rich history of reggae, this was a first.

A strong, tight relationship built up between the Saxon crew and the yard MCs. Back home, Saxon would play in areas in New Cross, Brixton, and Battersea with Jamaica's cream-of-the-crop MCs joining us on the mic, such as Super Cat, Peter Metro, Nicodemus, Papa San, and Sugar Minott, who lived in our local area. These artists were all drawn to the power of our Saxon energy: this is how massive our reputation had grown. Big-time Jamaican performers were flying across to play on our sounds—yet another historical first. I was on my way to a radio interview in Jamaica for RJR London, and Papa San was present. He was a genuine and welcoming character, and told me he was a fan of what I was doing with reggae back in the UK. Jamaican dancehall veterans Lieutenant Stitchie and Professor Nuts were also fellow Saxon supporters. The Jamaican singer Pinchers' reggae song 'Mass Out' features a snatch from my UK hit tune 'Hello Darling' (the lyrics 'Hello darling/Hello, good-looking'). I found some of the Jamaican performers either a mix of being well friendly or standoffish and not so approachable.

Trevor Sax, a central part of the sound system process and one of the greatest mixers and deejays in the reggae fraternity, speaks of his own Saxon experiences and what gave it strength:

My interest in music first came from the influence of my father, who named his sound system Sir Allen back in

Jamaica. My mum was a nurse employed by the NHS. I was born and raised in the borough of Wandsworth, south London, and grew up in Balham and Tooting. In those days, Black people lived in some big houses with high ceilings, many rooms and large basements. My parents and the local elders would keep blues parties, which we would call shebeens. Music would play to all hours, and there would be boxes of Cherry B. My father later moved back to Jamaica. My sister and I were invited to stay with him during our six weeks of school holidays. I attended Charlton Boys School, as I had moved to Greenwich—I believe the year was 1975—and on my first visit to Jamaica to see my father, after stepping off the plane at the airport in Montego Bay, I decided I was not returning to England— even though in Jamaica there was no electricity running properly at the time. For me, an 11-year-old, it was pure excitement.

So, I stayed, becoming a legal citizen, but in the eighties things took a turn for the worse on the island. During the 1980 elections there was gun violence; it was like living in a battleground, so I turned back to London. On my return, in my early twenties, I went to reside with my mum, who was living in Lewisham. I started buying records as soon as I got back on home turf, and would listen to new vinyl releases at a small Lewisham record store called One Little Corner. It was at this same store that I met Dennis Rowe and Owen Rowe, the founders of Saxon Sound System. I started getting to know them, and used my own deejay talents for Saxon while its main selector at the time, Lloyd Francis, was spending a bit of time in jail. This provided a chance to show my style. At that time in the UK Jah Shaka was pumping the roots and lovers' rock was the big thing, and I was coming with my own Jamaican-influenced style of mixing, using two turntables (Chris Goldfinger, another brethren from Asha World Movement, also played using two turntables, as he was grown in Jamaica). We from Jamaica would call this style of playing and juggling 'disco tech'. I also came with my own fashion style. Man in London were wearing leopard skin and snakeskin shoes; I was sporting Clarks footwear, just like my fellow Jamaicans.

I become good friends with Owen and joined Saxon as their DJ. From that point onwards I started playing all over, making big noises with Saxon. The DJs at the time were Papa Levi, Henry Prento, and Rankin Coolio, Smiley and Asha; later, Tippa Irie, Levi, Commander B, and Slater joined Saxon as our MCs. Saxon's reputation was second to none, so MCs from all over were drawn to join us like a magnet. I was working day and night to build up a vibe (our Saxon crew would not have been possible if Mrs Rowe had not welcomed all us guys into her home. I will never forget her love, kindness, and spirit. Mrs Rowe was responsible for what Saxon is today).

The likes of Coxsone Sound System were viewed as the seasoned professionals within the arena. At one dance at Deptford Crypt, Saxon was about to pack up early, but coming from Jamaican culture, I was taught that no man can make me pack up my sound. This attitude was ingrained: no packing up Saxon Sound until the dance was done. We would play out every single night of the week. We had packed-out dances from the Childers Street Youth Club in Deptford across the length and breadth of the country. One of Saxon's biggest followings apart from south London was in West London: we had great dances, rammed out, in Harlesden, White City. Over east side, the

Galaxy, Romford and the empty carpet shop in Tottenham on Broad water Farm. There would be not just hundreds of people in the audience, but a clear 1,000 people coming to see Saxon. My greatest memory of all time has to be winning the 1994 World Cup Clash, when Saxon were the winners of the competition.

We challenged anyone, anytime, and we played the best of the best. We would play regular nights at the Porsche Club in Birmingham, clashing the local Jungleman sound, and we became so popular in the area that we kept Saxon Sound and all our equipment in Birmingham. I had to work double hard, because sound system life does not pay a pension—I was responsible for my own pension in my later years.

The Almighty gave us a break, and we had strong standards and a reputation; we were on fire, compete and challenge anyone, anywhere. It was sinsemilla time, 'lickwood' mean 'rewind' and 'gunshot' mean 'forward'. Saxon contributed to the careers of so many artists, from Maxi Priest, Mikey General, Smiley, Tippa, Levi. Each individual performer had national and international hits. We had good foundation people working with us, the likes of Paul Robinson and One Blood Crew; Chris Blackwell from Island Records was also a supporter. Me and Maxi Priest would drive around, both of us crushed up in his black Mini, picking up or delivering records to Dub Vendor. Maxi would record his vocals raw from the mic to the dubplate recording.

Saxon; our unit was based on skill and togetherness. We knew each other so well, it was like there was telepathy between us, a magical presence, a sharpness. Jerk it up, pull it up, and then pass the mic, always possessing the element of surprise. One MC to the next. We had the top line-up. Levi was the squadron leader, and Tippa cemented everything together. We were so tight; even today, after 40 years, I am still brethren with Tippa; Daddy Colonel is godfather to my son, and Papa Levi is godfather to my daughter. Back in the day, you touched one of us, you touched us all. If you gave Saxon a problem, we would all come at you.

Tippa Irie has got longevity because he knows what it takes to stay versatile and to command an audience. Look at all the other MCs: Tippa has surpassed them, because he is professional and can manage the limelight. He has always been killing it because he was trained and schooled within the sound system environment with a required 100 percent work rate. Some artists sound good, clear and confident in the recording booth, but fail to cut it performing live on the road. Tippa had the both skills.

After so many years performing as an MC, I have mastered my craft. After 35 years, I have remained consistent, and I have to be—as I have said, the sound system does not pay me a pension, so I must be business-focused. Recently I spent two years in the States jamming with Wyclef Jean. After my years of experience, I have learnt that I don't do music for fame. but for the likes. Because you don't choose music, music chooses you. Be humble, think of today but, most importantly, with music and business entwined, think of tomorrow. Being raised in Jamaica taught me the good, strong values of longevity and hard work. I never wanted to be a man standing outside a bookie shop, looking to live off my bets and gambles. Our minds need to rise above the institutional ghetto mentality that holds so many of us back. We all need uplifting encouragement, 'cause as the elders in Jamaica say, 'Encouragement sweetens labour.'

In 1983, Greensleeves created UK Bubblers, a smaller, independent subsidiary record label with the declared objective of supporting British reggae acts, promoting what we were doing on a grassroots level. I was its first signed solo reggae artist. Greensleeves also aimed to build a studio based in London to further develop our sound. At this time, Greensleeves was the major reggae player in the record industry. Once again, sticking close to my roots, I wanted to lead the way and open the industry's tightly locked door, making way for the next reggae performer to step up. Before this, there had been no real interest or investment in British reggae, MC-style, within the closed world of major record labels and distributors.

Up until Saxon's time, all eyes had been focused on the energy and creative ability of Jamaican performers. British artists were used to being routinely ignored, and our talents dismissed. We were used to being way down on the record labels' lists; their focus was on promoting the multicoloured flavours of dance, pop, and rock. I sincerely wanted to change this situation because that was not going to be my road.

My greatest challenge was overcoming any mental negativity holding myself back. My aim was to bring UK reggae talent into the mainstream. Everybody would be given an opportunity to experience our music. Reggae music is always well received, and positively moves people across the four corners of the globe. Therefore, not marketing and promoting our music was not even a good business move, because in truth, it *sells*. In my eyes, hard-working, talented reggae performers should receive the recognition they deserve, and I was not about to allow record companies to block me, or try to imitate my work, or attempt to suffocate my talent. I was never going to accept a third-rate deal, accept being ignored or hidden away on the shelf, limited to one genre. I was not going to let the music industry marginalise my sounds. If they would not support me, I swore to myself, I would go it alone, independently.

My take has always been to let the public be the judges of what they want to hear; just provide us all with a fair playing field. I am UK-born, part of a new generation. All we were asking for as British reggae artists was just to be let into the party, instead of being left outside, staring in through the window. In the beginning, major labels frowned upon us, smirking with a patronising grin—but that was before Saxon bust in and we conquered, downtown, uptown, and all-around town.

Back home in the streets, yet another battle was bubbling—many of the ruling pioneer Lambeth sound systems, those elders who had held reputations for playing the best reggae, would not give us creative breaks, and even took pleasure in trying to block Saxon's destined path. Some tried to lock us new-flavoured youths out, seeing our growing success as a reason to try to hold us back. But we were not about to be denied a shout. The elders shared a strong collective view that the culture of the music must be preserved by sticking to strictly reggae music with Jamaican roots. This was the rule that reigned supreme before Saxon Sound System landed. The original sound system governors were giving us the very same trip about towing the line, the same old restrictions and boundaries we were receiving back in our homes, all those manners and rules put on us from our own Jamaican parents—tiring! They rejected our Black south London cockney twang mixed with yard patois. This was our own unique MC style. I was tired of feeling hemmed in by this small-minded territorial attitude.

My response was to chill out and say, 'let's enjoy ourselves.' I rode on the 'One Love' vehicle that became my motto for life's journey. This is another reason I left my home ground to start performing as part of Saxon. With my transition to Saxon, people from Brixton would throw bad word on me. I was used to having others try to hold me back through jealousy, competitiveness… whatever their reasons. Throughout my life I have never liked to limit myself or allow someone else to limit me. I was always searching for something greater, not for hype and the shallow trappings of fame, but for the longevity of my beloved music.

As a youthful MC I would shake up dancehall fearlessly and confidently. Coming from where I did, I was not about to let anything get in my way, and for all my sacrifices, I was not about to allow anybody or anything to take what was mine. It was full steam ahead. I was forward-thinking, steadfast, and motivated. I had become hardened and experienced as a performer, being on the frontline in competition clashes in my own country and elsewhere. By this time in my career, I was a highly trained warrior in the sound system arena. We all agreed, as the Saxon family, on what was required to make it work and what was required for us to step up a gear, maintaining a high level of performance, maximum stamina, and vocal output. Facing the challenge of the wider world, we knew we needed to move out of our comfort zone and at times step away from our own cultural norms.

Our record releases began to break open doors, providing us with greater opportunities further afield. I was fulfilling my goal. As Bob Marley sang, 'there's a natural mystic flowing through the air.' Once again, I was caught up in the magical energy of reggae. This was my life.

Rude Bwoy Monty, my good mate, speaks about his early days, the power of Saxon, and being a lifelong fan of UK dancehall culture:

> I am Rude Bwoy Monty, hailing from West Wickham, what those who come from south London would term 'country'. My parents are from the West Indian island of Saint Vincent. Where Jamaicans were formerly linked to Brixton through Windrush history, in my hometown,

it was migrants from Saint Vincent all around. I noted that Bajans—people from Barbados—were living around Reading, and in neighbouring Slough you would have a strong community of Antiguans. My early ventures were when my dad would take me with him to buy his smart party clothes, purchased from the famous Baron clothing store and the Big Apple hat shop, both in Brixton.

As West Indians in our home tunes, all manner of vinyl 45s would be playing on the gramophone turntable. Music was our tradition. Country, ska, bluebeat, reggae, calypso, and soca. At the age of 15, I was a selector in the Country Man sound system.

As a teenager, the sound of Saxon was blowing up all over through the wide distribution of cassette tapes. Back in our day, man would swap copies of sound clash cassette tapes. I first swapped a Jamaican sound tape I had in exchange for a Saxon sound clash session. When I listened to the Saxon tape, I was stunned by the nonstop delivery of the British MCs.

Next, I am carrying some food shopping; Mum was on the hunt, buying fresh meat from Petticoat Lane Market in East London. The golden rule as a West Indian child? You do not leave your parents' side. But out of the corner of my ear, I heard the tune pumping—'Mi God, Mi King', by Papa Levi. I had first heard his voice on my newly swapped Saxon clash TDK cassette. But this was vinyl. In a haste, I broke from my mum's hand and ran to the sound man in the market selling reggae 45s. Mum ran to follow and I begged and begged for a copy of Papa Levi's newly released hit song. Mum was so taken aback by my crazy enthusiasm that she purchased it for me. I carried the 45 disc all the way home with great pride, wrapped in a brown paper bag. I first witnessed Saxon playing live, clashing the Young Lion sound system locally. Jah blessed me 'cause the dancehall event was on my doorstep in High Wycombe.

I squeezed myself down the front. Within sound system culture, cassettes did not come with covers featuring any faces, just the date and the competitors, done. So, the only way you are to identify them personally is to go see them performing live on the sound. Then I heard the distinctive voices. Yeah, I could then finally identify the man dem, MCs. That one, Colonel; Rusty, over there. That one, Tippa. First time I put face to vocal, on the spot, I became a lifelong fan of Saxon. We called ourselves 'The Saxonites', a faithful part of the Saxon crew, treated as part of an extended family. There was a love of love and respect around the movements of the sound.

This was not Coxsone sound's time or any of the founding sounds' time. Coxsone were experts in importing the latest yard reggae tunes. This was purely Saxon down. The UK Black youth were the new kids on the block. The elders had to take a seat. The atmosphere was electrifying, totally thrilling. We all gathered around the Saxon sound. Tippa would step up, first MC on the mic: 'Unu, Ready?' Everyone would scream and shout out, 'Yeah!' Forward, the squadron of five, an elite set of MCs. To challenge these youths, you would need to swallow an Oxford Dictionary and a King James Bible.

I would get to meet the whole posse in person. It was thrilling to me, straight up. Meeting Musclehead was, for me, like meeting Michael Jackson. They were reggae royalty to me. You would see Musclehead dressed in leather and tiger skin, a beaver hat, driving a two-seater Mercedes sportscar. The only time I has seen a flashy car like that was being driven by J.R. Ewing in *Dallas*, on TV. I would travel in the van with the Saxon crew, 'cause them days man did not have car or transport. So, we caught a lift in the Saxon van—an essential part of a working sound system. Sometimes the sound would perform twice in one night.

In reality, it was freezing cold, a group of Black men squashed together sitting on mattresses, up and down the motorway. You would be desperate to take a piss, so you would bang on the side of the van with your fist, requesting a toilet stop. The sound man driving the van shout to you, 'No stopping! Piss in a Coke bottle!' If a man locally would have a car, a real rare ting of the times, about six men would pack in the car and hit the road, heading for Saxon, no matter the cost. We would all put hands in and split the costs for petrol.

As a sound man myself, I would be obsessive about the matter. Saxon and its silver preamps, distinctive sound mixing box, echoing, reverb, gunshots, and police sirens.

Notting Hill Carnival was another top event for the Saxon fans' annual calendar. You would see and hear the number of artists line up on the mic. The world went around. The night of the live sound clash recording of *Coughing Up Fire* was to be held in Paddington. There were no drivers locally. So, me and my brethren jumped on public transport and reached perfectly on time, from High Wycombe.

The dance was top-class. All the line-up were there, ready and hot for the Saxon LP later released on Greensleeves. So desperate was I to be present that at 4 AM after the dance ended, me and my brethren were stuck. We went to Paddington train station; the steel shutters were firmly locked and bolted. We both buttoned up our coats and went walking up and down to stay warm until the station opened again at 7 AM to get back home. This is how much we loved Saxon. We were committed, dedicated, loyal Saxonites. A little discomfort was worth the personal exchange, the buzz you received taking in the sound live. Nothing like it. The talent, drive, passion, and skill. Outstanding; there was no one like the Saxon crew on Planet Earth. Every individual MC was different. Saxon was unique. The draw for us: the MCs talked of subject matter we could relate to as Black youths living and growing up in the UK.

We knew the names of the places. The topics were ours; we lived them. Jamaican reggae talked of Clarendon, Kingston, or Negril. We could only mentally picture these faraway places. With Saxon, 'I love gal inna Brixton, police pull mi over inna Streatham': these were our places. So Saxon sound were part of our Black identity. Saxon could not be simply categorised as a Jamaican reggae sound or a British reggae sound. No, Saxon were uniquely crafting their own sounds. Masters of playing 45 versions, allowing the MCs to freely flow, synchronised in style and pattern, humour and dissing, roots and culture, lyrical poetry, making us aware of world issues and making sense of what was happening around us. They were the newsreaders of our generation.

Daddy Rusty was different from the rest, with a London accent. Daddy Colonel was a don of the fast-chatting style, another lyrical giant. Tippa Irie, with his distinctive style, high-octane voice, and perfect vocal melodies and natural flow. Papa Levi, killing the lyrics, verse after verse, reality, roots, and culture. The Saxon squadron feared no one and took on anybody at the drop of a hat. Miss Irie, Tippa's sister, came on the mic as a first female MC, joining the Saxon crew. This was a unique thing. Historically, dancehall was strictly man vibes. Saxon were the first again in breaking cultural norms and barriers, inviting Miss Irie onto the set as an equal part of the crew. Miss Irie had a magnificent, original flow. Big hair, big earrings... she had dancehall style and added a totally different south London spin. She was famous for being fierce, fiery, and a founding female MC.

Over 30-odd years on, I still faithfully follow the Saxon posse. Saxon founder member and selector Musclehead played at my birthday party, which was a true honour for me. I still see the great, versatile Tippa Irie perform with his live bands. I can't believe so many years gone by; I would be in front of him, just like the good old days, Tippa a teenage MC and I, a mad Saxon fan. I attended both the Saxon worldwide reggae sound systems sound clash competitions. Like precious jewels, I still have my original Saxon white-label vinyl and live cassettes. I've been present at the reunions. I am so thankful for being able to directly witness the emergence of Saxon, pioneers in the development of British Black people's music.

Today, I work with disadvantaged youths, as a music teacher. Once I brought a vinyl record to a lesson to show them, and they said, 'I know that thing, whatever it's called.' Sad to forget such an important part of Black culture. I notice something very distinctive with the youths of this generation. They are fearful of looking different; they follow the crowd. Back in the early Saxon days, you would pride yourself on being different, standing out from the crowd, not following everybody else.

Saxon was the first British sound system to be invited to play a dance in Jamaica. In 1985, we played on the legendary sound system operator Jack Ruby's lawn, alongside Sugar Minot's own Youthman Promotion. In 1992, Saxon was the proud winner of the UK Cup Clash. Later in 1994, we became the first UK-based sound system to win the World Clash. I had the privilege of being a part of this history-in-the-making as an MC with Saxon Sound, when we competed and won against King Addies, Kebra Negus, and Bodyguard. The venue where the World Clash took place was the Sanctuary Music Arena in Milton Keynes in, believe it or not, Saxon Street—so maybe we were destined to win. The atmosphere was electric inside, 80 percent men and 20 percent women. The sound ting, in reality, was a man ting, a place where brothers would get to let their hair down, have some male banter with each other. I liken being a sound system follower to being a football fan—it was that level of allegiance.

On the night of the World Clash, each competing sound crew had to set up their equipment beforehand—you had to have a good, powerful system to participate. Each sound would get 30 minutes to play against every other sound taking up the live challenge. It would go down to an elimination round, and all sounds would get 15 minutes each. During these rounds, the audience would decide which sound would be eliminated from the competition, and which should stay in the game, showing their reaction by cheering the loudest, or by a show of hands. Once a sound was eliminated, and we were down to two sounds, the final round would be called 'one for one'. This meant each sound played one tune, and the winner was chosen once again by the noise of the audience. On the night, Saxon won through the volume of the voting audience, and we received an engraved trophy—again, as in a football competition, like the FA Cup. The compere gathered the Saxon crew together and presented us with the cup, as the first British sound system to beat Jamaica's finest. The cup was kept at Musclehead's house (sound clash cups are trophies, and it was common to see a soundman's cups and accolades displayed proudly in his living room). It was a very proud night, and an event I will never forget.

In 1995, Saxon was the first UK sound system to tour Mother Africa, starting with a show in Zimbabwe. Saxon was also the first UK sound system to originate its own UK roots reggae festival, the One Love Festival. And today Saxon proudly stands the sound clash test of time, still moving the globe in UK dancehall style from generation to generation.

I truly appreciate the significance of Saxon. It changed the face of reggae music. This was the first time in the history of reggae music that world was looking at Black British reggae performers as the young stars of the industry as we began to maintain the talents, we had taken the baton—there has been no other time since when we are Black British artists were at the top of the game. The competition was fierce out there, and we did—and still do—carry the swing, with our ethic of teamwork, engagement, employment, and achievement. We were all equally respected for our multiple talents, and Saxon enabled our achievements in recording status. We were appreciated—and paid—as performers. All these factors were winning ingredients. I have had so much enjoyment, and memories of so many sound clash victories. I will always be proud of being part of a winning team that produced such successful results and engaged so many people.

So, as we say in dancehall culture, 'Rewind, selector, and come again.'

* * *

Just as my career as a deejay with Saxon Sound was blowing up, so was my own personal status as a solo recording artist. In 1984, I recorded 'Good to Have the Feeling You're the Best'. I penned these lyrics because I was coming from nothing. I had already made a hit with the number one tune that reached the top of the UK reggae charts. It made all the community around me proud, letting everybody know the sound system I was part of was also the best in the country. In these times we as MCs would describe ourselves as the best. Our motto was that if you believe yourselves to be the best, your hard work will lead you to success. This new track was laid down and mixed at Mark Angelo's studio and released on UK Bubblers. This 12' single was another big Top 40 hit, launching me onto another level of public exposure. I took great pride knowing that my music had reached the hearts of so many people in so many different ways. In the eighties, British Olympic javelin champion Tessa Sanderson CBE used this song as her motivation anthem.

As kids growing up, when we would play our music, it would not be long before we had complaints from the neighbours. It was commonplace (Aswad's movie *Babylon* shows how it was dealing with angry neighbours: the white racist woman, yet another complaining neighbour, telling Beefy—one of the characters—to go back to 'his' country. This was in fact our reality).

'Complain Neighbour', another hit of mine, was released 12 months after 'It's Good to Have The Feeling You're The Best.' The lyrics tell a true story about a friend called Deborah, a young woman who lived on a council estate in Islington, North London. I was going out with Deborah's best friend Hyacinth. During a small party gathering, Deborah was playing reggae in her home with three girlfriends and their toddlers, all enjoying themselves. Without any warning, a bunch of racist neighbours attacked her home, pelting a brick through Debbie's front window, shattering the glass—thankfully, neither the young mums nor their innocent children were harmed. This attack was traumatic for them, though, and gave them many sleepless nights. It led me to pen and produce 'Complain Neighbour'.

You could be born in England or Jamaica
You could live in Kingston or be a Londoner
You could be old or a teenager
There must be a time that you can remember
when someone knock at your door
'If you don't turn down the music
I will have to phone the coppers'
The complain neighbour, they sit on the
couch
watching Coronation Street and Eastenders
they wait till music to get louder.

Tippa Irie, 'Complain Neighbour'
from the 12' single (UK Bubblers
(Greensleeves Records), 1986)

It was in 1986 that my chart release on UK Bubblers of the single 'Hello Darling' came out. This track was produced as a reggae/pop crossover, with an attempt to reach audiences far and wide. 'Heartbeat' was my next single release. After 'Hello Darling' was released it cata-pulted me to an even higher level. The tune, one of my favourites, came about because one evening I was standing alongside the Saxon sound van after performing a clash in Parade Street, Paddington, at the Peoples Club, when a beautiful young lady came my way. I said, 'Hello, darling,' and she looked back in my direction and replied, 'Hello, good-looking.' Spontaneously, I thought, 'That's a good, catchy title for a new song.' I went back into the dance, grabbed the mic and started to put the words into a song, receiving good energy and reaction directly from the audience. As always, the guys in the sound asked me where I found those vibes: 'I bet it was some nice girl he was checking out outside the dance, that's how he came up with the lyrics.' They weren't wrong.

These were truly great times, we were blowing up with our own sound, recording hits on our own labels, and travelling to great success inter-nationally, but as I've said, we still lived in a marginalised community. It was tight one though, and at our best times we were rock-solid. We were in and out of each other's homes, in and out of each other's pockets. Within our local inner-city, working-class networks, word, sound, and news travelled fast. We gathered at youth clubs, sports and community centres, in church and at all manner of social gath-erings—music venues, house parties, sound system dances. We lived in social housing, in high-rise blocks; these were my first gathering spaces. I moved up and down the famous Brixton 'frontline'—Railton Road, Effra Parade, and Atlantic Road, reaching to the borderline of Camberwell, Coldharbour Lane. Back then, before the gentrification of Brixton, it was about strength in numbers; we felt secure walking the frontline. It was our local, safe Black haven, a place in our midst where we felt free for a short while from the prejudices of the general population and from racist police oppression (it was also a good place to buy a small draw of weed, which would be wrapped in newspaper).

The reality though is that inner city life in the UK from the Black community's perspective was like a two-edged sword, one side experiencing direct outright discrimination and on the other side a more subtle form of institutional racism. These same aspects in 1978 motivated many of us to share and respond to the challenges through our musical output. One example among many, was the British roots group Steel Pulse who titled their hit reggae LP *Handsworth Revolution*.

We were not joking, not my Black generation. We were experiencing so many hard aspects of Thatcherism, the racist sus laws, the racist education system, the lack of employment opportunities, the lack of any opportunities if you were Black and working class. The 1981 investigative report by Lord Scarman, alongside other studies and findings both government-commissioned and independent, had found the British police guilty of institutional racism. That was the match that had ignited the inner city. The neighbourhood where I lived and had grown up, along with the surrounding area, was now charcoal and soot. The community had been pushed too far, backed into a corner, and had been forced to come out fighting. It was not a pretty sight. This is engraved in my history; I testify to those times, to the riots and uprisings as part of my generation's struggles.

On September 28, 1985, I was informed through our local community hotline that the mother of my sistren and founding British dancehall MC, Lorna Gee, had been shot and paralysed by Brixton police. Me and Lorna moved and performed together during the same era and we were close, so this incident with her mother, Dorothy 'Cherry' Groce, especially hit home. Once again, the boys in blue had not learnt one lesson—not one—from the previous riot. Word passed one to another, sistren and brethren echoing throughout Lambeth streets that Mrs Groce, one of our beloved Jamaican elders, had been gunned down in her own home by the police. Mrs Groce's youngest son, then 11 years old, testified that the police had burst through the door; an officer later named as PC Douglas Lovelock, had shot his mother. The little boy, screaming with shock, was commanded by one of the officer's present to 'shut his mouth' as a gun was pointed towards him. The police had been searching for Dorothy's son Michael Groce, who was a suspect in an armed robbery case (though it was later found that those charges had been dropped prior to the planned police raid on the Groce family home).

This was the straw that broke the camel's back. Petrol bombs were lit; steel council bins circled our streets, filled with flames. The skies of Brixton were bright orange and red, smoke billowing out from every direction. It would be the second community uprising within just five years. The Thatcher government had continued with the sus law, racist treatment had continued at the hands of the Old Bill. The fury of the Black community was set ablaze yet again. Something was clearly not working; the system had failed us once more. The roads and smoke in our ends of SW9 were billowing from barricades set ablaze blocking police from entering Brixton, anything people could find to burn, it was set on fire. All around people having full on physical fights with the police. Stones and rocks throne, windows smashed and shop fronts robbed of their goods. Gangs of young men running down the roads ready for war against the racist forces of Babylon. It was get up stand up time, again.

My friend and old neighbour Neil gives his account, describing from a different cultural perspective the racism of the Met Police and the tensions leading up to the Brixton riot:

> Brixton was a nightmare, dealing with the Old Bill during
> the eighties. I used to love nice cars and loud music. I
> would blare it out of my flash motor. The police would be

on your tail, straight away looking to hassle and intimidate you. Even me, as a white kid from Brixton. We used to have a saying in Brixton: 'Black or white, stop on sight.' They would blatantly set you up. They looked to frame you as soon as your ID came up as SW9. We were treated like working-class lepers. Everyone was seen as a criminal. I even done a spot of bird, prison time, myself, after being framed by the local police for car theft. Having a history of growing up in care and being a Brixton resident was not a good identification mix for the ever-watchful eye of the boys in blue.

My brother, also a Brixton local born and bred, was sentenced to six months. Caught participating in the Brixton riot. Who would have thought? A white geezer nicked for rioting in Brixton. This was how we lived, alongside the Black community. Friends and neighbours, together. United, doing the Lambeth Walk. My brother even got done for affray as a white teenager getting into fights with the racists of the National Front who lived on the outskirts of south London. We hated the NF because they hated black and white races mixing together in harmony. Sorry, lads, this was us.

Even today, when you get your car insurance, Brixton is graded as a high-level trouble spot, still labelled as an area of crimes and thieves. I am still here, living today, and like Tony, we will never leave our SW9 roots. We have always been labelled the 'black sheep' of south London.

In my song 'Looking out My Window', I paint a lyrical picture of my street, my community and what I witnessed around me.

For the first time, my experiences were becoming twofold. I knew it was a transition. I could clearly see and feel my community's trials and

I was looking out of my window, chillin' in
my crib
Thinking about the ghetto in which I lived
Police used to beat us, with dem baton
Life so stressful, so rotten
Just like when fi mi parents, used to pick
cotton
This is Mr Tippa Irie, I have never forgotten
This is plain English I am speaking, not Latin.

Tippa Irie, 'Looking Out My Window',
Yeti Beats records, 2008

tribulations, but I desired positive outcomes for my life too, a progression for both me and my community. I wanted to show others that it *can* be done. To inspire. I wanted to achieve, to become a successful UK performer. In my professional life as an artist, I had put in the time and commitment. I felt after so much hard work, something big was about to bust for me. I truly felt I deserved a breakthrough.

The other side of the story is that despite all the odds against us, our success we achieved was real. I will close this chapter with one of my all-time greatest personal memories. My dad had left our family home to return to his beloved birthplace of Trelawny, Jamaica. In 1986 I flew to Jamaica in secret. As soon as I reached the island, I made a phone call immediately to my dad: 'Hi, Dad, it's Tony; you'll never guess where I am phoning from. *Jamaica!* I am here. I need you not to ask any questions, but tomorrow I will be calling a cab, pre-booked for you. The cab will bring you to me in Kingston.'

Dad, being a country man, was not too keen on the hustle and bustle of Kingston. Many folks who live and have grown up in the rural parts of the island have great suspicions in relation to Kingston due to its high-level crime reputation. I had also often wondered why, on an island that has so much natural beauty and so many churches, there is so much violence and crime. So, it took me a little while to encourage him. Thankfully, in the end, he agreed. Dad met me in the early evening in the city. It was such a great feeling, one that warmed my heart. I had missed Dad so bad. Next, I informed him that I would have to leave his side for a short while. Pops looked startled, then stunned when I took him backstage at Reggae Sunsplash. Dad was to experience his greatest surprise witnessing me flying past him up the stairs and jumping onto the main stage, microphone in my hand. To the eruption of thousands of cheers, I was billed as the UK hit reggae performer, Tippa Irie.

When I hit the stage, the first words from my mouth were: 'Lord, have mercy, mercy. Tippa Irie, in the party, party. Everybody come follow, follow me. Reggae Sunsplash, how ya feeling?' That was Kingston Jamaica, 1986.

Dad was so proud. He had never known how big his son's music career had become. Remember that my first taste of MCing was influenced by my dad's sound downstairs, back in my early days, dancehall, in the basement of our family grocery store in Brixton. As the elders taught us rightfully, plant a seed and it will grow a fruitful tree. Pops had planted the first seed in me, and now he was witnessing the tree mature. Tippa Irie, his son, was bearing fruit. For all these golden memories and so many more, I give thanks to the magical music journey I have travelled. I can also see now that my dad's persistence at following his ideals is definitely within me.

In front of my eyes, my popularity grew. Prominent Jamaican dancehall reggae artists were recording and releasing songs that mentioned 'Tippa Irie' by name, in their lyrics. Papa San's eight-minute classic 'DJ Business', released on the south London reggae label Fashion Records, describes the history of dancehall MCs. I had carved myself into this reggae history, given public recognition from such an early age. I reflected to myself, that if I put the work and commitment in, my musical journey would only get better. I was ready, and not waiting. I wanted to mould my own destiny, to live free and independent, to live the life I loved and to love the life I lived.

Chapter Four

Hello Darling,
Hello Good-Looking

I ALWAYS HAD LOVE FOR THE LADIES AND HAVE FOUND that there is nothing better than a great woman around me to provide a sparkle to my life. Public recognition as a renowned reggae MC definitely has its perks, and it has always, thankfully, been working to my benefit. Back in the day, I displayed six photographs on my bedroom wall, proudly, of my current female companions: Sandra, Karen, Sharon, Michelle, Claudette, and Karen Stewart, my real first love.

Music brought girls in abundance. Female spirit is something I had grown up with, having two sisters. I was the only man in the house after my dad returned to Jamaica. I felt at home around women; back in the day, in my era, that's how love was: joyfulness between man and woman, in a kind of old-fashioned way. Like brethren and sistren, or sometimes more intimate.

On the way home, sitting in the van that carried us and the sound system, I reflected on my interaction with the young lady, and in 1986, with the very same theme in mind, I wrote 'Hello Darling', the hit track that enabled me to break through and crossover immediately into the mainstream, hitting pop chart success with worldwide recognition. I remember the day like it was yesterday. I was slowly strolling and chatting through West London with my long-time friend Commander B (the same Commander B, Choice, and Vibes FM DJ with whom I had shared our very own Brixton Sound System as 'Tippa Graff' back in our school days). When we arrived at Greensleeves' famous record shop, I halted in my tracks, looking wide-eyed at the front window: the single's cover was everywhere, and so too were promotional pictures of me. Commander B, bearing witness, turned and looked me straight in the face: 'Tippa, you gone clear.'

Before this at Mark Angelo Recording Studios, I was having a problem voicing 'Good to Have the Feeling You're the Best', so I decided to take a break from the recording session. I sat in the vocal booth, disappointed with myself and wondering why I was struggling to sing this tune after I had sung it so many times before on the sound. But this was not the sound, it was a recording studio, and I had to get it *perfect* and *on point*. I sat on the floor drinking my regular orange juice, and what happened next changed my life forever. I started to sing, 'Hello, darling... hello, good-looking...' The next voice I heard was my executive producer Chris Cracknell's as he shouted out, 'What is that, Tippa?' I replied that was a lyric I was working on. Chris said, 'Go home and finish writing that song, because it sounds like a hit.' That is exactly what I did, and the rest is history.

In the production of 'Hello Darling' I was joined by first-class musicians. We had our first live rehearsals at Easy Street Studios and moved on to Mark Angelo's (he was the brother of top Page Three model Linda Lusardi). As one combined unit, we decided to create a commercial pop track, which would be formed by using a Linn drum machine and keyboards. It was co-produced with the skilful talents of Patrick Donegan, a former member of UK's top roots band Reggae Regular (which gave us hits such as 'The Black Star Liner' and 'Where Is Jah'), and the excellent engineer Lindel Lewis, who mixed several hit reggae songs including 'Can't Be with You Tonight' by Judy Boucher. I have to sing Lindell's praises; he was responsible for so much in the UK reggae scene. He taught me how to sing harmonies on 'Hello Darling' and how to arrange songs. I knew something serious was in the making: the feeling of the song was of a completely different musical combination. We had created the first UK fusion of jazzy swing, pop, and reggae.

I was happy with the finished product; it was fresh and unique, with a bright sound. The final mix featured Lindel playing the piano and programming the drums. Lead guitar was played by Ciyo Brown, and in the middle of the song, the track breaks with an amazing first-class saxophone solo by Ray Carless. My tune had all the ingredients for national chart success. Hearing the final mix, everyone involved knew it was going to be a record-breaking song within the music industry. I was working in partnership with some of the country's best musicians and producers in the reggae fraternity, and when those men got the feeling, I knew I was onto something special.

Little did I know my song would sell over 70,000 singles, busting Tippa Irie into the British charts at Number 22 and immediately to Number 1 on the UK reggae chart. The single release was accompanied by a music video featuring my debut acting, opening with a wolf whistle. I was looking sharp, dressed in a trilby hat, white shirt, and black tie, dancing around the pool table like Gene Kelly in between footage of me chatting up a beautiful brown-skinned girl (I believe she was a relative of someone on the film crew). I also invited my brethren Daddy Rusty to be in the video, dancing alongside me around the pool table.

I was now functioning on another positive move, ready to step up to the next challenge, the next level. I was a young MC from Saxon Sound System dances; now it was photoshoots, dance moves, and music videos. I felt proud of myself: in those times, it was rare for Black people to feature on TV.

In truth, I was already a hot artist creating a storm within the reggae community. I was already an established UK reggae performer, and an MC frontman for Saxon. 'Hello Darling' was just the cherry on my cake. As I have stated, with positive thinking and a motivated attitude, I had always been focused and determined to move upwards in my music career, never forgetting my roots, my culture, and where I come from. In 'Hello Darling', I no doubt gave Saxon Sound System an upfront mention in the first verse:

> *Hello darling*
> *Hello, good-looking*
> *I said 'Hi, baby'*
> *She said, 'Hey man,*
> *I hear you are the in thing.*
> *You're Tippa Irie from that Saxon Sound System.*

> *Tippa Irie,*
> *'Hello Darling' from the 12' single*
> *(UK Bubblers (Greensleeves Records), 1986)*

'Hello Darling' describes the story of my first trip to America, opening with me being drawn to a smiling, cool, sugar candy girl from downtown Brooklyn named Catherine. We started chatting, and she drove me to her home—she owned her own flat. We shared a finger-licking meal and drank champagne. I started chilling, relaxing, while she told me that she had no need to work because she had been left a million dollars by her Uncle Marvin. This whole experience was truly amazing. Catherine was my dream girl—such a slick chick.

As a reggae MC, I remained loyal to the roots and origins of dance-hall. I was a storyteller—'Complain Neighbour', 'Hello Darling'… all my songs are stories. This is the heritage of Jamaican MCs, the oral tradition of our African ancestors. I was mentored by U-Roy, the godfather. We were well-versed and highly trained poets of the spoken word. In the Saxon sessions we would all unravel a story. Smiley Culture's hit song 'Police Officer' tells of his experience being stopped in his car by the police, who ask him to give them his identification—until the officers notice that it's the famous Smiley, and request autographs before Smiley goes on his merry way. Once again, the Saxon crew brought our London experience to the table, our unique British reggae storytelling.

The road to the success of my release began at Greensleeves, where some major income was happening, and investment in studio time, musicians, and marketing. Mailouts went all over. Below, my manager at the time, Grantley 'GT' Haynes, describes the evolution of 'Hello Darling' and his role from the beginning of our early days working together. I first met Grantley as a promoter in Birmingham who booked me as an MC on dances. Grantley is a manager, producer, and founder of GT's Records. I immediately took to him, admiring his work ethic, character, and professionalism.

I approached Tippa Irie, asking if I could manage his creative affairs. The first question I asked was, 'What would be a sign to let you know you were reaching somewhere?' Tippa immediately replied, 'I would like to drive a brand-new convertible Volkswagen Golf.'

Greensleeves' management had created the UK Bubblers label. They were fixed on developing a standard reggae dancehall sound. My 'management mind' told me we needed something fresh and commercial, a musical brightness, a crossover energy that could reach a wider public audience, establishing an MC style that breaks all boundaries. My money was on the unique jazzy, reggae fusion style of 'Hello Darling'.

Tippa was first on the planet to use a combination of singing and MCing, sing jay, the vocal flow demonstrated on the hit track. In 1985, as one team, we went into Mark Angelo Studios in London. Lindel Lewis played keyboards and engineered the sound. Lindell was a great help and support to UK reggae artists, even providing coaching for up-and-coming new talent and helping Tippa by providing harmonies on his very own tunes. This team, which included Ray Carless on saxophone, Ciyo Brown, and Patrick Donegan, built the layers of what was to become Tippa Irie's national chart hit, 'Hello Darling'.

The radio and club dancehall exposure of 'Hello Darling' pushed my tune into the public arena. British DJ Kid Jensen was the first commercial radio DJ to support the sound of Tippa Irie. He heard 'Hello Darling' in a nightclub and told me he knew it was going to be a hit—and he was right. Thanks to Kid Jensen's show, I was featured on Capital Radio's daily playlist. In 1986, I was invited to be interviewed on Capital, live on David Rodigan's reggae show. I was interviewed by the independent pioneer DJ John Peel and by Tony Williams, who had been the first to play my music. Offering my first airplay on BBC Radio, they would take a keen interest in supporting and playing my new releases.

My musical career was finally rolling. It was a mental shift, an adjustment in thinking and being. I was now being interviewed not just about my music and creativity, but about my personal history. Fame naturally meant being under the bright spotlight. To be honest, I was simply buzzing, happy that all the hard work on the sound system circuit had started to pay off. Within weeks, I started to benefit from my song. With my first paycheque, I kept the silent promise to myself that I would purchase a white convertible Volkswagen Golf GT Sport. I vividly remember putting the key in the ignition for the first time and proudly driving my brand-new car out of the showroom.

I was still learning about how the music industry worked, and that is why I employed Grantley. He was a smart guy who could communicate with the label and help guide me through the future. He set up a publishing company for me and fellow artist Pato Banton, called Liftmoney. It's still going strong today—let's just say it's part of my pension.

As an artist, when my song was featured on the daily playlist, I knew that what I had created connected with the people. The listeners, thankfully, gave it a thumbs-up. I had moved a new style of reggae directly into the ears of the British public. This part of my journey began by doing PA performances. At the height of the tune, I was receiving a nonstop flood of live bookings. These performances involved me chatting on the mic live over an instrumental B-side version of my song, which would be played and mixed through a PA system.

I was still part of the Saxon sound system but due to 'Hello Darling' I was getting booked as a solo artist in my own right all over the West End, in London's most famous clubs, and was rocking crowds with my songs in top nightclubs such as Stringfellows, Limelight Club, Shaftesbury Avenue, and the Wag Club. The release of 'Hello Darling' supported my tour across Europe, as the reggae fever of Tippa Irie spread like an unstoppable forest fire. I performed live in Denmark, Finland, France, Spain… basically, every country in Europe. I developed a strong foundation through performing live. Prior to the release of 'Hello Darling', I'd had many years of personal endurance training as a veteran of the sound system circuit, clash after clash. So, when fame landed at my front door, I was ready as a performer for the hard work. I knew how to handle the circuit.

Touring live through the release of both hit songs, 'Complain Neighbour' and 'Hello Darling', gave me the chance to continue building up my reggae career. My hit single and my reputation led me to a tour of Jamaica, and in 1986 I performed at the famous Reggae Sunsplash, DJ Roll Call, and Sting. The founder of Sting was the legendary Jamaican policeman/promoter Isaiah Laing. He was *not* somebody to cross. People warned me in Jamaica, 'Tippa, be careful when you drive around with Laing, 'cause nuff man want to kill him.' But all the same, I felt safe around him. He looked after me and my sister Miss Irie while we stayed there.

I arrived at Norman Manley International Airport in Kingston and once I entered the terminal was faced with a large billboard advertising TIPPA IRIE. As a young Black man born into Britain's multicultural society, I had to adjust to being surrounded mainly by Black people; it was a shock for me. All around were people who looked like me. I loved it. I don't know *why* I was shocked—it was a Caribbean island—but I had never experienced that before. I can picture now, going to a dance in Jungle (West Kingston), and meeting some of my heroes such as the dancehall DJ Admiral Bailey, standing beside him as he passed the mic to me and my sister. The Jamaican audience was really staring at us: 'Who are these people from England, come to nice up the place!' They were just looking at us and knew straight away we were not from the island: we were not sun-kissed like the islanders and our clothing carried London vibes.

It was amazing to see Admiral perform his hit song 'Punanny' live. The atmosphere was a bit of everything—energy, crowd reaction, live gunshots (which could mean somebody in the dancehall was a policeman, or a soldier, or the area was showing its appreciation for the music). Curiosity grew as my sister and I took the mic and started to MC, especially because we were not born in, nor did we grow up in Jamaica.

You never know what to expect, being around reggae artists; as I anticipated, Admiral rose to the occasion, taking his performance to a higher level, not wanting to be outshined by the British performers coming onto his home turf. I did not want to leave the dance; in fact, we overstayed our time. Laing was not too happy because he wanted us to just touch the mic for half an hour and leave. We ended up performing for about two hours.

In Europe I experienced another level of live touring, performing on the mic to thousands of fans who did not look like me or even understand my language. This was the first time I witnessed the power and energy of reggae music, cutting clearly through all barriers of race and creed. I played in Europe with a whole host of bands, including eighties French pop group Bill Baxter, at the time signed to Virgin Records. Together we performed sold-out shows across France, headlining in Paris. I met Bill Baxter for the first time on a French TV show. We got on straight away when they realised who I was—the group members were quite excited because they loved 'Hello Darling'. Louis Primo, one of the guys in the band, was dating the famous pop singer Kim Wilde at the time—I thought this was cool, as I would see her on *Top of the Pops*. Bill Baxter asked me to do a tune with them, and I agreed.

In 1987, we came up with the hit single 'Bienvenu à Paris' ('Welcome to Paris'), which entered straight into the pop charts in France. We embarked on a promotional tour across the country, doing numerous TV appearances. I recall being dressed up like Sherlock Holmes on one show. I had a lot of fun with those guys, great memories. They were real characters, but no fools. Joe Cool, one of the band members, actually worked for SACEM, the French agency that protects the financial and legal well-being of performers and collects owed royalties on behalf of musicians (equivalent to the Performing Right Society in the UK).

When I returned to the United States to perform after my solo career had really taken off, I spent a lot of time on the West Coast. Roberto Angotti, a popular radio DJ, had a large audience on the US radio station KROQ based in Pasadena, California, with his popular show *Reggae Revolution*. Roberto was like the American equivalent of David Rodigan in the UK. He supported my music and helped me tour across the US. KROQ played Saxon and Tippa Irie from back in my early beginnings.

I entertained dancehall audiences right across California, working alongside reggae singer Pato Banton. In Los Angeles there was more of a Jamaican community, and reggae also had a large Mexican following, especially in places such as the Dub Club in Echo Park. I travelled down from LA to San Diego and played a lot in Solana Beach, at the Belly-Up Tavern. The audiences consisted of surfers and Mexican reggae fans—San Diego being located right on the border of Mexico. I had the pleasure of playing to Mexican people a few times, too; I liked Mexico City and Rosarito, and performed there with the Long Beach Dub Allstars.

I had fun in Tijuana, too, but what a crazy place. I recall leaving my hotel with personal security, 'cause in that place, if you are not careful, you can go missing. Driving to the gig, we had two accidents—one car collision and one motorbike crash. I started to wonder whether I was going to make it in one piece, but my night was just warming up. I did make it, and the show was epic, one of those nights you never forget. Anyway, afterwards there was a long queue of fans wanting to take photos with me; I had never taken so many pictures after a show in all my life. I finished the photos and was making my way to the exit when, all of a sudden, the promoter began pulling down the shutters to shield us from gunfire. It might sound strange, but it was nothing serious: no gangs, just youths showing off after having too much liquor. Let me big up TJ Fire Sound for introducing me to the Mexican people.

Roberto was the first person to bring me and Pato to the West Coast. We started by performing at a number of universities and smaller venues, and bit by bit our popularity started to grow. Going over to the States was like starting all over again. The masses there did not know Tippa Irie. For all musicians, America is renowned for being a difficult place to break through and become successful. Me and Pato worked well touring on the bill together, tight and always delivering a good performance. I liked Pato's professional outlook; as an artist he shared my motivation and drive. We were both willing to give it our all, working hard for our money. We also shared the same manager—Grantley.

In the eighties, BBC's *Top of the Pops* was a big thing in every household up and down the street. The music show hosted an array of the country's legendary artists performing for 60 minutes, and could attract up to 15 million viewers. When it stopped in 2006 it was the longest-running music show in the world (the first episode in 1964 featured the Rolling Stones, with the Beatles in the Number 1 spot). The rundown of the national hot Top 20 would have all eyes glued to it. The BBC presenters included Alan Freeman, Tony Blackburn, Simon Mayo, Noel Edmonds, Reggie Yates, and the now-disgraced Jimmy Savile. This was the eighties, so my generation had to suffer the racist comedy of Jim Davidson (with his 'Chalky White' character), or Les Dawson. So, I was truly thankful to see some black faces on *Top of the Pops*—Bob Marley and the Wailers, Marvin Gaye, Stevie Wonder, the Jackson Five, Musical Youth, Janet Kay, Eddy Grant... finally, reflections of my own self.

In 1986, I was informed by my record label that I would be performing on *Top of the Pops*. All my friends and family gathered around the television to watch. I recall Mum acknowledging that she was proud of her son's achievements as a recognised UK reggae artist, and saying to me: 'Well, so all that speaking and chatting to yourself in the bedroom has paid off.' I purchased some nice, trendy garments in Oxford Street and had my hair cut at my long-time Brixton barbershop, Ozzie's.

In truth, I found *Top of the Pops* a bit of a strange experience, a million miles from the sound system culture I came from. The studio was off Shepherd's Bush. I was brought into the changing room, where you have a wardrobe and make-up artist assigned to you. It was here that I first met Samantha Fox, the British Page Three model, who complimented me, saying, 'Alright Tippa, I like your music; looking forward to watching you.'

I spent the whole day alone, just chilling patiently backstage. I was the one sole reggae MC alongside the likes of Spandau Ballet,

Depeche Mode, The Cure, Sinitta, and Rick Astley. I was performing on the same bill as the cast of *Neighbours* and new pop idols Jason
Donovan and Kylie Minogue. On one side was onetime Wham! frontman George Michael, sporting dark shades and stubble with his hair
slicked back perfectly. The other dressing room held none other than
Boy George, with a painted face, false eyelashes, and multicoloured,
ribbon-filled dreadlocks.

Another strange adjustment was that once on the set, as my song
was announced, I was expected to lip sync in time with the swinging
beat of 'Hello Darling'. As a reggae artist, miming to my music was
the most unnatural way to perform. I stepped onstage sporting my
black leather, peaked cavalry hat—my trademark feature. I clicked my
fingers and grooved down to my song, dancing alongside an array of
young girls who, sadly, had little rhythm.

Although I enjoyed every minute of it, I found the experience
of reaching the top culturally alien. No disrespect intended, but the
famous lives of the people who were quickly surrounding me appeared
empty and fake. They seemed to be filled with self-importance. That
is what I saw of showbiz: it was a lot of pop and fizz, and not much
substance.

I was featured on all the major music shows on TV at the time,
with interviews and afterwards a performance of 'Hello Darling'.
Chris Tarrant's show *Tiswas*, I appeared on Craig Charles own show,
former lead actor in the TV series *Red Dwarf*. I was invited to be interviewed by Paula Yates on *The Tube*, and was the first reggae performer
featured as a guest on Terry Wogan's classic show. One 'first' for the
time was *Club Mix*, a TV show catering solely to reggae music. I audi-
tioned for host of the show, but my Saxon mate Smiley Culture beat
me to the post.

I would go into local newsagents and see photographs of myself
on *Smash Hits*, *New Musical Express*, *The Voice*, and *Black Echoes*, in addition to the reviews and interviews dotted across mainstream media.

Tippa Irie was famous in many dancehall circles up and down my local streets. An enlarged photograph of me was even displayed in WHSmith and HMV, as well as other large, mainstream record shops. In 1986, I was voted Best DJ of the Year by Radio London listeners as well as other accolades.

I would be eating in a restaurant, snatching some private time with my partner, and complete strangers would approach: 'Are you Tippa Irie?' By this time I had performed on *Top of the Pops* a couple of times and people would stop and ask for an autograph wherever I would go—filling up my car at the petrol station, shopping in the supermarket, out with my family, there was no escaping it: my face, and my music were out there. I was approached by major record labels such as Polydor, wanting me to sign.

I had already decided I would stay loyal to Greensleeves; my exposure was contributing to the increasing profile of UK Bubblers. I wanted to give back, because Greensleeves was the first major reggae label that had invested in me. I viewed our business partnership as a genuine relationship. I knew Greensleeves was a business, but it was an independent one, and I valued the arrangement more as a *trusting* relationship.

'Hello Darling' really did open the doors. Below, my Brixton childhood friend, neighbour, and marble-playing champ, Neil Sarisom, tells his story of 'Hello Darling'—and of our reconnection:

> I was in the kitchen at home one day in 1987 and hearing the beat of a great reggae tune coming from the TV. Then, as the singer started to sing, I heard a distinctive, high-pitched voice. I thought to myself, 'Surely not! It can't be...' Soon as I got to the screen, I could not believe my very eyes and ears. Wow, my old best mate from childhood in Brixton, Tony, being interviewed and performing 'Hello Darling' under his artist's name, Tippa Irie! There was my old buddy, live as day on GMTV.

I immediately phoned everyone I knew. 'Did you see GMTV? Bloody hell, it's Tony Henry.' The word went round like a hotline. I was so happy he had reached fame. I had been put in council care, so I did not even know Tony was doing reggae music. Fair play to him. All due respect. I had not seen Tony since our youthful days. But Tony has always stayed a local Brixton lad, like myself. So, I found out he had not gone far.

We got back in touch, and I was his chauffeur at his wedding. Anytime Tony is performing, he will call me, and I will arrange to collect or take him to the airport. Tony has the biggest heart; he will do anything for anyone. Even recently, I phoned him and shared a problem with him, and immediately he responded—in no time, he was straight outside my front door. This is the Tony Henry I know, a great mate. Our friendship together spans over 40 years.

One of the best things on reaching fame, apart from being noticed by the public, is that you are able to give back something financially to those who have been there for you, those who genuinely cared for you. During the period leading up to my national chart successes, good old Mum and I were sharing a flat in a housing estate in Streatham. Throughout my life I've been respectful of my elders, and my mum was the boss. She was my business advisor and personal mentor, and she told me: 'Don't get caught up with the fame business and, Tony, don't waste money on jewellery and vanity.'

I followed her words, obtained a mortgage and invested in a nice semi-detached property with a good-sized garden, an upgrade from our small council flat. We now owned a three-bedroom house, still in Streatham. My new home was full of happy gatherings of friends and family. My good mate from the Saxon Sound System, Maxi Priest, was a regularly welcomed visitor. All the good faces were welcome, with good, warm, loving vibes. Thankfully, I was beginning to reap the rewards of my talents, and I could feel life was now moving in a positive direction.

In 1986, I released a follow-up to 'Hello Darling' called 'Heartbeat'. During the eighties, electronic music was big. It was the time of Gary Numan, Soft Cell, and Frankie Goes to Hollywood, a time of New Wave and Goths. A new age of performers used more machines and fewer musicians. In this vein, Greensleeves also recorded and engineered an electronic synthesised track of mine called 'Panic, Panic'. I was always a versatile reggae performer but I was not sure about this pop-style remix. I believed it was too much of a risky crossover.

One hot summer day, I was called to the office by Greensleeves. On arrival, Chris Cracknell informed me, and several other UK reggae artists present, that from that day onwards the UK Bubblers would be no more. We were shocked. Chris was closing down the record label that had supported reggae artists from the UK. To put the final nail in the coffin, all there were told that the building of another reggae studio in London was being shuttered. Cracknell and engineer Gussie Clarke had their own ideas, and decided to build a studio in Jamaica instead, leaving us UK artists behind. Greensleeves simply switched on us. They baldly stated that they were now concentrating instead on Jamaican reggae artists. Wow, that hurt. I had believed this was a genuine relationship, with all the success I had given Greensleeves—'Tippa and the Colonel, Just a Speak', 'Good to Have the Feeling You're the Best', 'Complain Neighbour', and 'Hello Darling'. I thought, 'why is he doing this?'

This move was not even good business. UK Bubblers was a great platform, and it made no sense closing it down. UK lovers' rock artist Deborah Glasgow was smashing up the charts with her reggae hit 'Knight in Shining Armour'. Peter Spence, Tann-I Browne, and Annette B were also starting to do well as British reggae artists on

UK Bubblers. 'Hello Darling', alongside my other releases, provided Greensleeves with major exposure, and I made good income for the business again and again as the first British reggae MC to have a national hit released on their label. Remember, I had been approached before by major record companies, but had chosen to stay loyal to Greensleeves; it was my personal belief that we were all sharing a vision together, as a team. This was my first rude awakening in the music industry. There are no jobs, careers or lines of employment where the boss gives you only 24 hours' notice that your job is over. I was sacked and suddenly unemployed, my contract immediately terminated. No P-60, just shown the door. Yes, within the music industry this happens to artists, and I was now getting my first taste of it. Chris Cracknell was never my friend after all: to him, I felt like I was just another commodity, like Clint Eastwood & General Saint, who were on Greensleeves before the Saxon MCs. They too were kicked to the curb. Greensleeves just moved on to what was hot at the time.

In the beginning, my contract with Greensleeves was not a bad deal, but it was not great. I signed in 1984 for a payment of £250. In my early twenties I had decided to join the musicians' union. You were required to be a member to perform live on TV. I also received royalty payments through the Peforming Right Society (PRS) for radio airplay. I was now walking the path that so many artists had trod before. It was not an equal partnership; I had found out: it was solely business. In fact, I learned this when I had gladly attended Cracknell's wedding and also performed for the guests—but when I invited him to my wedding, he failed to show up. It was like that, and I began to wake up to the reality of it. The Greensleeves studio, called Music Works, moved to Jamaica, as did Gussie Clarke, the record shop closed down, and in the end, Cracknell and his partner Chris Sedgwick sold up their company and retired nicely from their reggae business.

Patrick Donegan, friend, guitarist, and co-producer of 'Hello Darling', is one of the members of the Tippa Irie crew still engineering behind the desk, and we have travelled the world together. Below is his account of events:

I was born within the most beautiful parish of Jamaica, Portland. My entire family are from Portland. I grew up surrounded by the energy of reggae music, ska, Dennis Brown, and Desmond Dekker, rocking the desks. My cousins were local selectors, and there were sound systems all around. At the age of 10, I left my island to reach England. At 15, I managed to save up while I was at school and bought a guitar. Day and night, I would practise; I am self-taught. I would jam with a fellow schoolmate, who played bass. I went on to become the guitarist for the prominent seventies roots band Reggae Regular.

Our talent resulted in a signing by the major record label CBS. Our relationship ended with CBS because we were a righteous roots band—they were not ready for us. We were looking for consciousness, and the label bosses were looking purely for cash cows. I realised that major UK record labels don't really want reggae to work. It was apparent straight away that UK studio engineers were only used to mixing and producing British rock and pop. Reggae music was a different world and culture from their own. The sound and mix of the pumping bass, the one-drop rhythm, and rhyming melodies. We were the only experts to 'music our own music'. We had the ears. This frustrated me.

One day, I watched a documentary on TV about sound engineers. Instantly, I was hooked. Later, I managed to be schooled by several engineers, giving me lessons on what knobs on the mixing desk to twist and time. I was also schooled by Mad Professor, who had a studio based in Peckham. I had lessons from Gooseberry Studios. Our band, Reggae Regular, became the original UK roots band, and worked with Greensleeves back in 1976. We began a long history together. Our band played the live backing tracks for up-and-coming Greensleeves artists. Later, I also co-produced Sister Love's hit 'Goodbye, Little Man' for the Cool Rockers record label.

Reggae Regular performed live on the same bill as Saxon. The dance was in Huddersfield, in Venn Street. This was the very first time I witnessed the explosive talent of MC Tippa Irie. Tippa was later signed to Greensleeves and was laying down an LP. Singles were being chosen from the LP. I was in the studio for one session when I started pumping the guitar, bom, bom, bom, de, de, and the hook line and melody for 'Hello Darling' were created. Tippa, in grand style, rolled with his lyrics, fitting the timing perfectly.

The rest of the Greensleeves team wanted to concentrate on strictly reggae sound. Once again, I felt I needed to guide the engineers, just like back in the old days. I was a Jamaican born into reggae; I wanted to produce, a swing jazzy, reggae sound that would break through the charts, an uplifting, bright tune. Crossover experimental style is what I tried. We worked at Easy Street Studios, and finally at Mark Angelo Recording Studios. Mark taught me so much as a musical mentor and engineer; he was always willing to help out and support all of us. There was great teamwork, reggae vibes. We were a unit. Everything was working perfectly to plan. We worked tight on the backing track, mixing, inviting the saxophone. I finally added a lead guitar, performed by Ciyo Brown. I co-produced, and the finished product was 'Hello Darling'. We, sat back in the studio, and everyone present knew: it was a bouncing hit. We had created something special.

Tippa Irie went on to fame, reggae featured in the mainstream. Tippa was born to chat on the mic. He has natural talent, is always on point, and is serious about music and polishing his talent.

The tune had done well for Greensleeves, reaching national charts. At this time, UK Bubblers had formed with the purpose of promoting strictly British reggae talent. We had all equally contributed to building Greensleeves, starting with the income from my own band back in the seventies. Tippa was hot, and now the label was promi-nent, mashing up the place.

You must remember that at this time, the eighties, British reggae was even more loved that Jamaican reggae. We had the crown, sound system champions like Saxon, live roots bands, and MCs. We had it all, at our door-step. The aim for UK Bubblers was to continue to build on our winning musical combinations. One strange day we were invited by Chris Cracknell, who informed us that he had decided to wind down UK Bubblers. Greensleeves was changing direction, building a studio in Jamaica with producer Gussie Clarke. We were all devastated—it was happening just as we were creating something unique. The rug was pulled from underneath us. Greensleeves went on to work with Shaggy, and a whole list of reggae artists on the island. We were dropped, no longer being the flavour of the day.

We all dusted ourselves off and carried on inde-pendently in our own ways. I built my own south London studio, Progressive Sound, alongside my independent label Progressive Records, still making dub and reggae. Tippa continues to entertain reggae fans across the world. He stuck to his roots, always professional, focused. Tippa has the creative talent to rock the globe. Today, after 40 years, I am still the one on the mixing desk, the engineer for Tippa Irie's live shows. Together we have stood the test of time. Music will forever be my life, and reggae, my vibration.

I view life's changes as something you just have to move with positively. Grantley and I met and decided to crack on with our own thing. Most times, you achieve very little by resisting change; I wanted success, so I just had to stay focused and keep marching on. Now that the relationship with a bigger record company had come to a sudden end, I tried to not let my new change of musical outlets get me disheartened. No major backers, no distribution deal: I was left with no choice but to finance everything myself, taking on all the business investment risk. Grantley had formed his own independent label, GT's Records, and he and I worked in partnership together on an entirely new project. I invited my original friend MC Daddy Rusty, and we recorded a track called 'Acid', themed around the birth of the UK acid house and rave scene. We recorded 'Acid' because a lot of mates we had grown up with in Brixton were some of the originals in the scene; later jungle was a branch that sprung of the trunk of the London rave scene. I attended the first early parties and dances, it had a large pull, young people attending, acid, ecstasy and high chemical lifestyle, that in truth but truly it was not a scene for me. This side of the independent road made my heartbeat stronger: I was free to develop any style I wanted, when I wanted. I was no longer limited to contracts and creative restrictions—I could work with whichever musicians and performers I chose. This was my life. As they say, one door closes, another one opens.

I am not a sweet talker, I am not a Casanova but the gals still rush mi, 'cause they know I am a super.

Tippa Irie, 'Lyric Maker'
from the LP *Is It Really Happening to Me* (UK
Bubblers (Greensleeves Records), 1986)

Chapter Five

Rocking Lovers

I HAVE ALWAYS BEEN STRICTLY A REGGAE FAN AND, most importantly, a dancehall MC. So, lovers' rock, UK-style reggae, this was something I was woven into. Much has been spoken about the era of lovers' rock. This reggae subgenre has featured in films and documentaries, and there is an extensive catalogue of great tunes. To know and understand the power of its musical and cultural influences, you would have to have been there at its height. Thankfully, I *was* there, at the beginning of the UK lovers' rock scene, and can bear witness to its magic.

It must be understood that the origins of Lovers' rock comes from Black British reggae, a sound created and founded on my very own doorstep. In essence, it was an escape from the outside world: a man holding a woman in his arms, showing complete respect. It was all niceness; this was a new energy, a British blend of reggae brought to our community. UK lovers' rock and the culture it established was an extension of the old-time blues parties and shebeens—once again, a part of my Jamaican heritage carried down through generations. It was great to mingle and meet sweet girls at house parties and dances: the energy of lovers' rock brought us together in oneness, good times, good vibes, and a party atmosphere. Dances were full of slow dance moves: you would rub out the pleats in a girl's skirt. After you had danced and grooved with a girl, you would move together so tight that the wallpaper could be rubbed off behind you.

I loved the energy of women, and equally loved the positive party energy of lovers' rock, lights down low, moving to laid-back tunes. The club scene was just so cool. I would rave all over London. In my neck of the woods the key clubs were Kings on the Rye in Peckham, The Podium in Vauxhall, Oasis and the Four Aces in Dalston, All Nations and Chimes in Hackney. I have memories of so many nice times, dancing at Night Moves in Shoreditch on a Sunday evening, or at the Apollo Nightclub in Willesden.

Getting ready for a night out at such clubs, I would hold a fresh (bathe), and splash on my best aftershave. I was not a money person, so I put on my Farah trousers and my pair of crocodile shoes, my Gabicci shirt. My sovereign ring and belcher chain and my one choperita. No need to go to barber's cause afro was in, so just brought my afro comb. I would be creative with my style adorning my calvary hat. I had a red Ford Escort, Mark 1, that was my personal mode of transport. I'd arrive at the club around 10pm, and I would be buzzing as a young man in heat. I was filled with excitement, ready and hoping to meet a new female. On entering the dance, I would scout and browse around to see what women were available and was not standing next to a man. I found it was better to head in the direction of a group of ladies 'cause you would have a better chance connecting with one of them. First thing I would do was make eye contact. If you look and get a smile in return this was an invitation but if you make eye contact and receive a cold screw face stare, it was a sign to leave it. I would discreetly and slowly move into a position to ask, 'how are you doing? Is everything okay?', 'Are you enjoying yourself?', 'Would you like a drink?' hopefully these questions would lead to a dance. If you had a good response and vibe was right, I could be dancing the whole night long listening to the sounds of lovers' rock.

I was 13 and it was the seventies when I first began to appreciate UK lovers' rock, with the release of 'The Man in Me', written and performed by the legendary lovers' rock producer, Dennis Bovell with

My father Steven
Alexander Henry

My mother Celeste Henry

My grandmother Josephine McNish

My cousin, Hector Henry, and
my granddad, Beckwick McNish

My mum with my sisters Avril
and Jackie

MISS IRIE aka
Avril Elaine Henry—my sister

My sister Jacqueline Henry

DESCRIPTION *SIGNALEMENT*

	Bearer *Titulaire*	Wife *Femme*
Profession	Dressmaker	
Profession	Reserve	
Place and date of birth	Trelawny	JAMAICA
Lieu et date de naissance	20th December 1939.	
Country of Residence	ENGLAND	
Pays de Résidence		
Height	5 ft. 5½ in.	ft. in.
Taille		
Colour of eyes	Dark Brown	
Couleur des yeux		
Colour of hair	Black	
Couleur des cheveux		
Special peculiarities		
Signes particuliers		

CHILDREN *ENFANTS*

Name *Nom*	Date of birth *Date de naissance*	Sex *Sexe*
Jacqueline Pauline HENRY	6.3.64	Female
Avril Elaine HENRY	9.12.67	Female

CANCELLED

Celesta Mae Henry

Usual signature of wife
Signature de sa femme

Bearer
Titulaire

Wife
Femme

CANCELLED (PHOTO)

Mum's passport

My dad in our corner shop

Me in my early teens

Me, age 10

Shabba Ranks, Miss Irie, and me

Me and Miss Irie

Me and Dad in Jamaica

Mum in the basement of our house blues dance room

Me and my sons Raphael, Micah, and Kash

Me and my daughter Rochelle at the Redway graduation

Me, my friend, and my son Micah

Me, Micah and the Ragga Twins

Me with school basketball team at
Beaufoy Secondary School–2nd year.

Me with the March Forth Kenya
Kids in Nairobi Kenya

Me, Smiley Culture and Asher Senator

Daddy Colonel and me

Me and General Slater

Me and Grantley Haynes

Me, Grantley Haynes and Pato Banton

Me and the girl from the 'Hello Darling' video

Me at the 'Hello Darling' video shoot

Tippa Irie & the Complaint Neighbour

Greensleeves promo picture

Me in the 90s

Me in my new Golf convertible car

Me in France

Me, Peter Spence and Sweetie Irie in Japan

Me on the road in the USA

Hector Cross, Dennis Bovell, Peter Huningale, Derek Cross, and me

Oneko Arika, me and Dr Ring Ding at METRO FM in Nairobi, Kenya

Me and Roberto Angotti

Me And Patrick Donegan

Me and Black Steel

Me and Crucial Robbie

Me, Pato Banton and Bob Burger

Me and Cecil Rennie
King Tubby UK

Me and Dennis Seaton
from Musical Youth

Me and Ali Campbell from
UB40

Me and Trininty

Me, Carroll Thompson and Kofi

Me, Janet Kay, and Peter Huningale

Me and Big Youth

Me, Dr. Ring Ding and Nadirah X

Me and Shaggy

Me and Neville Staple

his band Matumbi. Dennis was local and worked at Spark Side Studio in Brixton. He was responsible for producing artists such as Linton Kwesi Johnson and Janet Kay. He was also a soundman like me. His sound was named Jah Sufferer. Dennis later produced a song with me and Nadirah X titled 'Fight Fi the Roof'.

'Love Me Tonight' by Trevor Walters and 'Be My Lady' by Peter Hunnigale were two of my favourite releases. But when I watched Janet Kay perform her smash hit 'Silly Games' in 1979 on *Top of the Pops*, that was the first lovers' rock performance on a national level that really resonated with me. The song is a musical fusion: if you listen to the drum pattern played by Drummie Zeb, it is a reggae stepper beat that fuses with Janet's sweet voice—a perfect ingredient for a hit tune.

Lovers' rock has many varied patterns and combinations, both slow swing and rocksteady, fused with the one-drop drumbeat. UK lovers' rock has a very distinctive and unique sound. The music possesses a soulful, refined, toned-down style of reggae played on grand pianos or keyboards, a flowing pick guitar sound, a creeping, soothing soft bass line sometimes mixed with violins. Most songs feature upfront vocals and catchy choruses accompanied by soulful harmonies.

Several lovers' rock hit tunes were produced by south London's Mad Professor, on his own independent Ariwa Sounds label, which played a major part in the UK reggae scene. Ariwa song productions such as Sandra Cross's 'Country Living' and 'If I Gave My Heart to You' by John McLean, were classic lovers' rock sounds.

Carroll Thompson's (some consider her the Queen of Lovers' rock), first two singles were produced by Leonard Chin: 'Simply in Love', and 'I'm So Sorry'. I knew another skilful engineer called Bertie Grant who successfully produced some of Carroll's other hit songs, such as 'Hopelessly in Love', 'Just a Little Bit', and 'A Happy Song'. Carroll and Bertie went on to form C & B Productions, and later Carroll's Carousel label produced 'Dim the Light' and 'Daughter of Zion' by Winston Reedy.

In the late seventies we were blessed with the music of Audrey Scott, Michael Gordon and the Investigators, 15 16 17, Paul Dawkins, and Tradition, home-grown artists who all had several giant club hits playing lovers' rock. The vibes these artists carried inspired me musically. Their lyrics were centred on love, and the highs and lows of relationships. The words 'baby I love you' would feature in most lovers' rock releases. Themes such as *breaking up is hard to do, I am missing you,* or *I am leaving you* speak of love and rejection, with lyrics expressing heartbreak, jealousy, temptation, and one-night affairs. But the central themes of lovers' rock are falling in love for the very first time; the sparkle of romance; love at first sight; true love; the trials of young romance; marriage and commitment; building a home and family together. We were not afraid to express physical attraction—to me, it is a natural part of life. As Marvin Gaye sang, 'sexual healing… is good for us.'

It may appear strange to younger readers, and maybe I seem old-fashioned, but my examples of love and relationships were rooted in tradition that came down through my family, that were passed down through my Afro-Caribbean culture. As a reggae MC, I kept these true values, and committed myself to never saying anything derogatory about women in my lyrics. This is not how I was raised. During the period of lovers' rock, women were respected and valued, and this was expressed in the songs; they were viewed and treated as our sisters, mothers, and queens. Back in my raving days, women dressed with modesty, and were classy and glamorous. On the other side of the coin, men attending dances were smart, and went out to the lovers' rock clubs clean-cut, suited and booted. I would buy a pair of new slacks, shiny shoes, a pretty shirt. I routinely visited my local barbershop for a trim. Splash on plenty of cologne, and I was ready to go and dance the night away.

Instrumental in supporting our British lovers' rock scene were the great London-based independent reggae record labels: the likes of Fashion Records, Ariwa Sounds, Greensleeves, Progressive Sound, Groove & A Quarter. These labels provided breaks for up-and-coming UK artists. Thankfully, I had exposure from the best outlets, good-quality record labels, and first-class producers. London, once again, was home to many pioneering reggae producers. Making and conjuring magical sounds in the studio, these talented men were responsible for popularising the genre of lovers' rock worldwide. Dennis Bovell, Patrick Donegan, Chris Lane, Gussie P, Ruff Cutt Band, Mafia & Fluxy, Bertie Grant, Mad Professor, Peter Hunnigale, Lindel Lewis, Drummie Zeb and Tony 'Gad' Robinson from Aswad, Paul Robinson *aka* Barry Boom and his brothers from One Blood. Remaximum and Easy Street were among the studios where the hits were created. The likes of Dennis Brown and Freddie McGregor recorded lovers' rock songs with British record labels, produced on our soil. My long-time brethren Peter Hunnigale went on to produce his first LP independently on the Street Vibes label, titled *In this Time*.

Radio deejays Tony Williams and Ranking Miss P gave the first airplay to British lovers' rock music. Their support opened doors for me, and I gained wider exposure with their help. There were several sound systems that promoted and played our lovers' rock music, making this reggae genre their chosen vinyl on the decks: sounds such as Sir George, Sir Lloyd, Gemi Magic and Diamonds, a Girl's Best Friend.

Anthony Brightly from Sir George also managed the Chimes nightclub in north London where I had many a good night. The club was filled with all kinds of characters, but the vibe of the music drew me there. You had a whole heap of yardies (Jamaican born) who still thought they were back in Kingston and the local Londoners who never connected with the yardies; all the women dressed up to the nines like Xmas trees. A night would not pass by without a visit from the police and inside the clubs were always plain clothes, undercover police. Well, they thought they were undercover, but we knew exactly who there were.

Our dances were a bigger extension of our house parties, the opposite to the male-dominated sound system culture. The love tunes and themes alongside a softer form of reggae attracted girls in abundance. Lovers' rock dances were lights-down-low, truly intimate affairs. The fact that so many women attended meant the men were sure to follow: a guaranteed audience.

Female UK lovers' rock artists who successfully featured on the reggae charts from the seventies through to nineties were hitmakers such as Louisa Mark, Jean Adebambo, Judy Boucher, Audrey Scott, Janet Kay, Carroll Thompson, Donna Marie, Sandra Cross, JC Lodge, Kofi, Sylvia Tella, Winsome, Deborah Glasgow, Paulette Tajah, and Janet Lee Davis. Male artists included Peter Spence, Lloyd Brown, Phillip Leo, Peter Hunnigale, Winston Reedy, Don Campbell, Richie Davis, Nereus Joseph, Vivian Jones, Victor Romero Evans, Trevor Hartley, Roger Robin, Bitty McLean, Dennis Bovell, Trevor Walters, Barry Boom, Michael Gordon, Trevor Dixon, Maxi Priest, and Mike Anthony. Lovers' rock bands included Arima, the Administrators, Tradition, the Investigators, and girl groups such as Charisma.

My lifetime friend and musical partner, Peter Hunnigale, explains more about the music:

> Lovers' rock is a subgenre of Jamaican reggae, so we cannot play it the same, can't make it the same; we don't have the Jamaican ear, we don't have the Jamaican experience or technique. As UK reggae musicians, we are emulating a sound but using different chords, a more colourful, melodic, and varied range. It's a bit sweeter in the sound. Jamaican music tends to use more root notes. In the UK we were singing about love and relationships, Jamaican artists focused more on poverty and the hardships of

growing up—hard times, what was going on within their social structure and society.

Jamaica still would have its lovers' music—great songs from artists such as Freddie MacGregor, Delroy Wilson, and Sugar Minott. I took my influences of vocal harmonies from the Abyssinians and the Mighty Diamonds. Back in the day the UK studios drew reggae artists such as Dennis Brown, Sugar Minott, and Gregory Isaacs. During the time they spent living in the UK, our music had an effect and influence on them, and we should be proud of this history.

Ali Campbell speaks about the ups and downs of the music industry.

In Jamaica, the birthplace of reggae, we tried to educate and support foundation reggae artists who had not been paid for their work, showing other artists what we had learnt as UB40 and encouraging performers to join the PRS and musicians' unions, to find out about rates of pay and how to protect and value yourselves. When I met Lord Creator in hospital, he was broke; UB40 covered 'Kingston Town'. After the release, he started getting paid his royalties, enabling him to build a big house and settle his private hospital bills. UB40 also established reggae recording studios on the island.

What had been happening was that reggae performers on the island needed money, and would accept a cash advance payment. This would be paid by the producer or record label to the artist—and that would be the last bit of cash they would see. The music might go on to sell thousands. In our beginnings, as a band, we had learnt from my dad's experiences in the music business. Even though we were only getting £7.80 on the dole, when we were offered an advance payment of £150,000 we turned it down, stayed independent and went on to reach Number 2 on the UK albums chart. The Jamaican foundation artists were paid a pittance instead of getting a fair and just percentage.

Points, percentages, royalties, owning your masters, have always been the ways to protect your art. Today, within the industry, downloads are killing our music. We must press on and continue to adapt to these changes. Live music is our only real way of earning as a performer.

To create a hit, first I would have to have the perfect tune, the right beat mix and sound, to capture the right energy at the right time. Growing up in south London I had the added benefit of being surrounded by so many talented producers and reggae and lovers' rock artists. I was out on the road weekend after weekend, doing PA performances. Later in my career, I performed lovers' rock with a live band. I had four hit singles 'Stress', 'It's A Love Ting', 'Baby I've Been Missing You' and 'Raggamuffin Girl' all on the British reggae charts, collaborating with several prominent artists in the movement. I won numerous musical-recognition awards and was part of, and witnessed, the evolution and explosion of the music we call lovers' rock.

I am not 100 percent sure—correct me if I am wrong—but I believe I was the first British dancehall reggae MC to put a combination of MC and lovers' rock singers together. Back in the day, you would have the vocals, and the toaster would feature at the end of the tune. We had tunes from Daddy U-Roy such as 'Soul Rebel', which blended his style around the singers. My style was completely original, adding my cheeky-chappie vibes and my ability to adapt to any form of music. This gave me the Midas touch. I interacted with the song,

Step up Mr Honey Vibes and tell them what a
gwaan, Lord have mercy
Rice and peas and chicken stuffing
any girl that me get she have fi raggamuffin
Rice and peas and chicken stuffing
any girl that me get she have fi raggamuffin
From the way that she talk, she a raggamuffin
and from the way she walk, she a raggamuffin
From the things that she do, she a raggamuffin
I man love her for true, cause she a raggamuffin
girl
Cause when she whine an go down, she a
raggamuffin
When she whine and come up, she a raggamuffin
When the girl do the duck, she a raggamuffin
and when she whine and stuck, she a ragamuffin.

Peter Hunnigale feat. Tippa Irie, 'Raggamuffin
Girl' from the LP *A New Decade* (Mango (Island
Records), 1991)

ad-libbing in and out from the start. This provided a new energy that complemented the smooth singers, both male and female. I was the final piece in the puzzle. My involvement and talent got the result that was needed: a hit song. My first single release in this style was titled 'Raggamuffin Girl'. This collaboration with Peter Hunnigale reached Number 1 on the reggae charts in 1989.

Peter Hunnigale, *aka* 'Mr Honey Vibes', describes the time we both made 'Raggamuffin Girl', our first unique lovers' rock/dancehall fusion hit:

> It was in 1986, and my lovers' rock release 'Be My Lady' went to Number 6 on *Black Echoes'* reggae charts. Locally, people would now recognise me in my own right as Peter Hunnigale; attention from the ladies, it was great, but I never took my eyes off the musical prize. I stopped doing the live bands and concentrated on my own ting.
>
> At the beginning of the nineties, Delroy Clarke, fellow musician and one of my brethren, had just come back from Jamaica and advised me to take up some dancehall reggae music vibes, branch out with some collaborations. So, I had a little drum machine and created a beat and played the bass on it. I played it to the Choice FM DJ Paul Blake (Commander B), who was my schoolfriend and engineer Fitzroy Blake's younger brother. Paul was a schoolmate with Tippa Irie; all four of us grew up in Helix Road, on the block together.
>
> Paul then invited Tippa, who at the time was famous through Saxon and 'Hello Darling', with chart success. I had already laid down the vocal pattern, 'Walking down the road the other day'… Tippa joined me and came with his original style, his rolling MC catch line chorus 'rice and

peas and chicken stuffing'. All around us could not understand what the vibe was, so I was getting a little fight; I was
known as strictly a lovers' rock singer, and people in the
media and music business were like, 'what is this 'chicken
stuffing' business', but the twist of it in the end is that our
song, 'Raggamuffin Girl', went on to become a Number 1
hit in the UK reggae charts. Even in Switzerland, it went
to Number 1. It was a great hit for us, and we went on to
do a combination LP together, *A New Decade*, and a second
LP, *Done Cook and Curry* with Rebel MC.

In 1981, UK lovers' rock artist Trevor Walters reached Number 27
on the UK charts with 'Love Me Tonight', crossing over to the mainstream. He had further hit song with 'Stuck on You'. In 1987, Maxi
Priest, with his hits 'Wild World' and 'Some Guys Have All the Luck',
rose to smash-hit status—'Wild World' peaked at Number 5 on the
national charts. This represented another one of our own crossing
over and signing successfully to a major label (Virgin Records). Lovers'
rock began to fly.

In 1990, I had a hit single with Peter Spence, 'Girl of My Best
Friend'. Peter was always good to me, and we got on very well. I met
him through Grantley, our manager in Birmingham, who organised
our musical connection. Peter was a ladies' man; he was deadly. You
would *not* want him around your girlfriend. Together we formed a
great team. Most memorable was a show we did together for PCRL,
the Birmingham community radio station. We actually smashed the
place to pieces, performing our hit song. As soon as we walked on
stage, the young ladies were screaming and trying to maul us and pull
us off stage. We could not even get through our song due to the excitement of the ladies present. We had to keep pulling up our hit song and
started again, the atmosphere was simply electric.

This same song took me to Japan—my first time ever reaching that

Ring a ding, ding ding
Cause mi say what's the matter with him
make you wanna love my girl so
One thing mi no, mi na gonna let her go
You think you are a go get fi mi girl just so
Well, make I tell you something, nothing no
go so
The two of we grow up down in the ghetto
Mi never once look pon your girlfriend so
and soon as you see me girlfriend, name is
Coco
You start gwaan like you a Romeo.

Tippa Irie and Peter Spence, 'Girl of My Best Friend' from the LP *Original Raggamuffin* by Tippa Irie (Mango (Island Records), 1990) part of the world. 'Girl of My Best Friend' was an Elvis Presley cover we produced in reggae style, and featured on my 1990 LP *Original Raggamuffin* (Mango), alongside another cover version: 'Stand by Me', originally sung by Ben E. King. I was surprised by how much they loved the old tunes in Japan; they were drawn to our classic covers. This helped sales of the LP.

When I arrived at the airport in Tokyo, I found the technology so advanced in every form. The weather was nice and warm; the food, up and down. Truly, I was not into sushi and Japanese food—I have never been into the raw fish ting. The people who brought us into the country gave us the five-star treatment though, and we did five shows in total: two live performances in Tokyo and three across Osaka and Nagoya. The fans were genuinely into my music; it was amazing to see Japanese audiences singing along to our songs. The live band was tight—I used a backing band from Birmingham, with Steve Clarke on drums, Peter Spence on guitar, and Preacher alongside Ryan on keyboards. MC Sweetie Irie opened the show for us as the supporting act.

I was a little bit nervous, but my nerves melted away as soon as I saw the smiles on the faces of the people in the audience. It was like they could not believe I was there in person. That made me want to give my all. The shows all went well, and the promoters were very happy. I found it amazing the way the people were disciplined at the end of our show; everything was immediately packed away, and the audience had gone. The production teams and our itinerary were on point, with no stone left unturned. I was impressed by the profession-alism. I was again blown away when I went to Club Jamaica, a reggae club in Tokyo—it was like being at a Saxon dance back home, or a Stone Love dance in Kingston, the clothes and everything. And the Japanese girls had rhythm—they could dance. I found that everything the Japanese liked or followed, they would replicate exactly, and reggae music was no different.

* * *

Lloyd Brown: I had known him from back in the day. I first saw him performing at People's Club in Paddington, and he sang with the Exodus Sound System. I recognised his talent back then. Together we released our UK reggae-chart Number 1 hits 'Stress' and 'It's a Love Thing'. We recorded an LP called *Combination*, released by Tex Johnson on Discotex, his record label. We also recorded the single 'Baby Mother', which was our first release together on a major label—Arista Records. Chris Hill, one of the deejays at the sell-out Caister Soul weekenders, was responsible for signing us to Arista. It was really an experience for me: at Arista we were introduced to two white guys who were part of the A&R team; they both really loved and understood 'urban music'.

They then introduced us to a Black guy whose role was to push our musical careers. We were initially over the moon, because we thought we had a brother in our camp, but the only thing he was focused on at the time was TLC and their hit 'Waterfalls'. He did not help us at all, and clearly did not understand how to market reggae music. In the end, strange as it may seem, it was the Black promoter who *least* understood our UK style of reggae. We made one video and one single, and that was the end of our relationship with Arista.

For Fashion Records, I added a dancehall vibe alongside the vocals of Janet Lee Davis on the release of 'Baby I've Been Missing You', a cover of Bunny Maloney's classic tune. I first met Janet at Fashion's A-Class Studio with producers Chris Lane ('Mr Cheerful') and John MacGillivray from Dub Vendor. Their studio was based in Stanstead Road, Forest Hill. Chris was a miserable sod, but always told you the truth no matter who he upset along the way. I can never forget Gussie P, who started off as an apprentice engineer but later rose to become one of the key members in the Fashion camp. Gussie was a character,

Honour for yu body girl
honour for yu shape
and for your nice little face.

'It's a Love thing', Tippa Irie and Llyod Brown,
Groove and a Quarter record. 2005

Now ever since we kiss this girl I can't resist
This girl miss me so much I can't resist
Mr Irie and Janet Lee Davis
Why the girl a miss the Tippa because me
have the charm,
mi no stop love her from dusk to dawn
I will water the lawn, sow the seed pon the
farm
when she sees Tippa a come, she just sounds
the alarm
We a go sound the alarm loud and clear
because we have the ting that she wants,
year to year
Although I am not always there because of
mi career
I believe my woman is very sincere
I am going to tell you why the girl love the
Tippa and ting
cause I am a youth man who is very genuine
Mi a loving, caring and sharing
and exciting when we get skin to skin
Well, me a go tell you why the girl, just a love
the Tippa
because me have the ting the doctor ordered
Them say absence makes the heart grow
fonder
because she love the DJ, she don't want
another.

Janet Lee Davis and Tippa Irie, 'Baby I've
Been Missing You' from the 12' single
(Fashion Records, 1994)

always with the jokes and spliffs in hand. He took no prisoners and would laugh in the face of performers who did not reach the required standard. Fashion had a vast back catalogue of British reggae hits. Fashion knew the game well, they were a good quality team, totally dedicated to the music.

Now let me move on to Miss 'I-Don't-Pick-Up-My-Phone' Winsome, my fellow performer in the house, the go-to woman inside the Peforming Right Society (PRS), the Chief Advisor, the Princess. I have so many names for this woman, so bubbly, cheeky, bursting with character... and the girl can sure sing. In 1989, my MC vocals complemented her track 'Superwoman', produced and released by Fashion Records. Winsome did justice to this Karyn White classic we recorded. Our tune was put together by the legendary Sly Dunbar of Sly and Robbie fame. Whenever these great musicians came from Jamaica, John from Fashion would capture them and see what new tunes and beats they had up their sleeves. Sly and Robbie worked alongside Fashion, our UK label, re-recording tunes in reggae style.

I created music with lovers' rock royalty, featuring, for instance, on Janet Kay's LP *In Paradise*. I was on a roll—who would believe I worked alongside the Queen of Lovers' rock, who I had first watched on my TV screen in 1979? Later in 2013, we recorded a track titled 'I Want to Know', produced by Junior Giscombe. Working together, I learnt another valuable lesson: make sure everything is clear and written in stone when it comes to agreements; *have a contract*. Unfortunately, there was a miscommunication. I wanted a publishing percentage for my lyrics, but they were offering a one-off payment only. I was not happy with this decision, but I really wanted to work with Janet—so I let it slide. But it did teach me something I will always remember, and it made me wiser and better prepared for the future.

I did many a show with Janet Kay and her husband Victor Romero Evans, and we have become very good friends over the years. I admire

Janet's longevity, how she and Carroll Thompson have managed to keep their careers going; they are real role models to me, and I respect them in every way. I believe they should enjoy more recognition for the contributions they have made to reggae music.

Below my good friend Janet Kay, the Queen of Lovers' rock, describes her history, giving testimony to the era:

My parents come from the Jamaican parish of Saint Thomas. I am directly connected to Paul Bogle. My great-grandfather was one of the first Baptist deacons in the Morant Bay church, and my family lived opposite the courthouse where the statue was erected recognising Paul Bogle a as a national hero. He was a leader of the 1865 Morant Bay protesters, who marched for justice and fair treatment for all people in Jamaica.

I was born in Willesden Green, North London to strict West Indian parents. Our family would attend the local Baptist church. I spent the majority of my schooling in North London, but for a short while our family moved to Barnet, where me and my brother were the only Black people in the entire school. Thankfully, we moved north-west, and I attended secondary school in Kilburn.

My first exposure to music was listening to pop; the artist Lulu was great, and singing along to the Beatles' chart hits and listening to the sweet voice of Andy Williams, and to Dionne Warwick, Ginger Williams, Gladys Knight, and Marvin Gaye. I loved all the Motown acts; the Jackson Five and little Michael were my favourites. Seeing them perform on TV was the first time I really saw anybody else looking like me in the British media, performers that were representing Black music. When it came to reggae, Dennis Brown was the one for me.

I really enjoyed the acts featured on a seventies TV programme on Sunday nights called *Live at the Palladium*. I looked forward to *Top of the Pops*—I would be glued to the screen, singing along to the words of the latest pop entertainers. I would buy a magazine called *Disco 45*, and it would feature the lyrics of the latest songs. I was that girl who sang in the mirror, using my comb as a microphone. I was a big *Top of the Pops* fan, taping all the shows on our family VCR.

I sang at the Girls' Brigade and in my church choir. One day, my best friend from school, the lovers' rock artist Sonia Ferguson—who at the age of 14 had a hit song titled 'Ooh Baby, Baby' (I provided the backing vocals for the song)—invited me to a rehearsal session with Aswad. The studios were situated in Harrow Road, connected to a record shop called Gangster Ville. I saw the microphones plugged in and I sang a few words, the first time I had ever sung through a PA system. Tony 'Gad' Robinson from Aswad heard me, and was impressed. Tony said there was a tune Alton Ellis was looking to record, and that I could be right for the part. The release was a cover of Minnie Riperton's song 'Lovin' You'. I went home to ask my parents, and they said no to the idea straight away. For days and days, I pleaded and begged. My father would have to meet the people who were inviting his daughter to their studio. Alton Ellis agreed to come to my family home and speak with my parents. Alton went into the living room to discuss the plans with my father; we as children were not even allowed in that same living room!

As a teenage girl in 1977, I recorded 'I Do Love You' and 'That's What Friends Are For'. I sang a version of 'Silhouette' and Louisa Mark's 'Caught You in a Lie'. Together Alton Ellis and I recorded a hit duet together titled 'I'm Still in Love with You'. Our song reached Number 1 in the UK reggae charts. Working alongside a producer named Delroy Witter, all my lovers' rock releases made it to Number 1 in the British reggae charts.

In 1979, Dennis Bovell produced 'Silly Games'. We recorded at Gooseberry Studios in the West End, near Chinatown. Drummie Zeb from Aswad would play the live drums on the track. The single was originally released on a white label. 'Silly Games' was first supported by the North London reggae sound system Sir George. The song then caught on, and was played everywhere. It was a hit. 'Silly Games' would finally be released and distributed by Arawak Records.

Lovers' rock is a unique, strictly UK style formed during the early seventies. I would describe it musically as a fusion of pop, Motown, and R&B, mixed with ska, rocksteady, bluebeat, and reggae. We were young girls when we were singing this music. As teenagers, we wrote about our first loves, falling in love, and breaking up. Our music's central focus was on love. Our British lovers' rock sound became so big that it drew attention from Jamaica. Top performers such as Dennis Brown, Sugar Minott, Gregory Isaacs, and Alton Ellis all came and worked in London, through the love of UK lovers' rock style.

For me, Sharon Forrester was one of the founders of lovers' rock. In 1973 she recorded her reggae hit 'Silly, Wasn't It?'. In 1975 came Louisa Mark's hit song 'Caught You in a Lie'... The Black British female trio Brown Sugar released 'I'm in Love with a Dreadlocks' featuring Caron Wheeler of Soul II Soul.

From the beginning of the eighties, Carroll Thompson became a great lovers' rock performer. Back in those times, the bands and performers were majority-female. Lovers' rock possessed a strong female foundation.

I was away on my first holiday… and received a telephone call that I must come straight home. My song 'Silly Games' had started to climb up the UK national charts, and they wanted me to perform on *Top of the Pops*.

I could not believe it; it was my dream come true. I had been a weekly fan of *Top of the Pops*, and now I was to perform on the show. I had no budget for clothes, so I looked around my bedroom to see what I could wear. I took out a knee-length, pink t-shirt that was in fashion at the time—we used to tie a knot in the side. I wore my hair in a natural afro, and I chose to wear a flowing headscarf with sequins sewn on it.

I come from humble beginnings, the eldest daughter of eight children. I had never received any special grooming; I had not attended drama or dance school. I never had singing classes or vocal mentoring. What I had was a strong ambition and inner determination. I had a dream that I wanted to manifest as a reality.

On arrival at the *Top of the Pops* studio, the programme management informed me that I had to mime to the words of 'Silly Games'. I had never practised lip syncing before, so I sang live. I was scared but determined. I had never even performed live before—*Top of the Pops* was my first time! To think that in front of me and the audience were millions of viewers, watching me sing live…

I would perform three times on *Top of the Pops*. 'Silly

Games' reached Number 2 on the UK national charts. I was also featured in the *Guinness Book of World Records* as the first British-born Black female performing a reggae track to reach the pop charts. I became the first artist to make lovers' rock cross over to a wider audience.

Even though 'Silly Games' reached the top of the national charts and the single was played everywhere and sold in the millions, it would not end up being a good deal for me. I would never see any financial reward. I was never involved in any contract or licencing deals, or in any management agreements. I was a young girl—I did not have any knowledge of the legal side of the music business. I don't really like discussing that situation, so let's move on.

My disappointment and dissatisfaction with the music industry led me to take up several roles as an actress. I was on the set one day of *Babylon*, the movie featuring Brinsley Forde from Aswad, and I asked Victor Romero Evans how I could get into acting. Victor introduced me to his network, and I had my first acting roles featuring in a TV show titled *No Problem!* on Channel 4. I also played a part in a theatre show, *Mama Dragon*, produced by the Black Theatre Company.

I first met Tippa Irie on *Top of the Pops* in 1986, when he was performing 'Hello Darling'. Tippa is a fantastic reggae performer, so talented and gifted as an MC. He established a unique UK fusion of Jamaican and British music. I did not know Tippa from the early Saxon days, 'cause in truth I was never really a raver. I invited Tippa to perform a track on one of my LPs. It was a combination singer-and-MC duet called 'I Want to Know'. Tippa, as usual, delivered his great dancehall verse.

Tippa Irie brought a fun side to reggae and lovers' rock.

Now, once bitten, twice shy
I am simply that kinda guy
Now I know that you're kind of confused
but my heart I don't want to lose
Well, you say you check for me
but me check for you too
But to be quite honest
mi know not what to do
Before I met you, I was in love with Sue
and she took mi heart and broke it in two
Well, you say the loving that you have
but this DJ no wanna end up sad
I know you are the number one pon the chart
but I don't want you to break Tippa heart
Mi say each and every time
but I don't want you leave mi behind
Once bitten, twice shy
I am that kinda guy
and I am not sure if I wanna give love a try
I know one day I gonna have to try again
but the question is when.

Janet Kay, feat. Tippa Irie, 'I Want to Know'
from the LP *In Paradise* by Janet Kay
(Sony Music, 1996)

A wonderful entertainer. We have been on so many shows together, and after so many years we are still close friends. Tippa is so honest and friendly; I simply love him.

In the nineties, I worked with Beats International on 'Burundi Blues'. My songs were being played all over Japan, too: 'Silly Games' became Number 1 in the country. It was a bigger hit in Japan than it was in the UK—I was not made aware of any of that happening to my music.

One day, I received a phone call from Sony Music inviting me to sign a deal and produce an LP. The previous Janet Kay LP they had produced didn't even have me on the front cover of the sleeve—it featured another Black girl. In over 40 years in the music business, I had never been signed or approached by any British recording company. I had never been offered a deal. So I could not afford to lose this Sony break, in Japan, but at the time I was eight months' pregnant. Thankfully, the label was supportive—and the management was female. Two weeks after my son was born, I spent four months solid recording *Love You Always*. The front cover even features a photograph of me and my new born son.

To date, I have recorded over 15 LPs, and I am still performing lovers' rock after 40 years. I believe that for new artists coming up, the way forward is music downloads, internet exposure. You can be your own boss; you don't have to sign to any record label. You can be in control of your creativity, and remain independent. Create yourself and your own chosen image on social media for free.

I am thankful, with all the struggles that I have been through, that I am still here, alive. I have learnt that life is a forever-learning process, I will never stop learning the lessons life continues to show me.

Back in the seventies and the origins of the genre, as Janet Kay attested, it was common for young girls to be exploited by the record bosses. These females were vulnerable, innocent teenage artists. They were just coming up, trying to get a break. The companies left the performers high and dry while the industry skimmed the cream. What happened to Janet Kay and '*Silly Games*' is, sadly, another mainstream music industry story.

Greed is once again the main feature. The record companies function for themselves, not the artists. Several prominent UK lovers' rock performers who released major hits ended up being ripped off. Another example of this is Felix Da Silva, who wrote, produced, and arranged 'Can't Be with You Tonight' by Judy Boucher. This hit song should have been Felix's lifetime lottery win, but he signed a bad recording deal and lost out on thousands of pounds, if not millions. There are no friends in business, as I had learnt from my experiences at Greensleeves.

Our music was also held back. Lovers' rock should have been released and marketed through the mainstream. Why were the likes of Jamaica's Beres Hammond or our own UK favourite Peter Hunnigale not being featured on Smooth Radio, or Magic Radio? Sadly, once again it is the same old story: as performers we always lack the recognition we deserve within the music industry.

From my own experiences in the music business, I knew that for me to maintain my public presence and remain in my chosen career, it was essential to stay ahead of the game. I had to remain on point, focused, and professional.

Despite the challenges, British lovers' rock of the nineties saw a resurrection and rebirth of the original flame that had been lit in the seventies. I knew the music was getting big based on the size of the venues I was playing, such as MCing at sold-out shows in the UK in places such as Brixton Academy, and the Hummingbird in Birmingham. In fact, lovers' rock gave me some really varied experiences. I would dress up, suited and booted, and perform at all types of events, even beauty and fashion shows.

'Girl of My Best Friend' and 'Stand by Me', both with Peter Spence, provided us with wider public exposure through Capital Radio airplay. We performed live in UK roadshows, entertaining large crowds. I began headlining global tours, travelling across Japan with Peter and Sweetie Irie, playing to audiences in the thousands. I also performed with Peter Hunnigale, catapulting our lovers' rock music into the heart of Australia. I did live shows in America as well, with Lloyd Brown, Don Campbell, and Peter Hunnigale. We were smashing it. It was such a pleasure to watch packed audiences grooving to our hit songs. Lovers' rock had reached international status, creating fans all over the world.

On my travels, I also found that small West Indian islands are crazy for our UK vibe. Lovers' rock is massive; people love it. Janet Kay is huge in Japan, Brazil, and Hawaii. Donna Marie is a giant artist in Brazil. Maxi Priest is huge in Hawaii and has fans across the Caribbean. But the small-island audiences—they are really drawn to the old-school reggae sound. And I have always felt that lovers' rock has a small-island vibe attached to the energy and sound of the music.

With roots that stretch deep into the Caribbean, Peter Hunnigale knows this as well. Below Peter describes his own tales of the times, digging deep into the memory bank:

My parents come from Redland, an area back in Jamaica's Trelawny Parish. I have loved music all my life; music was as important as our dinner. Growing up in a Jamaican household, I listened to my parents' playing tunes in the home: Wilson Pickett, Fats Domino, country and western, Jim Reeves. There were tunes on the turntable like, 'Wand'rin' Star'. I was a sixties baby, so reggae music had not yet been birthed. The music was ska and bluebeat. On the radio, we had pop music, and we loved this genre—Spanky and Our Gang, Herman's Hermits, PJ Proby, Dusty Springfield... Desmond Dekker with his ska tunes featuring on the charts and on TV. Music was all around me; such great times. My creative inspiration was infused with all different vibes of music.

I went to the Tulse Hill School, a secondary school in Brixton. From school days, sound system culture was bred into us, like joining up with your favourite football team. Coming from Brixton I was exposed by nuff sound systems all around, spoilt for choice: Coxsone... Neville and Danny King... King Tubby's... Matador... This culture was a central dynamic in our lives. As young people we would jam together, making our own speaker boxes. Dancehall motivated us to be involved. Boys would bounce around, showing off their new sound system cassettes. My first exposure was at school assemblies and talent shows, where you could sneak a little exposure. 1975 was important to me, watching the birth of British lovers' rock. Girls from the surrounding schools of Tulse Hill, Norwood girls, girls from Dick Sheppard, they were first at putting their singing groups together. Tunes around in the day included 'I'm in Love with a Dreadlocks' and 'Black Is Our Colour'.

I learnt to play my first three chords at guitar class with our music teacher. In my classroom, I linked up with a few like-minded friends, and we agreed to form a reggae band. Fitzroy Blake was my schoolmate, one year senior to me, and when he left school he got a job as a tape operator, reel-to-reel, in a top full-on studio in Wardour Street in the West End. I would beg him to give me a bit of free studio time; he agreed, so I would cut some dubs with me on vocals and Fitzroy as the engineer. After recording, we would cut dubs at LTS with John a mate of ours who worked there. It was good experience, as 16-year-olds. To this day, I still have a musical partnership with my old spar Fitzroy. He left his studio job and linked with Raymond Simpson and his brothers, forming a studio called Vibes Corner in Loughborough Junction. We taught ourselves and shared skills; we were our own youthful mentors. I was getting known as a local artist, men on the Brixton front-line would call out my name—'Yo, Peter, go mash up the studio, nuff respect, nice youth, nice and easy!'

Al Campbell had come over from Jamaica with Stereograph Sound System. I was the guitarist in the studio, and we would all create music together and with Fitzroy as our trained, experienced engineer. Apart from loving the music, there was such a vibe being amongst the musicians, such lovely, creative people. The camaraderie in music is second to none; it was gold to be a part of that community. I had always been drawn to music as a full-time career, playing instruments, singing and produc-ing reggae. Choosing music as my vocation saved my life: growing up, Brixton was a hard, tuff place with so many different distractions as a young Black man… it was rough. I needed a focus.

Barry Simpson, Raymond's brother, designed our own independent record label, Vibes Corner. We clubbed together, and our first record was released, called *Dancing Time*. It gave us a little name out there. 'Girl on the Side' was my first song from my earliest LP… 'Slipping Away' was another early tune of mine, and 'Got to Know You' I released on the Street Vibes label, the next label with the Simpsons and Fitzroy Blake. I wrote a song called 'Giving Myself Away' that reached Number 24 on the *Black Echoes* reggae chart. I loved music so much, running along this same time I was playing bass with the original live band The Pioneers and The Chosen Few; I moved with Mafia & Fluxy, Reggae Bubblers, Trevor Fagan. To think that as a young man in my early twenties…

With experience I learnt I had to be flexible—listening, opening myself up, exposing myself to different songs, multiple styles, and varied genres. Throughout my life I had always been a deep lover of music, so this was no problem, trying something different: versatility was my second name. I loved the challenge of stretching my skills, always looking to build on my talent, mastering my own unique MC craft. This challenge has been, and always will be, faithfully alive and well in me.

Now hear this
we apply the DJ to the rhythm
they coordinate and bring melody
Well, I man come to tell you about the latest
hits
the youth them a-say it a rip up the market
Well, all over the world in every district
a new kind of music, the acid a-kick
On Top of the Pops, a-where me first hear it
them talk something and it goes like this
Acid, a new style a kick, everyone talk bout
it.
I man Mr Irie can't believe it
how acid it did come out of the woodwork so
quick
every club you go in and every club you visit
you're guaranteed to hear this acid music
Well, acid gets big and gigantic
and all of the youth dem love it
Some a-take the E and some LSD, so take my
advice and don't do it
'cause it a-make you sick, put you pon drip
then you find out it never worth it
Follow your friends, take ecstasy
the next time you might end up sorry
This is a message to the public:
leave out the drugs and deal with the music.

Tippa Irie and Daddy Rusty, 'Acid'
from the 12' single (GT's Records, 1988)

Chapter Six
Rumble in the Jungle

A NEW GENERATION OF BRITISH YOUTH WAS ON THE rise, having switched from the old-school reggae we had all grown to love. The teenagers were now listening to something very original, fresh, from right here on our very own streets. This music, originally termed 'dance', 'acid', 'rave', and 'drum and bass', moved swiftly into a brand-new flavour called 'jungle music'.

In 1987, the next genres of music I was to ride the mic over were dance and jungle. Daddy Rusty and I were the first British reggae MCs to pen the lyrics of a song ('*Acid*') in recognition of the new dance/reggae fusion called 'jungle music'. I had first heard my songs, as well as samples of *Coughing Up Fire* and extracts from Saxon Sound tapes, being sampled in these tunes; artists such as Fatboy Slim were using them in their tracks. In 1989, I recorded a jungle white-label track titled 'Hyper Hyper'. This was around the birth of London's acid-house warehouse raves. The British public, tired and bored, working nine to five, had a desperate need to escape on the weekends, and took cheap return flights from London to Ibiza. The Spanish rave parties were attended by thousands. The emblem of this dance scene was a yellow, happy, smiling face.

This new electronic genre of dance music was not good for the employment of live performers and musicians; in front of my eyes, digital machines rapidly phased out the need for human beings. The need for a campaign to keep music live was reignited.

I was born into reggae, so I knew what it was to be authentic; all routes came from Jamaican styles of dub, from Kingston's King Tubby to hypnotically creative mixes from engineers and producers such as Lee Scratch Perry, and in the UK, Jah Shaka, Mad Professor, Jah Tubby's, Adrian Sherwood, and Nick Manasseh. Reggae is where the origins of UK jungle musical arrangements came from, featuring a fusion of dub, exaggerated basslines, lower-level frequency electronic beats, and a hardcore industrial backbone with synthesised digital percussion loops. It had a 4/4 drum pattern, leading to the central ingredient of the breakbeat or drum solo. Jungle tracks sampled and abstracted sounds from a mixed genre of music—slices of soul, rare groove, jazz funk, roots reggae, dancehall. The patterned drum machine beats were originally sampled from sixties American funk, soul songs such as 'The Apache' and 'The Funky Drummer' (alongside other James Brown samples). 'Amen Brother', by The Winstons was an original classically central drum hook, contributing towards the evolution of UK drum and bass.

Back in my day, the selector's talents would be assessed by how they mixed the tunes, left to right, turntable to turntable—this was the founding art of sound system music. Vinyl was mixed live on the night by human hands... not machines. Dancehall mixes were never pre-recorded; that would be forbidden. Rap and hip-hop music, all these genres hail back to reggae dancehall, where their teachers, mentors, and musical forefathers originate, into the early 1970s when DJ Kool Herc brought his Jamaican reggae sound system culture to the Bronx, live mixing and sampling on the decks.

Back on my own soil, Maggie Thatcher became notorious for introducing laws in Parliament clamping down aggressively on illegal raves. Police possessed new powers to shut down house parties and heavily fine promoters, seizing equipment as the Old Bill had done previously with its closures of pirate radio stations and dancehall night-spots. The state would enforce its control over anything independent and DIY by any means necessary, using its powers—an extension of the sus laws aimed at working-class Black communities—to close down dance parties. In the late eighties and early nineties, the free festivals and rave movement were targeted by the British police as well. Raves up and down the country were disrupted; vehicles and ravers were turned back at stop points on the M4 and M25; venues and squat parties closed down, with equipment seized and destroyed. Under the Criminal Justice and Public Order Act (1994), anyone putting on an illegal free rave would face six months' imprisonment. This Act specifically mentioned electronic music, so dance music with repetitive beats could be identified by police. From this time forth, across the four corners of the country, the Freedom to Party campaign was born.

Recognised legends of this new jungle movement were DJs Fabio and Grooverider, alongside Jumpin' Jack Frost and the Ragga Twins. Fabio and I grew up together in the same manor, Brixton, and even attended the same primary school. I was around the pioneers of jungle music from day one, witnessing the music evolve. There was a whole new catalogue of fresh new artists arising from the drum and bass sound: D and B was more of a straight techno sound with a few samples and vocals. UK Jungle was a merging of reggae, roots and Dancehall musically weaved into Drum and Bass. The key artists in this new emergence were: DJ Kenny Ken, Roni Size, DJ Solo, DJ Hype, Nicky Blackmarket, Mickey Finn, Navigator MC, Stevie Hyper D, Redman, Skipper D, Dilinja, Top Cat, Tenor Fly, Rebel MC (later to be known as Congo Natty), and UK legends Goldie and Chase & Status. Independent, homemade, DIY record labels carried and promoted the latest tunes within the genre: Ibiza Records, 3rd Party, Shut Up and Dance Promotions, Bassbin Records, Digital Soundboy,

Kemet Records, Paradox Music, Ministry of Sound, Suburban Base, V Recordings and Moving Shadow Records. Later, the major labels (Sony, BMG, etc.) took up distribution of jungle releases.

The pirate stations promoting early jungle and drum and bass included Sunrise FM, 88.3 Centreforce, Dance FM, and Rude FM. Dances were advertised by word of mouth—then it was off to large warehouses, industrial units, empty houses, woodlands, or the green fields of Essex and Kent with the whistles, glow-in-the-dark illuminated tracksuits and wristbands. The raving posse was growing up and down the UK, with dances and festivals everywhere. In fact, dance festivals would not take place without promoters having their own jungle stage and arena.

The British rave scene was massive. Through the warehouse dances, nightclubs, and the mainstream Jungle Fever festival, the UK rave scene evolved into a profitable, independent business venture. Venues began to welcome, with open arms, the new sound. In London, venues such as Camden Palace, the Astoria, Jungle Mania, Roast, Brixton Jamm, Vauxhall Arches, Roller Express, Telepathy, the Hippodrome and Bagley's. In the north of England there was the Eclipse, the Hacienda, the Sanctuary Music Arena, the Que Club. All these venues and others hosted sold-out, popular jungle rave nights.

One weekend, I ventured into one of London's most famous dance club, Ministry of Sound, to check out my first jungle rave. It was a lot different from sound system dances, which were populated mainly by Black audiences. In this event, I felt like a fish out of water. The predominately white audience made me feel a little uncomfortable. A lot of the behaviour on the night was alien to me: the absence of weed, people endlessly going to and from the toilet, and a lot of people high on cocaine and pills. I thought to myself, 'With this type of monotonous beat, you would *have* to be taking something.' A prude like me—or, you might say, a wise man—did not take any hard drugs. I just rolled my little herb spliff, and that was good enough for me.

I was curious to see how everything worked at these raves, though. The deejay would be mixing, and the MC would hype up the crowd— very much the same formula as at one of my regular sound systems. Jungle had limited vocals, mainly samples. My reggae sound would play a full vocal, and then I would MC over the version on the B-side. The atmosphere in this rave was electric, though. It was good to see Navigator MC and the Ragga Twins doing their thing. They had moved on from traditional sound systems to this new scene, and it was a good platform for them to find a new avenue, to get themselves out there. They did just that—and became very successful. The environment was sensorily intense, with flashing strobe lights and wild illuminated backdrops.

I found the sound of jungle heavy, and I knew in my heart that this music was not for me. I was born and raised on the foundation of dancehall reggae. In fact, jungle was a child born from dancehall, and uniquely engineered in the UK since the days of the 'Sleng Teng riddim', when reggae engineers and producers began shifting digitally within the music world. I never personally connected with or gravitated to this music.

In the beginning, there was a saying that an MC who could not make it in reggae would switch over to jungle, kinda like a dig at failing dancehall MCs, but a bit silly and childish, I thought, 'cause music is music—the objective as an artist is for you to find what makes you successful, feeding yourself and your family.

Dance beats, samples, drum and bass, a techno sound with faster engagement and more beats per minute, a higher tempo—thankfully, jungle had reggae music sampled throughout its tunes. And I had no need to cross over: I was a reggae superstar in dancehall, in my own world, coming from a different seed—the root, the foundation. Rave and dance music were simply not in my DNA. And again, I found the rave scene hedonistic, fuelled by drugs, crack cocaine, and an array of powders and pills guaranteed to have you up on your feet, dancing like a zombie from nightfall to sunrise. The central connection of ecstasy to acid house culture struck me in the same way that trippy-hippy sixties' culture was connected to LSD and mind-bending hallucinogens. Simply: none of this was for me.

I would not really frequent the London jungle rave scene often; I'd just pop my head in and out. With the likes of Shy FX and Nicky Blackmarket back in the beginnings of the movement, I was watching it grow. But I never fully identified myself with one particular scene and genre, never wanted to limit myself and restrain my MC talents. I stepped and moved in and out of scenes, as an artist in my own right, as it suited me. In my relationship with jungle music, I am content that I have given my all when offered any jungle track to ride the mic over. I had to be versatile to pay my bills, in reality, to be able to live. So, I would go on any rhythms thrown my way.

In 1988, Soul II Soul's unique sound caused a massive storm both on the streets and within the music industry. This started with their first releases 'Back to Life' and 'Keep on Movin', performed by Caron Wheeler and Jazzie B, the Funky Dred. The theme of this new dance generation was captured in Soul II Soul's motto: *A happy face, a thumping bass for a loving race*. The nineties soon arrived opening a new technical era with new inventions. DVDs were in, VHS was out; CDs were in, vinyl was out. Out with the home-phone landlines; in with the mobile. I found myself entering head-first into a new world of technology, where everything was becoming slimline and more compact.

In the world of politics, British working-class people rioted in protest against Thatcher's Poll Tax, leading to pitched battles with the police in Trafalgar Square. In 1990, my hero, South African freedom fighter Nelson Mandela, was released from prison, ascending in triumph to the presidency in 1994 and bringing to power the African National Congress.

This era also began churning out processed, manufactured, mass-produced bands. The Backstreet Boys and Spice Girls were all the rage. Pop had Oasis and East 17. Prince and Michael Jackson kept making chart-breaking songs. In 1991, the country's Number 1 rock band, Queen, was in mourning over frontman Freddy Mercury who died from AIDS-related pneumonia. On my radar, American R&B, hip-hop, and soul were becoming massive, with the likes of KRS-One, 2Pac, Biggie, Public Enemy, Boyz II Men, Jodeci, R Kelly, and Mary J Blige. On the UK reggae charts, British lovers' rock was holding its own in the Number 1 slots. Essex boys The Prodigy were popular underground and would later go on to capture the ears of the mainstream.

There were big tunes in the grassroots world of jungle, with the latest independent singles hitting the dance floor with the likes of 'The Helicopter Tune', 'Burial', 'Sound Murderer', 'Limb by Limb', 'Dark Age', just to name a few. Later, as the jungle movement grew, labels released compilation LPs. The popularity ensued. UK Apache's and Shy FX's tune 'Original Nuttah' entered the UK national Top 40. In 1994, jungle crossed over with General Levy's and M-Beat's track 'Incredible', which was produced by Fashion Records. The tune was a UK dancehall MC smash hit, a breakthrough (M-Beat, its producer, said: 'Yo, General, we want you on this track.' He replied: 'Incredible.' And the tune exploded). In the same vein, I was invited by will.i.am of The Black Eyed Peas for 'Hey Mama', which become a hit song. Next thing I knew, I was on a plane to Hollywood.

I knew General Levy from back in the late eighties. He featured on a north-western sound called Tippatone, in the times of Robbo Ranx. General Levy would spar with Junior Dan. As a young man, he travelled down south to watch me perform with Saxon. I linked with up-and-coming British MC Sweetie Irie when he featured on the hit tune 'On and On' with Aswad. Sweetie Irie coined the 'Irie', part of his name after me; I view him as my son in the reggae fraternity. He was part of the One Love Sound System that was run by Steve-1 love, who used to move with Jah Shaka.

I believe it was positive that 'Incredible' crossed over into the mainstream. General Levy became famous, and it enabled him to buy a car and a nice house, to have money to look after his family—a great thing. At the time of the release of 'Incredible' there were haters from inside the jungle scene, hating on General, jealous that he made it and they didn't—the usual stuff. I heard a rumour that General had proclaimed he was one of the originators of jungle; others called him a bandwagonist jumping on the back of jungle music, snatching his slice of fame. There were two minds: commercial jungle versus grassroots, underground and independent. Anyway, I thought, 'good luck to you, General, my brethren.' It was good to see jungle music empowering brown, black, and white, young British working-class musicians from out of the ghetto. To provide another youth from the streets a living? To me, that's got to be a good thing.

The nineties delivered to us a new London sound with the birth of jungle, a fusion of old meets young, bringing the heritage of Jamaican dancehall and roots reggae to a new generation born into the party vibes produced by electronic sounds and beats. As a teenage artist at home in your bedroom with keyboards, sampler and mixer, mic and drum machine, you're set and ready to go. Doing it yourself: the new standard. Teenage mastermind engineers living in council tower blocks arranged and produced a line-up of banging dance tunes. This underground jungle movement rejected the mainstream music business, music contracts, and record bosses. This time around, young people were feeling in control of their own destinies.

I first knew Congo Natty when he was known as Rebel MC. I joined him when he was doing some community projects, helping, and supporting youths during the nineties. I remember doing a show in Bristol when Congo Natty first came out under that name. There was barely anyone on the floor on which he was performing, so he came down to our dancehall floor, which was packed, and in the end, he joined me onstage. It was good to see him do his set for the first time. Congo Natty was not popular then, but steadily made a name for himself as a jungle DJ.

Later, Congo asked me to work with him on another project, joined by Sweetie Irie, General Levy, Top Cat, and Daddy Freddy, honouring us as recognised forerunners of UK dancehall. We collectively rode a junglist tune, 'UK Allstars'. The song was recorded and engineered at Sleepy Time Studio, Lewisham, with Unit 137 Sound System. Our tune became a hit. It was very easy for me to record with my fellow MCs; we had worked together for up to 30 years, and the vocals session was done in no time at all. There were great vibes in the studio, and we all got along. Congo let us do our own thing. Most of the time, when I do work like this, they send me the raw beat, and I put my vocals on the track and leave them to mix it. The same applied to the '*UK Allstars*' project. Our video was filmed in the same studio in which we did the song. In the jungle scene, our tune went huge; it blew up. We started headlining at massive festivals such as Boomtown and were the main act on its Lion's Den stage. We were the supporting act at sold-out shows for the nation's favourite ska band, Madness, and performed at the House of Commons Festival in south London.

Sometimes working with different characters can be very frustrating. Egos step in and personalities clash. Being in the studio is cool, as you just do your thing and leave, but when you start to perform in live shows with people, their true selves are revealed—and this can be disappointing when you expect better. I prefer good organisation when I am working, especially when doing a large show. As a performer, I require professionalism. I don't go onstage and wing it—I only improvise if and when the occasion requires it. Working with Congo, my only disappointment was that production took too long; at times he said he would complete a project, but sometimes never did.

Boomtown was my favourite live show with the UK Allstars. Whoever thought of this gathering was a wizard: it was like going to Hollywood… but in Winchester, rural England. The first time I stepped onto the Lion's Den stage, it was situated inside a giant marquee. I played there live with my band, and I remember my manager at the time, Dominic Walch, saying he did not know what to expect; but to me it was just another gig. I met it head-on and as always, delivered my best. It's not easy playing at the Boomtown Festival, as there are so many acts on different stages—so when people come to see you perform, they must be true fans, because they have another five acts or more to choose from, all performing at the same time.

Dominic helped me a lot with my music career, and we travelled to a lot of places together, including America—but my favourite experience was playing live in Kenya with Dr Ring-Ding. Dominic helped me get a publishing deal with BMG in Germany, and also linked me up with George Powell of GHP Music, who collected my Phonographic Performance Limited (PPL) royalties. You need people like these as part of your team. I don't mind giving them their 15 percent, because 85 percent of something is better than 100 percent of nothing. Me and Dominic went our separate ways, but still remain good friends to this day.

I have worked alongside an array of jungle engineers, performers, and producers on songs such as 'Law of the Jungle' with Booyaka Crew and 'Pass Me the Rizla' with Deekline and General Levy. Benny Page and I wrote a joint jungle tune, 'Hot like Fyah'. Troublesome, D Fly, and I released another jungle song, 'Always There'. By popular demand, Deekline—a great producer and a fan of my music—created a jungle/drum and bass remix of 'Good to Have the Feeling You're the Best'. The video of the remix featured me acting as a proud, grinning parking enforcement officer giving out tickets to vehicles along my path. It was really funny and I enjoyed filming it in the heart of the West End.

In 2021, I received a call from Voltage and British jungle pioneer Shy FX, inviting me to ride a new track with him. I also engaged with a fellow MC, Apache Indian, through my independent business Dubplate Central, and Apache and I co-produced a jungle tune. This dual-culture combination is yet another sign of how far dancehall reggae and jungle have reached people. The power of dancehall reggae to draw talent from the Asian community in the UK with the likes of both Apache Indian and junglist MC UK Apache. This cultural melting pot was overflowing with talent; British dancehall reggae and jungle were even fused with bhangra.

I give thanks. It is amazing that I have been performing my style of reggae for four decades, and that there are still Tippa Irie fans in this generation. I love fusing and mixing different genres. I still feel fresh and young inside, motivated to face another day. I am alive when I perform my music. I love seeing the audiences light up. Jungle music puts a smile on people's faces; it produces an energetic, positive, and joyful energy.

Much has to do with my versatility. As DJ Jumpin' Jack Frost noted:

'Tippa Irie is the living proof of versatility coming strictly from the sound systems, moving, and adapting his MC talents into drum and bass, jungle. The eighties, working with King Tubby and Saxon, today working with the likes of Congo Natty and myself... this is the art of his longevity within the business. He can vocally ride on any track you give him.'

That said, young people still request my eighties anthem 'Hello Darling' at jungle raves. They see which artists are on the bill and study their musical back catalogues, and when we come to the show, even if our song is not jungle.

Unfortunately, I witnessed the rave scene become like a secret inside party, where at times performers could forget where they came from, feeling they were above others. I found that the drug culture negatively affected people, but to each their own; it was not for me. I was clean and did not want to be contaminated by that lifestyle. I would not get invited to the after parties, of course; when people are doing drugs and you're not, they do not want you around.

We in Britain need to be proud of our musical history, in which reggae MCs with origins in dancehall could fuse with jungle music. The up-and-coming selectors were influenced strongly by the musical vibration passed down by elders of the Windrush and sound system generations... and dubstep, UK Garage, grime, drill—these popular youth genres and sounds are also the result of a fusion of cultures, featuring the MADE IN THE UK stamp, an extension of all our potent talents.

Below are thoughts from my long-time friends the Ragga Twins (RTC), Derman Rocker and Flinty Badman, who were part of the foundation of jungle music. The Ragga Twins were responsible for bringing underground jungle music to the ears of the mainstream public, riding their MC talents over jungle rhythms.

> We both were raised in East London, in Hackney, and have always shared a love for all genres of music. The UK is a melting pot, with mixtures of so many musical strains, be it reggae, R&B, or dance. Reggae was our first love. In the seventies we were influenced by the tunes of Big Youth, the

Mighty Diamonds, U-Roy, and I-Roy. Our parents were from the West Indies, Dad from Dominica and Mum from Montserrat, so music was always playing at home. The musical influences were so strong that back in our school days, we built our own speaker boxes, and in the eighties we worked on our own sound system, Unity Sound.

It was back in those good old days when we first saw Tippa Irie in Edmonton over our sides. His talent shone, performing with the legendary Saxon Sound System. It was the time of Smiley Culture, Asher Senator, Ricky Rankin, Peter King, Tippa, Rusty, Papa Levi, General Slater, and Tenor Fly. We had great admiration for these guys. We will never forget witnessing British dancehall history as Tippa mashed up a dance at Dick Sheppard School in Brixton. Saxon was clashing Coxsone on the night. To us, Tippa Irie will always be the General: he has the MC ability to chat on any rhythms. Tippa always puts his heart and soul in his performances. We will always respect and honour Tippa as one of the UK dancehall pioneers. His longevity in the music business is on account of his lyrics and delivery, and his showmanship and charisma.

We took the MC dancehall skills and vocals we had developed on the sound systems and crossed over into the jungle genre, which was in its foundation stages at the time. Jungle was an extension of acid house, and from its birth had British origins. So, we felt at home with its combination of dance music and drum and bass with dancehall reggae. The deejays spinning the tracks were the likes of Mickey Finn, Kenny Ken, Groove rider and Fabio, DJ Brookie… One of the main pirate stations promoting jungle in its beginnings was Rush FM. Jungle music bust massive, with giant raves taking place, so we adding vocals and lyrics to the forefront of this new genre. From its beginnings in the early nineties, we ended up taking jungle worldwide.

From the successful release of our singles, 'Spliffhead', 'Wipe the Needle', 'Hooligan 69', and 'Mixed Truth', we went on to produce a track titled 'Shut Up and Dance' alongside the release of our LP, *Reggae Owes Me Money*. The Ragga Twins received a record contract, signing with a subsidiary of EMI. It was a major deal, and it taught us a lot about the workings of the industry. It was a 360 deal, but we found the experience very controlling and restrictive in terms of our independence and choices. Your professional creativity and control as an artist become undermined. In the end, we made a joint decision to go independent. We could be who we wanted to be, and collaborate with who we wanted, when we wanted. We have been independent ever since, and never looked back.

So many endless memories, raving at clubs and jungle events such as Roast, on Sundays at Linford Film Studios in Battersea, Sunrise, Centre force, the Orange Club, Jungle Mania, Jungle Fever, Desert Storm, World Dance, Living the Dream, the SW1 Club, Roller Express, the Hippodrome, and the Coliseum. Jungle nights at the Astoria were unforgettable, and Germany held some of the biggest raves at the genre's beginnings, with thousands attending. Coventry equally carried great jungle vibes.

Our advice for new artists is to make music how it makes you feel, because nobody knows your vibes, only you. Be yourself and be original, by owning what is yours. Music has been a central part of our lives from day one, so we learnt about both how to perform and how to manage our business within the industry. We know that music has changed our lives, enabling us to tour and see the world. The more exposure we received, the more the experience humbled us both. We felt blessed and we never took anything for granted, leading us to put in the hard work required.

Chapter Seven
Big Tings a Gwaan

MAXI PRIEST MADE BRITISH REGGAE FANS AND artists proud of his legacy by putting our music on the map. Who better then to describe Maxi's journey to fame than Maxi himself:

I was born and bred in Lewisham, and grew up in a large family as one of nine brothers and sisters. My parents were Jamaican, hailing from the beautiful parish of Saint Elizabeth on the south cost. My mother was a faithful member of the local Pentecostal church. This brought a light into our home. It was a Christian home, and as children we were raised with songs of praise, 24/7, giving thanks to the Almighty through song and prayer. We walked and talked in the way of the Good Lord. I can only describe my childhood within my family environment as, awesome. Hallelujah. Amen. Great times, my family childhood memories. In our house dwelt the Holy Spirit, providing the positivity of life's purpose. We kids grew up with self-surety and hope.

This was my foundation. I felt the joy and happiness that rejoicing brings to one soul. My family members were all baptised, serving Christians. In my own self as a youth, I rejected this concept. My belief was that it was not right to baptise a child, so young and impressionable. Wait till one has grown into a teen, then one should be free to decide. I said no. I was proud of our culture, heritage, and Blackness, but I had my own determined, conscious, youthful mind.

My brother was a member of the Black Panthers. We all stood strong as Black people. We were upright, rebellious youths. We knew ourselves, who we were. No need to be led. I had my own mind; I walked my own way. It was a radical time, 'Get Up, Stand Up' times.

At the age of 14, sadly, my dad died. From that point onwards I was tasked—as a teenager—with becoming a man. Early on in life, this was the road carved out in front of me. I had started to embrace the faith of Rastafari. I was truly the first youth in my school to natty up my crown. I felt this to be just a spiritual, organic transition, given the way my mother raised us. Raise a child in the way of the Lord, and he shall not depart. I moved on to higher plains. Rastafari was I man church.

I was true, red, gold, and green. One hundred percent lionheart. Rasta was my fortress, my guiding light. Back in the day, it was dred to be identified as a natty, a Rasta. Schoolteachers, police and even your own elders would try to stress you. I remember one morning, to my shock, awaking to the fact that some of my locks had been trimmed. A chunk of my natural hair, missing. In the night, while sleeping, both mi granny and mother crept in my bedroom, in the dark. Trying to scalp me, truly, for real.

I would work day and night. My family grew into tradespeople. Building, carpentry, decorating, whole heap of gathered skills and trades. Working on the site by day, by night selling an abundance of top-class ganja. This was how the flex had to be. Dad dying in my early teens. I had to grow up quickly; we all did, in our teens. Main objective, first reality, putting bread on the family table. Income. Yep. Talk is cheap, so dollars have fi run.

It was serious times for Rasta, identified as public enemy Number 1. I was a lion, a bold warrior, fearless, protected by His majesty. I walked the streets of south London freely, chalice in hand. From early on, I developed a rebellious spirit. Born in June and moving alongside the Twelve Tribes of Israel, I identified as tribe of Levi, the house of the royal priesthood, called for serious works. See it now clearly: Maxi Priest. Originally, I was called 'Levi', but progressed into using the title 'Priest'.

I was raised as a spiritual child, guided by the hand of the Most High. A child of June, summer love. I was drawn to the sunshine rays, hibernating during the cold winter months. Gone—you would not see me. As a child, family members would always ask me to sing Christian melodies. I loved music, and the chance to sing out, loved and cherished this powerful energy, a gift I was reassured that the Lord had bestowed unto I. Everyone in my inner circle would ask little Maxi to sing praises of rejoice. I would sing to myself, lyric after lyric rolling off my tongue. Humming melodies in my head, I was always full up to the brim. My cup, overflowing with melodies. Later, on the turntable, I sang praises to Jehovah, praises unto His name. Early out, I had my own sound system, Gladiator Sound. People would call on the 'Priest, Priest, Priest', for I, to take up the mic and sing. Rastafari was my journey. In the beginning, I was the Lewisham Ras, moving with Gregory Isaacs and Dennis Brown, burning herbs, singing and jamming with the big reggae names. I was on fire, no stopping the Priest. I moved with all manner of Rasta mansions. Twelve Tribes, Nyabinghi, Ethiopian Orthodox church vibrations and Ethiopian World Federation. Yes, this what me, lionheart, Rasta, called by the King of Kings, Lord of Lords for life works. Summoned through my talent to serve Jah. I have always connected my faith and life works to the knowledge of the Conquering Lion. We as sons and daughters of the Most High were called to use our inborn blessed talents, to do our best, be our best, in all things we do. Reaching out to the highest places in the name of the Almighty, we have the birth right to live in His glory, our achievements taking us to better places, striving forever to improvement. The works of Marcus Garvey called I to serious tings, and wealth is also our God-given right. Haile Selassie was crowned with a solid gold crown. Wealth is inherent to our culture, mindfulness and productivity creating our personal wealth through serving the Almighty. Advertising our talents, not to hide one's skill under a bushel. Let your light shine. Yes, let it shine.

The first time I came across Tippa Irie was around Brixton sides. Tippa was performing on King Tubby's Sound System. Those times, we were all about as performers, making our stand. Tippa, from his beginnings, has always been a serious artist, and he was drawn to Saxon vibes because we were into serious business.

Tippa and I have been tight for the longest time, bona fide family. He is an original MC performer in his own right. His love of music comes first—he has no choice. Music is his heartbeat, drawing him in like a magnet. He can't live without the fire, and music is the fire. I share that very same fire. You may turn away for a while, but the fire will call you back, saying: 'You can't go anywhere without me.'

Island and Virgin, all was good, but major record labels never really understood where we were coming from and where we wanted to reach to, like having your wings clipped when you wanna fly.

I brought singer-and-DJ-fused combinations to the world, building hits with great performers such as Shaggy and Shabba Ranks. I co-founded the Madhouse record label alongside Dave and Tony Kelly. Working with the likes of Jamaican artists Daddy Screw and Terror Fabulous, I wanted to bring my love for dancehall to the mainstream, producing a bright, sharp, commercial sound. Where there was pop and R&B, I wanted dancehall reggae in the charts, adding a different melody, new flavours to the ingredients. I started by practising on an MP-60 drum machine, organising new breaks and beats.

Back in the early days, when we all started to get breaks, I would see Tippa and we would look at each other like, 'wow, did this really happen?' Our dreams had come to pass. Seeds bore fruits. We gave thanks, for many are called, few are chosen.

Music is like a large umbrella, encompassing so much and so many. The connection to people, the power of music in all its forms. In the Scriptures, King David sang psalms for the whole of the Earth. He sang songs of the Most High to yellow, white, black, brown… one and all. Connectivity, covering the whole of we. Different levels making spiritual connections. Music enables us to educate and help people, to know their culture through the messages, delivered.

Tippa is a bundle of happiness and joy, but always serious and professional about his work. Longevity is about professionalism, and when you witness him deliver, you know. He has done his homework. In life, we all start somewhere. By learning versatility and open-mindedness, our progress takes us higher. Many I know have tried to sway him from his musical journey, but Tippa knows his craft; I know he will never give up. Singing with his head held high, he is destined to doing his ting. I have great memories of us touring together, performing live in Long Beach, California. Of recent, we have worked on some joint ventures and vocal combinations.

Life and economics are entwined. In truth, you can't do shit without money. It does not mean you sell yourself; you sustain economics to empower yourself. Everyone to get fed. It is a two-pronged approach. First, grow your finances, empower yourself, and in turn you can support your community. Like planting a seed: it grows, its branches reaching out from the trunk. Same with life, ourselves, and our communities. His Majesty taught us: spiritual and material, work hand in hand. Not one without the other.

In my life, I have walked with a whole heap of famous cats. I have moved through the ghetto amongst the evillest, dog-hearted men. I have been blessed to trod to Ethiopia, to stand alongside the King's throne within the Royal Palace. I have walked alongside the royal black lions. In truth, from my family upbringing in Saint Elizabeth, I was two feet away from being a man planting veg and farming goats. In turn, the Most High, forever, blessed and guided me throughout my entire life. I could have got where I am no other way. Most importantly, I have learnt in life that you must nurture your talents like a good friend. Look after yourself, and what the Most High has provided for you.

Maxi Priest is a towering figure in UK reggae. And so too is UB40. I have been mates with Ali Campbell and his fellow UB40 bandmembers since the eighties. Below, Ali describes his own journey into the history books:

I was born in Birmingham, and grew up in a working-class area, one of the poorest areas in Europe at the time, called Moseley Village in Balsall Heath. The area was identified as a tenant yard in the UK, nicknamed 'Sodom and Gomorrah'. At the age of nine, I ran errands for local prostitutes. The community was multicultural—Jamaicans and Asians had a great presence. I was raised watching the best Indian movies, and reggae was the music playing from our local cafés and dances; reggae was all around me. From a young age, me and my brother would sneak into shebeens without our parents' knowledge. I loved the curry goat juice and white rice.

My dad was a famous Scottish folk artist, Ian Campbell, who recorded 27 LPs and managed a club called The Jug O' Punch, one of the biggest folk clubs in Europe. I had Irish rebel folk musicians such as the Chieftains and the Dubliners in my presence growing up, and even Billy Connolly and Paul Simon. I remember one day witnessing Ronnie Drew of the Dubliners taking a piss outside our front doorstep.

My grandad was from the Shetland Islands, and my dad was born in Aberdeen. They were both strong union men, members of the Communist Party and the Campaign for Nuclear Disarmament back in the sixties. During the seventies, my dad's political affiliation resulted in him being banned from entering the US. He had always been anti-America; I found this a bit strange. How could you hate a place if you had never set foot there?

My musical influences came from a very different place;

in fact, I hated folk music. When I started listening to reggae back in 1969, it had just formed itself, coming from ska and rocksteady. Originally as a kid, I loved Michael Jackson, and I was a big Jackson Five fan. I had JACKSON FIVE on the back of my denim jacket. In 1974, I went to see them perform at the Birmingham Odeon. Later, I even went to see Bob Marley and the Wailers perform live at the very same venue. It was the best experience; those events musically changed my life. I would sing along to the Jacksons' tunes 'ABC', 'I Want You Back'… I could reach Michael's high-pitched tones until my voice broke and my balls dropped.

The first reggae LP to deeply influence me was *African Herbsman* by the Wailers, produced by Lee 'Scratch' Perry. I was a bit of a weird kid; I would walk around carrying the sleeve proudly under my arms. Roots reggae music reverberated around in my head. No other schoolkids at the time knew much of reggae, just me.

Yes, I would be so proud, well-done London. These UK reggae artists had made reggae music accepted by the British public. Tippa created a light-hearted commercial style of reggae for the UK. His amenable character and style would encourage and welcome white audiences and listeners. That is why I call these times unique; this British-sounding reggae music was first of its kind. Prior to that, reggae had been underground, and many around the music were very protective and puritanical about it. As British reggae artists, we were opening doors, promoting reggae on the charts, and carrying our love for the music worldwide. In the beginning, I had wanted to become a drummer, but could not afford the kit. I lived in a working-class area of Birmingham with mass unemployment. I would famously fail to wake up and get out of bed, always arriving late to sign on at the local dole office. My brothers would sign on in Moseley town centre, 8:30 AM. We would get chatting to guys in the line of the dole queue, and we shared our interest in reggae. This is where the name 'UB40' came from: an UNEMPLOY-MENT BENEFIT 40 form. This was the document we used to sign on with, and this is where the title of our first LP came, *Signing Off*. No more dole—we were a working band now. Sly and Robbie and I rehearsed, playing along to 'Mr Know It All' by Sly and Robbie , building ourselves as UB40. So, we signed off from the dole queues. The rest is history, a new beginning for all of us.

We formed in 1978, after rehearsing at youth and community clubs. Our first single, 'King'/'Food for Thought', was a big hit, and was recorded in our mate's bedroom, in his flat. We were strictly independent, controlling our own opportunities. I was a big fan of dub music. I loved it. This is where you hear the dub reggae influences in our early releases *Signing Off* and *Present Arms*. The dub we performed was once again unique, this echoed sound that UK audiences responded to.

As I have said, at the time reggae music was very puri-tanical—only 'genuine' reggae was deemed authentic, only when it was recorded and produced in Jamaica. So, when UB40 came on the scene, they were like, 'Who is this little white fucker whose band is playing bad reggae!' We were termed by many as a 'white reggae band'. Our Black bandmembers took great offence at this label!

We were creating our own sound alongside Steel Pulse, Aswad, Misty in Roots, and Black Slate. We went on to sell over 70 million records globally, so upon reflection, we were just in the right place at the right time. Why shouldn't reggae music sell? If it's good enough, it deserves to be sold and distributed worldwide.

Some of my greatest memories touring across the globe were in 2007 playing to a crowd of 80,000 in South Africa. We sang our chorus, 'amandla awethu', meaning 'power to the people', calling out, 'Amandla!' with the audience responding, 'Awethu!'. UB40 had upheld the cultural boycott against the racism of the apartheid system for many years. It was great to be a part of, and witness, the freedom of the people.

We were invited to perform in the Solomon Islands and met indigenous tribes with bare bums, carrying bows and arrows. On our departure, they played their flutes to the tune of one of our hottest UB4O songs. In 2004, Goldie Lookin Chain featured a song with UB40 in a mention.

In 1985, we invited reggae artists to collaborate on our LP, *Baggariddim*, including Tippa Irie. This independent UB40 project was a way of us helping and supporting unknown or not-so-well-known UK reggae artists. On our *Labour of Love* tour in 2000, and on several other tours, Tippa Irie was invited to be UB40's supporting act. Tippa, being such a warm and friendly character, transfers his happy vibes to the audience. His vibes make it easy to follow. Tippa is always great support to have around.

I have learnt from travelling that in truth, all people are the same. All we as UB40 have been doing is carrying the love mantra of reggae music.'

Who would have ever thought that I would be travelling, socialising, and performing with reggae heroes like Maxi Priest and UB40, or in my early days with legends such as Dennis Brown and Gregory Isaacs?

I must confess that I was a bit starstruck at the time meeting me child-hood musical influencers. I have performed live shows on the Jamrock Reggae Cruise with Damian Marley, and several festivals shows with Julian Marley. The Marley family has always paid me respect as a fellow reggae artist. I became close, respected friends with Ali Campbell, noted above, and Astro, also of the legendary UB40. They were just great, ordinary working-class guys from Birmingham. My manager GT had grown up around UB40, coming from the same side of town. One day I was walking through London's West End when I heard my name: 'Hey, Tippa!' It was Ali. He pulled out a half-ounce of weed and clutched the inside palm of my hand while informing me it was the best high-grade sensi. That's how we used to roll, back in the day.

As a reggae MC working for over 35 years on the circuit, I have rubbed shoulders with and performed alongside many celebrities all over the world. During an interview on Capital Radio, David Rodigan—the world-renowned reggae ambassador—said of me, 'Tippa Irie takes planes like taxis.' True, Europe, Jamaica, America, Russia, Central America, Brazil, Japan, China, and Africa: my music, and the name Tippa Irie have taken me all over the world. Thankfully, I am still trav-elling with my first love, reggae.

I was featured in lots of newspapers and magazines. My first appearance on TV occurred in 1983 when I was filmed talking about British reggae in a record shop called Peckings situated in West London. As my songs earned greater exposure, I was invited to perform and be interviewed on BBC TV. I appeared as a guest performer on BBC Radio's *The Craig Charles Funk and Soul Show* and TV's *Club Mix*, hosted by my old Saxon mate Smiley Culture. I also performed several times on *Top of the Pops*.

I recall sitting in a TV waiting room in France. The gentleman alongside me, dressed sharp in a pinstripe suit, asked: 'What are you going to do tonight?' I told him I was going to perform my song. He said, 'good luck.' He was then called to the stage to a rousing round of applause. It was only *Gene Kelly*—I had been chatting with the man that gave us 'Singing in the Rain'! who would believe it.

I also appeared as a BBC guest reggae artist on Saturday night's *Wogan* show, performing 'I Know Love' in front of millions of viewers with my old mate Maxi Priest. Maxi had originally recorded the song with Jamaican dancehall artist Tiger, who could not make it. So Maxi called me last minute to join him, and we performed the song. Our duo went down a treat.

After all these amazing life experiences, another dream would come to pass: this was another positive lesson, a fulfilment that your visions and gaols can become a reality in front of your eyes, if you seize the moment. As I have described in the early chapters, I am a crazy mad sports fan. In 1993 my football team Arsenal were going forward to challenge Sheffield Wednesday in the Football League (Coca-Cola Cup) and FA Cup finals. Let's remember that I have been a staunch fan of the Gunners since junior school. I had an idea to write a song in tribute, with my long-time brethren Peter Hunnigale. We produced the track, 'Shouting for the Gunners', in his bedroom using a small mobile studio. This is the song that I dedicated to my team.

I was already known by the Arsenal players, having either gone to school with them or they were Saxon Sound System fans. They were local south London lads: Ian Wright from Lewisham, Kevin Campbell from Brixton, and Andy Grey, who played with Crystal Palace FC. Kenny Sansom, born in Camberwell, and Paul Davis, who I also knew from my secondary school, Beaufoy. I remember our school days, when Paul would run me around the gym giving me pointers on how to improve my football skills. Paul was a very humble dude.

Who would believe that we would record our song with backing vocals sung by the Arsenal team in person—Tony Adams, Lee Dickson,

Arsenal team them no have no mercy
pon the opposition them have no pity
They have Paul Merson and Lee Dickson
Alan Smith, Paul Davis and Tony Adams
Mr Winterburn and Mr Hillier
and Mr George Graham, well, him is the
manager
and Mr Seaman who deh in a-the goal
and have everything under control

> *You got to see it, Arsenal, team in a red and*
> *white*
> *see to believe it Mr Kevin Campbell and Mr*
> *Ian Wright*
> *Poetry in motion, Arsenal team is such a*
> *delight*
> *We got the spirit, a very, very, very big part*
> *of my life*

> > *I know that you know, shouting for*
> > *the Gunners*
> > *I know that you know that we are*
> > *gonna win the cup*
> > *I know, that you know, shouting for*
> > *the Gunners*
> > *I know that you know that we are*
> > *gonna win the cup.*

Arsenal FA Cup Final Squad
'93 feat.
Tippa Irie and Peter Hunnigale
'Shouting for the Gunners'
(London Records, 1993)

Nigel Winterburn, Ray Parlour, and Steve Bould? This was one of those icing on the cake things. For me, a lifelong Arsenal fan, life could not get any better.

Producer Charles Bailey was responsible for the original idea. After we mixed the tune, I contacted my local Arsenal-supporting radio DJs—Commander B, Jigs and George Kay from Choice FM, Pete Tong from Kiss FM—and they gave our song daily airplay. Peter Hunnigale and I signed the tune to London Records. 'Shouting for the Gunners' went mainstream and entered the British national pop charts. George Graham, the Arsenal manager, would not permit the players to perform our song on *Top of the Pops*, so we created a video. The song became Arsenal's winning FA Cup anthem. The end of this tale is that I was all-out victorious, with a treble win: another national chart hit song, and Arsenal's triumphs in both League and FA finals.

* * *

Peter Hunnigale, my old friend, collaborator, and partner on 'Shouting for the Gunners' reflects on our friendship and musical partner, alongside his own experiences within the music industry:

> Tippa? I have witnessed him do this on so many occasions: his MC contribution makes the song. Tippa's injection makes the difference. He done it with me as an artist, Lloyd Brown, Janet Lee Davis, Papa Crook, Winsome, Peter Spence... Tippa has constantly, throughout the years, achieved this, even been invited to record with The Black Eyed Peas. Record labels working with white reggae bands invite Tippa for their work to have authenticity.
>
> Tippa, born who he is, doing what he does, his fusion in the work making the magic happen... he was made for

the job. He plays like a Number 1, First Division football player; everybody loves his style.

We are still working together today. So many memories over the years, touring together from California to Australia... Power Cuts reggae club in Sydney, even performing in the Nevada desert. We toured across Australia for one month. Tippa has a good business head; he knows what to expect and is expert and experienced, informing other artists how to go forward. His knowledge over the years is golden. In addition to his talent and skill, his business sense is what has helped him maintain his longevity as a global MC.

Being my great mate, I know Tippa is a hooligan—he's strong-willed, and knows what he believes and stands for. He is a very generous guy, never wanting to go out of his way to hurt or wrong anyone. I have lived and grown with him. When I have been down, or Tippa on a difficult road, we have been there for each other, true long-time brethren. As he appears, that is who he is: genuine. If I look behind my back or over my shoulder, Tippa is always there for me. We are just ordinary people; our lives are entwined not just as colleagues for 40 years, but also brethrens. When my mum passed, it was Tippa's mum who stayed up with me throughout the night, frying fish and consoling me. I was invited to sing at Tippa's mum's funeral, but I could not— it was far too close to me. It was Fitzroy's and Commander B's mum, my mum, and Tippa's mum all together, living alongside each other's houses... our families were also entwined.

I have been a producer for many years, and I have been blessed to work with so many artists; Musclehead from Saxon Sound System came to my house in Streatham and brought the legendary Dennis Brown with him to voice a tune. At the time, I was recording in one small room, like a shoebox, so tiny you could not even change your mind there, but I had fitted a backing studio and keyboard. The room was so small, we could not even fit a vocalist, so Dennis had to sing on a tune I produced, 'Cupid', on the narrow landing. That's how we used to work back in the day… that was a crazy experience (there was no one like Dennis Brown: a beautiful, spirited person, he gave you a smile every time you saw his face. I am sure everyone who worked with Dennis, the Crown Prince of Reggae, would testify to his wonderful nature).

I have worked on the production side alongside artists such as Freddie McGregor and Frankie Paul; on the UK side, with Tippa Irie and Maxi Priest and even the world-famous Gilbert O'Sullivan, when I was with Down to Jam Records. I was one of the artists who would be known for taking UK reggae worldwide. As a British reggae artist there is a huge disadvantage: even though we have a massive number of talented artists and musicians, we are not recognised. People may think lovers' rock is big, but this is not the case outside of this country. Lovers' rock and UK reggae are not seen to be 'authentic' up against Jamaican dancehall music; from back in the day the word has been, 'if it is not Jamaican reggae, it's not cutting it', that the home of reggae is Jamaica, just like America is where you will find the best R&B and gospel music.

They say money is not wealth, ownership is, and it was important that what we had created was part of us. We never got the exposure and recognition and endorsement as true reggae artists. Yes, Janet Kay and 'Silly Games' are big in Japan, but I do not know where else Janet has toured internationally. I was fortunate as an artist to have played live in so many countries. I call Tippa 'Marco Polo', reggae explorer of the world, because I am sure he has circumnavigated the globe at least a couple of times; but Tippa's travelling is really unique as a British reggae MC, having so much international exposure. I give thanks to DJ Tony Williams, who set up a foundation recognising UK reggae, homegrown talent; he must be recognised himself as a pioneer for his role in promoting me, Tippa, and many others. This was Mr Williams's own initiative within the music industry.

I have been licenced through major record labels, but truly, all my life I have been working independently. I don't care what anybody says: it is essential that you have a contract. It does not matter what an artist does, the talent and the contacts—nothing better than having a record deal. You can't make it solely alone. It's the machinery behind the record label that moves records. Tippa and I have experienced this; we have taken a track straight to a label that has gone into the Top 40 on the national charts, and we have not even sold a single record. It's the network and the machinery that makes it for an artist; an artist can't do that alone.

Tippa has always been a full-on networker. One night he was out at an event, and Charles Bailey approached him. Charles said he had the rights to Arsenal's FA Cup anthem. Tippa, being an Arsenal head, jumped at the chance, and we beat out a track together. We built the catchphrase, and I thought of the terrace atmosphere and created the tune. We recorded and laid it down in my house in Streatham, completed and mixed it. Then we played it to Charles, and he liked it but did not know what to do with it. Tippa and I had radio DJ contacts, so we gave it to Jigs on Choice FM, Steve Jackson on Kiss FM... they promoted it, as they were Arsenal fans. In the background, something else was brewing—the BBC phoned Pete Tong from London Records and said, 'What the fuck are you doing? We are supposed to have first dibs on any Arsenal anthem.' The tune felt had the combination of making a good hit and got sent over to the BBC.

It was the 1993 Arsenal football team, Coca-Cola and FA Cup finals anthem, and we got through the door. This experience taught me about the strong links between football and the music industry. Arsenal fans within the industry would just have the power to make things happen, as long as you were a Gunners fan. It was just business—that's how it works. We were supposed to do a *Top of the Pops* feature live with the players, but manager George Graham would not permit it. Our Arsenal anthem got onto the national charts, in the Top 40.

In 2003 I was performing live at the Belly-Up Tavern in Solana Beach, near San Diego. I took a call straight after the show from a very good friend, Shelly Roots. 'Tippa,' she said, 'will.i.am wants you to record a track with his group The Black Eyed Peas.' Within the same week, I had voiced a tune with DJ Motiv8, who was a close friend of the band; I believe this is where the contact originally come from. In the evening, I went back to David Monaco's house, in La Verne, California, where I was sleeping on the settee in his front room (David is the lead singer of the band Better Chemistry). In the morning, David drove me to Los Angeles. There I met will.i.am and Fergie of The Black Eyed Peas at the band's studio.

will.i.am and Fergie informed me that they were working on releasing an LP titled *Elephunk*, and will.i.am had produced a track that they wanted me to voice. I listened to it in the studio one time and took the instrumental track with me back to La Verne. Through the night, I vibed with the tune and created the lyrics for my verse and melodic chorus. The next day I contacted will.i.am and we met in the studio; he could not believe that I had mastered the track in such a short time. I went straight into the studio booth and laid my vocals down; will.i.am was grinning and gave me the thumbs-up. He mixed there and then and gave me a first listen. Just as he had been impressed by my speed laying down the MC vocals, I was equally amazed by how fast he mixed our joint track.

I witnessed first-hand how talented will.i.am was—a multi-talented musician, he played every instrument; he was a top producer specialising in a range of genres such as pop, dance, and hip-hop, crossing over musical barriers. *Elephunk* was a fusion of flavours. We shared the same work ethic, being eager and motivated to get the job done. He was friendly and welcoming, making me feel relaxed and at ease. Straight-up business, too: he paid me a nice little fee for my MC contribution, and our agreement included a percentage of the publishing.

'Hey Mama' was to be the third track released from *Elephunk*. The first single release was 'Where Is the Love?', which was a worldwide Number 1 smash hit. I was halfway through my tour of the States when I was invited to the video shoot for the LP's second single 'Shut Up', linking up again with Will and The Black Eyed Peas. Sitting alongside me was Kanye West, who had just been signed by Jay-Z and Damon Dash from Roc-A-Fella Records, before he became a billionaire hip-hop superstar.

'Hey Mama' went straight into the Top 10. The The Black Eyed Peas were signed to Interscope Records, managed and owned by Jimmy Iovine, who was also working with master rapper, engineer, and producer Dr Dre.

I returned to London and was chilling at home when the phone rang. A voice said: 'Is that Tippa Irie? We want you to come to

Cutie cutie, make sure you move your booty
Shake that thing like we in the City of Sin,
and
Hey shorty, I know you wanna party
The way your body look really make me feel
naughty.

The The Black Eyed Peas feat. Tippa Irie,
'Hey, Mama' from the LP *Elephunk* by
The Black Eyed Peas (A&M, 2003)

Hollywood.' It was The Black Eyed Peas' management, booking me to take part in the filming of the video for our hit song. The following week I flew out to LA, and was put up in a very nice hotel on Sunset Boulevard. On the day of the shoot, they sent a car to chauffeur me to the location. At the film studio, I was directed to the makeup and wardrobe area and chose my clothes. There was plenty to choose from, but I was drawn to a brown velvet tracksuit, a nice red shirt, and a trilby hat. I found the vibes a little different from when I had been in the studio with will.i.am. The band's team, film crew, and choreographers they were cold as ice towards me. Unfortunately not the best time I have had, I did not rate their unwelcoming energy at all.

apl.de.ap, Fergie, and Taboo were as nice as always; will.i.am was cool, but strangely I felt that he did not seem like he was happy for me. I did not read too much into it and carried on doing my job—it was such an important event in my career, and I was not about to let anything or anyone spoil it. The shoot went well and the song took us on numerous TV shows across the world. We even performed 'Hey Mama' together on *Top of the Pops*.

Touring with The Black Eyed Peas also taught me a lot, apart from taking me to parts of the world I had never ventured into before. It was a real eye-opener: they had a lot of people working for them, for example, a business manager, general manager, road manager and, for the gigs, a production manager. They did not have a huge band, but they were able to reproduce their music very well when performing live. I went from Ryanair, EasyJet, and the occasional British Airways flight to flying first-class, and on private jets. When you are hot, everybody wants a piece of you. Sports companies such as Puma would want you to wear their products. Marketing, sponsorship, and endorsement deals started to flow my way. At every stop, I would reside in top-class hotels and receive goodie bags as gifts. It was wonderful to feel valued and appreciated as an artist, and for me, a hard-working MC, it was well overdue.

The live shows were exciting. I did a 10-minute spot every night, opening the show, and had the audience eating out of my hand without fail. I would do my thing and then introduce The Black Eyed Peas onstage; then I would leave, and on the second song into their set, they would call me back to perform '*Hey Mama*'. That would be it for me—my job was complete for the night. I enjoyed the rest of the show, and when it was all over, we would repeat it. It felt like *Groundhog Day*: rise in the morning, check out of the hotel, get on the tour bus (we were either driving to the next part of town or being chauffeured to the airport to jump a plane to another international destination), arrive at the hotel, check in, get some rest, eat some food; next, it would be time for our sound check. We would normally do one if The Black Eyed Peas were doing the gig on their own. If we were playing live at a large festival, we would only need to do a line check, ensuring that the instruments and vocals were set by the engineer at the right levels.

Being on tour as an artist, around so many other famous faces you get to know people on a more personal level. I found will.i.am eccentric—one minute he was cool, and then at other times, a bit vague and distant. I guess having the responsibility of being the leader of a popular band can take its toll. Dealing with groupies, management, marketing, and all the other people around you non-stop, needing your ear, requiring your time. I know this kind of pressure from my own global touring experiences.

Fergie was a beautiful girl both inside and out, always respectful and loving towards me, full of vibes. She had respect for my talent and longevity as an artist in my own right. She was like a sponge, eager to learn all she could from me, and I was willing to help her in any way I could. apl.de.ap and Taboo were also very respectful and apprecia-tive of my own talent. apl.de.ap was from the Philippines, and I had performed twice in Manila, at a dub club.

I did not realise it, but apl.de.ap was short-sighted. The way he dances and performs onstage, you would never have thought it. I really liked him—he was a very friendly guy, as was Taboo, who came from LA and was also a multi-talented dude, and a wicked dancer. In fact, everyone in the band was an excellent dancer: they came from American hip-hop culture. My spirit took to Taboo the most; he understood what I had experienced within the industry, and we had a few conversations about my past. He was very happy for me, getting this break. All in all, I got on with everybody on the tour, kept my head down, and did my job like a pro. Right on time if it's call time, present at ready in the hotel lobby or prepared when time came to step onstage. I was *always* ready, 'cause if you miss the bus, no one is waiting for you.

The success of *Elephunk* led to a British and European tour. All the venues were sold out, from my hometown Brixton Academy to the London Forum in Kentish Town. Also, numerous large festivals. We supported acts such as the Sugababes, Mary J Blige, Pink, and Roots Manuva. My touring as part of The Black Eyed Peas in 2004 opened many new doors, giving me another closer look inside the music industry, sharing the red carpet with the likes of Puff Daddy, Busta Rhymes, Britney Spears, Jay-Z, and Beyoncé.

During my time performing in the States, I experienced the world of underground grassroots rap. In New York, I worked in the studio at the same time as the great rapper KRS-One. The next day we would be performing on the same bill in Santa Cruz. Back home, I performed live on stage with LL Cool J at Wembley Arena in the presence of thousands; at Glastonbury Festival, backstage in a giant tent, I played pool and had a giggle with Pink (and of course, I would win every game!). I found Pink straight down to earth. Also at Glastonbury, I was supporting Sir Paul McCartney, who was headlining the main Pyramid festival stage the very same day.

A serious mind-blowing memory I will never forget took place in 2004, while sitting at home chilling and watching football on the TV, I received a knock at my door. I was pleasantly surprised to be presented with a gold envelope, recorded delivery. I signed, and upon opening it, I got the buzz of my life: it was an invitation to the 47th Grammy Awards, as a nominee. I was going back to Los Angeles for the ceremony. Yet another addition to my musical journey, which I shall never forget. The The Black Eyed Peas and I received a prestigious ASCAP music industry award for 'Hey Mama'.

Another personal buzz was being invited to the prestigious Ivor Novello Awards ceremony, honouring music industry songwriters and composers. There I received a tap on my shoulder: 'Yeah, love, do you know where the loos are, I am busting to go.' It was Amy Winehouse, all high heels, tight dress, and jet-black bouffant hairdo.

The following year, The Black Eyed Peas produced their fourth album, *Monkey Business*. will.i.am again invited me to MC on a track titled *'Dum Diddly'*. This time I was offered a one-off payment for my involvement, with no royalties. I did not really like this, but I agreed—as Mum used to say, something is better than nothing. It left a bitter taste in my mouth, but I was still thankful. I had thought I was part of the team by then, but it was the same old game of unfair play within the dog-eat-dog music industry: very little love but plenty of harsh business deals, where the artists rarely benefit equally.

One of the tracks I was part of would be used in an advertising campaign and featured on TV and radio; on one occasion, our song was used to advertise Apple's iPod, and while all the band members had been given free iPods along with other Apple gadgets, I was left to point out the fact that I had been gifted with nothing. I always lived by the principle that fair is fair, and you should treat others as you wish to be treated yourself. Of course, if you don't speak up and ask for what is rightfully yours, you won't get. So, I spoke with will.i.am, and my Apple items suddenly arrived. Another lesson from the music business: if you don't know, they are not going to tell you: people will try to pull the wool over your eyes.

* * *

As I've mentioned, one of these perks of fame came in the form of the most beautiful women who have ever been drawn to me. One of the first times I realised this fact was in 1984, on the night Saxon recorded *Coughing Up Fire*. As I walked through the crowd on the way to the front, I received an uninvited pinch on my bum; as I flinched and looked back, I saw it was a young girl who proceeded to give me a flirtatious wink. She informed me her name was Catherine, as she looked me up and down. No messing around, just plain and simple, Catherine said: 'Tippa, let's meet up after the dance.' This became a regular occurrence in my life—females showing their appreciation publicly. In truth, I could leave a Saxon dance with a different woman every night.

Being in the limelight provided me with numerous girls, which led to a lifestyle of pure excitement. As an artist who chose music as a full-time career, it was very difficult for me to maintain a long-term relationship. I found that either your partner would have to be a 100 percent dedicated reggae fan, or my loved one would have to stay at home alone without me on most weekends, rain or shine, 12 months of the year—in fact, even during the week. It works for some: as they say, absence is supposed to make the heart grow fonder. But in reality, the music business lifestyle can disrupt your relationships. I required the energy required to have a full-time relationship put into my career. Our routines and disciplines can be hard on your family's life, and my momentum was all part and parcel of my dedication to achieving success as an internationally recognised artist. I *wanted* to be single, to be honest, because it was a buzz for me having so much female attention.

Before I had a good time with any woman, I was always honest, and let them know from the outset—well, most of the time, anyway— that I could not manage a relationship that was too intense, and that commitment was not on my agenda. All I required from people around me who were sharing my company was to be easy-going; relationships were casual, but at the same time always respectful. My lifestyle made it truly difficult to commit to one person. If any ladies wanted to hook up and choose for us to roll together but without anything too serious, I would be cool with that.

As Dr Dre said, 'California knows how to party.' I was now personally experiencing this and found that this sun-kissed American state had some of the prettiest and sweetest women—yeah, an abundance of beauties. I was at the beginning of my 27-day tour across the US. At the first venue I performed, I hooked up with a cute woman who dropped everything she was doing, career and all, literally putting her life on hold to join me every night, sleeping alongside me at each hotel. That's good-old California for you.

I am thankful to have had a life full of fun, engaging with a lot of different females across the world, women of all colours, races, cultures, shapes, and sizes. And even though I have had the opportunity to experience dating women who are rich, I have the strongest love for working-class women from within my own community: I find that, most of the time, they are more emotionally stable and secure in themselves, depending on the individual.

At times, the women I have had relationships with appeared to be unfaithful, superficial, and selfish. It was not just men around me who could be deceptive, but women, equally, could lead double lives.

Travelling so many diverse destinations from one side of the globe to the other has exposed me to so many different cultures. I found Brazilian women very attractive, looking like supermodels; and I experienced Swedish women as free-spirited and very adventurous. I found the culture in Sweden to be relaxed about sexual relationships between adults. We British view sex as a taboo subject, and in fact, we are conservative in our outlook regarding adult relationships—unless you're an Essex girl or Yorkshire lass... pick your choice, them all nice!

During the time of my Number 1 hit single *'Raggamuffin Girl'* with Peter Hunnigale, I flew to Sweden to do a show for Dr Alban, who had a hit single titled *'It's My Life'*. He had his own record shop, and upon entering, I saw a beautiful woman working behind the counter. I said in passing to Dr Alban, 'What a lovely girl.' And left it at that. He showed us around his recording studio, got us some food and then it was back to the hotel. I was relaxing, getting ready for the show, when there was a gentle knock at my door. I opened it to find the lady from the record shop standing in front of me. She was even more stunning up close and personal. We had drinks and polite conversation. Then I informed her that I needed a shower, and she replied that she would come with me. I thought to myself, 'Okay, then!' She was very confident and forward, and led me to the shower, where I was washed and foamed all over; the rest is history. The next day, Peter Hunnigale asked me why I had such a big smile my face: 'What a-sweet you so?' But I did not say a word. Me and the record shop woman kissed and hugged and went our separate ways. I was then onto the next destination.

A little story about Asia. I really love this part of the world; I love the vibes of Thailand, the Philippines, Cambodia, Vietnam, and India. In Japan, I played my first night of the tour at Tokyo's famous Club Jamaica. On arrival I was greeted by a petite Japanese woman, who informed me that she was my tour manager, promoter, and publicity officer. All I can say is that she took very good care of me, in more ways than one. She became smitten by me, and decided it was going to be her mission to tire me out, night after night—one hour working onstage, and another hour of me working in the bedroom. She was relentless in bed; when I thought I had given her my best, she would look at me as if she was Oliver Twist, asking, wide eyed: 'Can I have some more, sir?'

During the time of my signing with Arista Records, I was invited as a guest to a company party. I was dressed to the nines and looking sharp in a black velvet suit. It was a big dinner-and-dance event, and everyone was looking immaculate. Everyone danced the night away, and I felt a connection with this artist arising. Next, she asked me to join her back at the spa area of the hotel. Once inside the spa room, I had a pleasant surprise as she proceeded to invite me to join her in the hot jacuzzi situated privately at the end of the hotel. Let's just say that things got very hot indeed. We then decided to take it to her room and made love. Then she got up, and I got up and left—exactly how she wanted it, just to be pleasured through the night. As Frankie Valli and The Four Seasons sang: 'Oh, What *a Night*'.

Upon reflection, though, I found the mansion of fame a lonely and empty place. I was raised by strict Jamaican parents, and I was from humble working-class beginnings. I was always taught to take people as I found them. Being in the presence of famous figures, travelling and touring with hundreds of artists and musicians, I have been exposed to mega-stardom, and yes, so many of these people did believe they were 'superstars'. I found this level of ego led to a nasty level of selfishness, looking down on others—as if these stars had been born special. If you did not feed some performer's ego, you would witness grown adults having tantrums like spoilt children. I saw this numerous times, especially when they couldn't get their drug of choice. One time I was with a guitarist who could not find any sensi to buy, and he was a living nightmare to be around. At after-show parties the people present immersed themselves in champagne and cocaine, but this was not my style; a spliff of nice, natural weed would be just fine for me to chill out with. After a while I even cut that out; I had written and recorded some great songs under the influence of herbs, but I realised that I could also perform as well without it.

And each music industry after-party seemed like just another opportunity for people to show themselves off, all designer clothes and fake smiles. Back in the eighties, when I first started touring with famous artists, I was disappointed to observe their desperate relationships with Class-A drugs. Some individuals had serious white-powder addictions. On account of my refusal to partake, I would not be invited back to these after-show celebrity parties. That was fine by me; in truth, I preferred to jam on my own, back at the hotel. I had always been straight up: what you see is what you get, man of my word.

I saw, first-hand, drug addictions taking over the lives of some legendary performers. I saw how big egos and self-centredness led to downfalls, big crashes. These negative, toxic behaviours, alongside drug cravings, I witnessed the addictions making people lie and cheat even to those closest to them. With fame, I was surrounded by yes people— the music industry is full to the brim with fake souls. Everyone loves you when you are at the top, and when you are no longer at the top, they suddenly experience amnesia: you are immediately disregarded, treated like a commodity, a business product.

Working with famous performers I noted that the more popularity they received, the more the fame would go to their heads, transforming them into 'swellheads'. Nice, decent individuals crossed over into self- ishness, with the expectation that all must focus solely on their wants and needs. The root cause of this? Forgetting where you come from. Instead of sticking to their roots, humbling themselves and giving thanks, they served the all-consuming monster we call *ego*.

I was the first British dancehall artist to tour Africa during the eight- ies, performing with the Ruff Kutt Band, and later I was backed by my own musicians. Gambia was the first destination I performed in as part of my *Motherland* tour. I felt like a diplomat there on my way to the stage, escorted by armed military guards. I felt at home in Gambia. En route, my tour bus drove through crowded shantytowns, and we received a warm reception at every stop. Being privileged to be the first British dancehall artist to reach Gambia was, for me,

I wake up in the morning and turn on me TV
Well, crowd of people, tell me what you see?
All these groups them who are manufactured
by A and R people, who don't know no better
Instead of them invest their money pon the street
On the youths them who really know how to do it
invest their money in a total crap
and Tippa I don't respect that
They have no talent but them a-make all the money
It is not a joke, it's not funny
They have no, no talent but them a make all the money
It is not a joke, it's not funny.
First thing they do is have some auditions
them send out request all over the land
It don't even matter if you can sing
so long as you're good-looking and you're trim
Then they give them some pretty routine
and I am sure, crowd of people, you know what I mean
Then they promote them all over the place
Everywhere you go, you see them in your face
What the hell do we have to do
to get a slice of the cake and go through?
How long we have fi wait
to get a piece of the cake, that we a-bake
Well, is it a black thing, why the youths can't earn two
shillings?
Well, Tippa know it's a sin and it a-really hurt my feeling
Well, they don't like the youth because the youths speak
up the truth
and Tippa talk from the heart, there is nuff idiot tune in
the pop chart.
Must be because we are not funny, why they don't want
we make no money
Tippa knows it's not fair but we know they just don't
care.

Tippa Irie, 'No Talent' from the LP *I Miss*
(Lockdown Productions, 2015)

such a personal achievement. At a time when most reggae artists only mentioned Africa in their lyrics, I was actually touring it as Tippa Irie and Undivided Roots.

On arrival at the airport, sporting jeans and shirt and wearing my leather black cap back to front in dancehall style, I was received by rows and rows of dancing and Jamaica flag-waving Gambians. Speakers outside the airport had been erected, blasting out the music of Tippa Irie. After getting through Customs and Immigration, we travelled in a traditional African minibus along the dusty, scorching-hot tarmac roads. The experience reminded me of transport back in Jamaica. Alongside us were several motorcycles, a mode of transport fans used to follow our minibus. I wanted to experience real African life, so I passed through the local ghettos and crowded markets, moving amongst ordinary Gambians. Giving full respect to the culture, onstage I performed in a traditional outfit, sporting a black and gold trimmed hat.

In Botswana, I was minding my own business, taking a stroll along the beach, when I proceeded to take a couple of pulls of my small spliff tail. Two men approached me suddenly and asked, 'What is that you are smoking?' I thought nothing of it, until they posed a second question: whether or not I was in possession of a dangerous drug. Then they enlightened me as to their profession, introducing themselves as plainclothes policemen. The two officers arrested me. Crowds began to gather around, protesting and making noise. The crowd shouted at the police officers: 'You can't do that, this is Tippa Irie, who has come to play to the people of Botswana.' The officers did not blink an eye as they put me in their Land Rover, then drove at speed to the local police station and put me in a shithole of a small, concrete cell with just a small bucket to wash and piss in. There was no one else in the cell. Confronted with a stern-faced sergeant, I thought, 'what the fuck have I got myself into now?'

I could not believe the police were locking me up for half a joint; I could see that all they wanted was money, though. It was ridiculous, but these officers weren't joking. I had to phone my manager, Grantley. Fortunately, he was able to make some street negotiations, bribing the station police. The cash exchange ended with me being released without any drug-related charges. I wiped my brow, opened my cell door, and walked to freedom. Anyway, I put that experience behind me, went back to my hotel, and built another joint, then had some food and a nice shower and caught a little rest. Then I went to do my show, and it was a real eye-opener: it was situated in a diamond mine.

The miners worked so hard, but when they got their pay all they would do was drink. It reminded me a little of Friday night boozing in Newcastle. I felt sorry for these miners—I could see that this was their life, working down the mines and drinking to ease the stress. They were paid little for their labour.

Once we hit the stage, the audience would not let us off. It must have been one of the longest shows I have performed, lasting two and a half hours, but I was not going to argue with a bunch of drunk miners. It reminded me of performing with Saxon at blues dances back at home from 10 PM to 6 AM. The Botswana tour was very successful, and I performed seven shows up and down the country, all well received.

Later in my career, I was booked to perform at a fundraising benefit in Kenya for a charity, along with my friend from Germany, Dr Ring-Ding, and my manager Dominic. We named the tour Come Back Alive, because driving in Kenya comes second in danger only to driving in Mexico. At night, Nairobi was like a ghost town, with not a car in sight. Dr Ring-Ding had a huge tune in Kenya called 'The Needle'; to this day, they still love that song there. It was a version of a Lord Kitchener soca tune.

We arrived at Jomo Kenyatta International Airport in Nairobi. The people who managed the charity, called March Forth Kenya Kids, were Lynn Rossetto and her husband Oneko Arika. We developed a trusting relationship—and today Lynn is my manager.

I passed through Kibera, the ghettos of Nairobi, and played one main show at a venue called the Jeevanjee Gardens, where I dressed all in white, looking sharp and feeling good to be in Africa again. We had a safari and took a flight to Mombasa before accepting Oneko's invitation to visit his hometown of Maringo, where I was honoured to plant a tree. Back in Nairobi, I went dancing with some locals at the Monte Carlo Club, where I was introduced to other selectors with Papa Charlie and the King Lion sound system. Me and Dr Ring-Ding blessed the house and smashed it up with some lyrics—they loved it, and could not believe we were there. Kenya will always have a special place in my heart; hopefully I can return again.

Throughout my life, I have always identified as African. I recognise that my origins are from the continent. Travelling to Africa in my early twenties was another of my life's ambitions come true—to reach the place of my ancestors, to have the experience of actually seeing it, living it, breathing it. I felt connected to Kenyans, because I knew we shared the same roots, to me it was simply going back to my roots, a heritage and cultural calling from within. In 2021, I released a song titled 'I Am an African', depicting the same journey I have just described, also in 2022 the same song became the title track for my independent self-released album.

Below, my friend and percussionist from Kenya, Oneko Arika, reflects on our friendship and our experience together in Africa and America:

Growing up in Nairobi, Kenya in the 1980s, the simple act of listening to reggae music was considered rebellious. Reggae was not very much appreciated by the powers-that-be. It was too radical. You would rarely hear reggae on the radio. I had friends who had family in London, and they would send us cassette tapes which were from pirate radio stations in the UK during the time when sound system culture was taking off. It was taking off in

Kenya too from the influence of the UK toasters. There were dances at night in big clubs where only grown-ups could go. I was only about 10 years old at the time, but I would always try to sneak into the dances. I felt an attraction to this reggae music from a very young age. A few of the musicians I heard on the pirated tapes really stood out to me, in particular Tippa Irie and Pato Banton.

We could identify with the lyrics and the vibe of the UK MCs. What they were singing about was exactly like our experience in Africa. We were surprised to learn that Black people in the UK seemed to have the same struggles we had in Africa, despite our leaders being African. Through these tapes, I learned so much about reggae music and the ideas and experiences that other Black people had in different parts of the world. It felt like these artists were our African brothers. Tippa's song 'Hello Darling' was doing very well during that time. We played it over and over. We would just play and rewind and play again. If you told me back then that someday I would travel to the USA and actually meet the man behind that mic, Tippa Irie, and he would become my close friend, no way I could have believed it. Decades later, I found myself at the legendary Dub Club in Los Angeles on the very night that Tippa Irie was performing with the man from Germany, Dr Ring-Ding, who also had a very big hit in Kenya. His song called 'The Needle' is one of the biggest reggae hits of all time there and we all thought he was a Black reggae artist. After the show, I met Tippa and we immediately connected, like we were old friends. He used to call me 'the Dread with the vibes' before he could master my name. The night we met, Tippa invited me to his show the next day at the Coach House in San Juan Capistrano where he was playing with

Pato Banton. Just like that, I was standing next to two of the legends who had changed my view of the world outside of Africa with their lyrics. Tippa introduced me to Pato. Three months later, I started touring on percussion with him, and now after 14 years, I still share Pato's stage.

Shortly thereafter in 2010, my girlfriend and I invited Tippa and Dr Ring-Ding to come to Kenya to perform at an event under a nonprofit that we run called March Forth Kenya Kids. Tippa barely knew us, yet he trusted us enough to come to a foreign land, under our care, and perform a free show for the people. That's just the kind of guy he is. We had a week of events, along with some crazy, funny, and memorable experiences, and of course he mashed up the place. It is now more than a decade later, and the people of Kenya are still talking about the time Tippa Irie and Dr Ring-Ding were there. We kept in touch, we saw each other every year, and became very close. He became like family to me and my partner at the time. So, we invited Tippa to come to America for our wedding and I asked him to be my best man. He flew all the way to California just for our wedding and he actually carried my wedding rings for me which is a really special thing. I will always have Tippa's back and I know he's got mine. We have travelled the world together and share a bond as brothers, and also as artists, that is unbreakable.

These stories from all over the world come back to me with so much love in my heart and pride for my accomplishments. I never imagined I would visit the continent of Africa one time, let alone the multiple countries my career has taken me to see. Likewise with the USA. I have been blessed to see much of that great continent and now, after over 38 years of touring, you can imagine I have endless stories. There's one, though, I can't forget. The year was and the band was booked into a redneck town in Alabama. The musicians around me were extremely fearful about facing the audience in this famous town with so much racist history. Visions of white sheets and burning crosses were playing on their minds. I thankfully persuaded the band to come along. 'Look, guys,' I said, 'we have signed a contractual agreement.' I had never been to Alabama, so I wanted to take a look. Coming from London, I had not had anything like the type of experiences Black people might have faced in the States; I was oblivious. So, we trod on, packing our instruments in the van and off we went.

The gig was situated in a large barn. I started to laugh out loud: 'Really, it's a bloody barn!' A middle-aged woman greeted us, and the hospitality was wonderful. We were all made welcome, and by that time the band performed tight. So, the show was fabulous. It was a mixed crowd, but a mainly white audience, and they were all rocking to our reggae. When the show was over, we sold some merchandise; a few drinks later, it was back in the van, and we hightailed it out of Alabama. Even though the vibes were welcoming in the venue, outside we were still 'niggers', and did not want to take a chance on running into people not so welcoming.

On my travels, I have always found that America, with its 50 states, has a very different vibe depending on which state I ventured into. I performed in Yuma, Arizona; the temperature reached 115 degrees Fahrenheit. It was so roasting that I could only stand out for five minutes, and had to return to the air conditioning, The temperature rose as if I had been in Dubai. It was the total opposite when touring Colorado, where I was performing in Boulder, up a mountain, ice-cold in sub-zero temperatures. The mountain area that the gig was held was at such a high altitude, we had to have oxygen by the side of the stage.

In Chicago, my sister Miss Irie and I went to get a takeaway from

McDonald's—and it was so cold that by the time we got back to our transport, our fries and burgers were literally frozen. But we ate them anyway, we were hungry.

One of the downsides of being on the road is that you end up eating a lot of junk food—which is why some Jamaican artists on tour walk with dem chef, unless they are like Big Youth and cook the meals themselves. When performing alongside Big Youth, he would remind me with his words of dietary wisdom. 'Tippa, I don't eat food from the road, and I don't eat from anyone.'

Touring America always reminds me of the long, heavy road trips, driving for three days from New York to Las Vegas, performing and travelling through the states with my backing band. Seven hours here, nineteen hours there. People don't really see this side of the music business—it becomes a full time dedicated job, not like a nine-to-five lifestyle and we are not paid overtime for additional hours worked, it's just expected of you, it's what we do.

I love California. What a beautiful place—but, like every other state, it has its good and bad elements. There are a lot of plastic, superficial people there, and when you are hot, the flavour of the month, and have something they want, they will be all over you. But when things are slow with not much going on, they don't want to know you. In California, when or if you make it, you can make it real big—but for some people, it's like being on a hamster wheel: it's very expensive to live there, and there's a lot of competition. Everybody wants to be an actor/celebrity, but many people are fighting to keep their heads above water. I guess that's just the way it is in that part of the world—Tinseltown.

In Los Angeles, you will find the Dub Club, where any reggae artist of any substance has played; you name it, they have featured at the Dub Club. I have to big up Tom Chasteen, the promoter and his team, for what they have done for reggae music in the area, and within the local community.

I have crossed over into so many beautiful towns, such as Santa Barbara, where I performed at Soho. In Orange County, one of my favourite venues was the Coach House, another iconic place that has covered every genre of music. The hospitality there was second to none. I really felt at home in San Diego, because of my good friend Carlos Culture, who was a schoolteacher by day and a local radio DJ by night. I have never met a person who was so much in love with Jamaican culture as this guy. Carlos knew all there is to know about reggae music, be it European, Jamaican, or elsewhere in the world—he would know all the artists. Before I performed onstage in San Diego, he would select his finest reggae tunes to keep the people happy. Carlos was also very close to my ex-manager Roberto Angotti. It was because of Roberto that I met him. I will really miss Carlos: he passed away suddenly in 2020. May he rest in peace.

I worked alongside numerous top-level musicians and bands, travelling with Jurassic 5, was a very interesting experience. In general, I find working alongside bands difficult: you have so many different personalities and getting up to six very different characters to agree and be on the same page can be a pain in the neck. Jurassic 5 are cool guys, though, especially my mate Chali 2Na. I have worked on a few tunes with Chali; together we released a song called 'Come On', and we also did a tune with Better Chemistry in La Verne, recording a song called '6 Foot Shorty'. In 2021 we worked with the Nextmen, releasing a tune titled 'Chicken of the Sea'.

Below is an extract from the Tippa Irie 1999 tour diary. It provides an example of my work rate and schedules when performing as a professional artist.

I have just finished a two-week tour of the Big Apple, and a sweet showdown in Mexico in Rosarito with the Long Beach Dub Allstars. On to San Diego, my second home, and then I move on to LA. Last night I nice up the people at St Mark's, right beside Venice Beach, then on to Reno, Nevada. The Allstars and I rocked the people at the Snowboarding World Championships. I then made my way back down to LA for a photoshoot for my new single, 'Divide and Rule', to be released on Who Dun It Records in June. Me and my friend Ras Shiloh are also working together on a riddim track called, 'Been There Done That'. Well, after doing tonight's show and shooting a video, the next plan is for me to find a 24-track studio to finish two more tracks with the Long Beach Allstars, one track titled 'Sensi' and a second song, 'It's All Good'.

Two days' time I shall be returning back to San Diego for my final show at the Earth Day festival, where I will be headlining with my band Jah Soldiers. It's a wonderful show, people coming together to respect the Earth and look after the planet we all live on. In truth, after touring the States, I did not really want to come back to gloomy England, but such is life and work has to go on. On reaching back, two days after I am doing a show in France with a sound called Baba Boom, and I have just finished recording five dubplates for different French sound systems. I also recorded for a French label called Night & Day, and I recorded 'We Don't Care'. It was another busy weekend in Paris, the way I like it.

On my return from France, I chilled out with my family and got some rest, ready for my show at Subterania in Ladbroke Grove with David Rodigan and on to Porky's nightclub in Peckham for the Pure Jam Crew. In May, back in the USA, doing a show in San Francisco with Jamaican reggae artist Pinchers, and then start all over again with a show with my old sparring partner, Pato Banton, in San Diego. Then off to East Coast. I have a few festivals in places like Detroit, then Toronto, Canada.

The biggest venue with the largest crowd that I have performed for was on the main Pyramid stage at Glastonbury in front of over 200,000 people. Another who-would-believe-it moment, Tippa Brixton boy on stage with the most legendary ex-Beatle. We went on just before Sir Paul McCartney.

I have played all over the world, and I've mastered the art of adapting to whatever size the venue—be it a smaller, intimate place or a massive stadium. I put in the same energy every show: this is my work principle. I will always give my best. In a larger show, you must connect and communicate in different ways. I supply my own form of camaraderie, building on audience motivation and participation. If there are only 10 fans, or 10,000 people in the audience, I always give it my best. I believe the fans deserve that: it's work, and the customers are the audience. It's all about focusing on delivery. I am no longer shaken by the element of surprise; large crowds, festivals or stadiums, I just try to ride life humbly the same as the next person, even though I have fame. I am still no different than anyone else, just sticking to my roots.

I give thanks daily for how both the public and the music industry have honoured me over the years. In October 2015, Black History Month, I was invited to attend an event at Number 10 Downing Street as a Black role model in the music industry, and I had to meet Prime Minister David Cameron on the day, Simply: what a prick is all I have to say.

Flexibility and connectivity are both required professional requirements when touring as a successful entertainer. I perform in Jamaica differently than I'd perform in Thailand; people in various countries have different cultures, so I entertain in different ways, adapting to the movements and needs of the audiences. For example, in Jamaica

I perform a sharp and snappy set to match the crowd's expectations. Nations outside reggae's origins don't have that kind of expectation; but in Jamaica, the birthplace of reggae music, competition and audience expectations are fierce. They are not easy to please, and you'd better be on top of your game—ask my mate Maxi Priest.

I have hundreds of great memories from live touring, traveling to all manner of countries, being away from home for long periods of time and at times with short notice. The wonderful team sprit between musicians that make a live performing band. From the time management, dedication and commitment of rehearsals, practises leading to the major buzz of performing in front of people from hundreds to thousands. The reaction of the audience making it more than worthwhile. I am still hungry and always ready to perform, I am as eager toady as I was over thirty years ago. I still possess the fire to entertain in my belly. That's music for you and life on the road, nothing better than making such a powerful connection to people.

Chapter Eight

My Greatest Blessing and My Worst Nightmare

MY LITTLE SISTER AVRIL HENRY WAS BORN IN EAST Dulwich Hospital on December 9, 1969. I was her older brother by three years. I thought it was great to be the only boy in the family home. Having two sisters, I was well spoilt, waited on hand and foot, and we had so many fun times, filled with innocent, joyful memories. Avril may have had two or three dolls, but she preferred to play pat-ball. Throwing a ball to the wall and it bouncing back, my sister always caught it with speed on the rebound. I would be outside, also playing my favourite games—marbles, or penny-up-the-wall, with my neighbour Neil, with the occasional knock-down ginger (where you knock on people's doors and run away), and of course, football.

We shared many common interests together; we were so close growing up. My little sister was a tomboy. She was no easy cookie, and would take no prisoners. Avril was outspoken and could stand up confidently for herself from a young age. She was one of the rocks of our family and had my back in any given situation.

Avril would observe me chatting lyrics, and at the ripe age of 13 she announced that she would like to be like me—a dancehall MC, or a DJ, as we called it back then. I would become her ghostwriter. Avril would come up with the theme and an idea for the tune, and I would put together her lyrics. I can recall one of Miss Irie's first songs:

she boldly declared the lyrics 'mi na push no pram'. Back in my early teenage years, young girls would look forward to settling down with children and a family—but this was not for my little sister. Avril was looking for freedom and independence to match her colourful personality (so much for that idea: she went on to be a mother of three children). I guess that at the time she wrote those lyrics, that's how she was feeling. As MCs, that is what we do—write about how we are feeling, express ourselves through our lyrics. She was no way ready for kids then.

Little Jackie, my cousin, looks back on one story involving Avril that really captures her spirit back then:

> Just to give you one experience that would show you Avril's spirit: one night we went out raving, it was me, Tanya, a close long-time friend of the family, Jackie, the eldest sister, and Avril. We put our best outfits on and our hairstyles were looking fine. We realised that we had been out together longer than expected, so the plan was to creep back into the family home before any of the elders recognised that we were still missing into the early hours. We managed to make a plan; I saw that the toilet window was slightly ajar, so we hoisted up Avril in her best garments to climb through the window.
>
> Avril managed with her skinny self to get through the window gap. Ten minutes passed by, with no sound or sight of Avril. Twenty minutes went by, and Avril still had not crept down the stairs—this was the plan we had all agreed on. We tried to get her attention, but to our shock, Tippa's mum slowly opened the front door, giving us the hardest stare and some choice words before letting us all inside. Avril had dropped asleep after climbing through the toilet

window, in the process, forgetting we was all outside shivering in the cold. Avril was an original, stylish rude gal.

I would encourage Avril to push herself further, supporting and motivating my sister to reach her goal. The downstairs basement of the family grocery store was her beginning. Like me, my little sister practised for the first time on Daddy's sound system, Musical Messiah. She became very good, chatting over different reggae versions. I witnessed my sister's vocal talent evolve in front of my eyes; it was just organic and natural. As I have said, my family, the Henrys, were all equally born into the spirit and energy of dancehall reggae vibes.

At 15, my sister launched herself as a new, fresh UK female reggae MC. She followed in her brother's tradition, going by the name of 'Miss Irie'. We would go together all over, to see live reggae artists perform. We would look at each other, giving the thumbs-down sign if the performer was not on par, not cutting the cloth on the night. At the age of 17, I was confident that Avril was ready to perform alongside me.

When Avril launched herself as Miss Irie, there were few female reggae MCs and DJs brave enough to take up the mic, such as Lady G, Lady Mackerel *aka* Macka Diamond, and Sister Nancy, Brigadier Jerry's sister from Jamaica. From America, we had Shelly Thunder, Miss Lady Linda, Lady Ann, Lady English. From our UK family it was Sister C, Muma Allie and Cinderella. Ranking Ann and Lorna Gee both worked with Ariwa, Mad Professor's record label.

I introduced Avril to Saxon Sound System, who I was working with at the time. On the mic, Miss Irie had a big presence, just like her loud and bossy personality. Her lyrical performances were sharp, exciting, and on point. She had the banter. It made me so proud seeing my sister so self-confident and talented.

Miss Irie's loud identity matched her vibrant and electric character. Always and every day, my younger sister was sharp-dressing and fashion-conscious, unique, original, always creative with her style, wearing dangly, giant, gold earrings while sporting red or blue hairstyles. My sister was a south London bashment queen. She was a hustler. Avril could take milk out of coffee; she was a right Arthur Daley from the eighties TV series *Minder*.

Avril reinvented herself constantly, never wearing an outfit a second time. My sister also ventured into a bit of catwalk modelling, working alongside my cousin Little Jackie, who is a professional hairdresser and clothes designer. Little Jackie is another successful, talented, and creative member of the Henry family. I have a photo in front of me as I write: Avril has brilliant white hair in it, with blue dyed tips. Flamboyant Miss Irie pushed up a new style, in more ways than one.

As with Irie family values, she was taking her MC craft seriously, right to a highly competitive standard. I would take Miss Irie to join me at any sound clash I was in. We joined as a brother-and-sister MC combination. I passed the mic to her like a baton. Saxon was famous for being original, and so it was with their welcoming of a female MC into the sound. Sister C was another female MC performing as part of the Saxon crew. This was a unique stand for Saxon in the male-dominated sound system culture of the eighties. Saxon removed the barriers and boundaries by flinging open its doors, welcoming female MCs for the first time in the UK to take up our joint dancehall tradition.

When Saxon started to become popular, playing outside the country, I took Miss Irie along. Performing with Saxon Sound in Jamaica, Canada, and the US, she was in her element, moving around with fellow MCs Lady G, Lady Linda, and Lady English, the very same artists my sister was listening to on her turntable at home. Now, in the flesh, she was rubbing shoulders too with likes of Shabba Ranks and Papa San. Next plane out together we were touring the States, playing in several cities including Long Beach. The colourful dancehall queen Avril was so happy and felt so at home. She was having the time of her life.

Yes man, settle. I am better, hotter than the rest
Mind who you call, come settle and rest
My name is Miss Irie, I stick out mi chest
'Cause mi a-better, rougher, badda than the rest
No big show-off gal, want to come test
I am the only woman in a Saxon gang with the mic inna mi hand
When Miss Irie come through, session have fi ram
Mi a-settle the rhythm, like the rings pon mi hand
Mi wheel and turn, juke and mi jam
I rock the man; I rock the woman
Mi, I am the DJ, Miss Irie from London
Mi parents from the Caribbean, all our ancestors are African.

Miss Irie, Saxon Sound System, Peckham Rye Park, south London, 1987

On our return, I offered Miss Irie a combination track on my new LP *Ah Mi Dis*. Our joint track was titled 'Mi Never Go Down Deh So'. In 1989, on Saxon's Hit Factory label, Miss Irie recorded 'Man Na Work'. Avril went on to work and tour with Ariwa Records and Mad Professor. I also introduced my sister to my manager Grantley Haynes. Both Mad Professor and Grantley helped her as they had previously helped me. In 1990, doors opened further as my sister recorded a single titled 'DJ of the Future', released on GT's Records. This track was a female response to Sweetie Irie's hit track, which he had released with Aswad.

In the nineties I had a Number 1 hit on the UK reggae charts. It was a duet with Lloyd Brown called 'Stress'. This provided me with a perfect opportunity to offer my sister a recording break. Miss Irie and Paulette Tajah produced a female response tune titled 'Vex', released by Groove & A Quarter Records. Miss Irie recorded and successfully released a total of five hit reggae dancehall singles. It was strange for me to see Avril performing; it was like seeing a reincarnation of myself on the mic. Just as in the beginning, I made a pathway to support the MC dancehall birth of Miss Irie.

I was her big brother, and she was always so full of positive praise for my music, encouraging me, telling me how proud she was of what I had achieved. I would go to her in times of need for guidance and advice. Avril was my go-to person. I would confide in her and she in me; we would rarely be seen apart. She was also my security guard, my defender, and protector. No one would dare trouble me when Avril was around. My little sis was my guardian angel. We were flesh and blood on tour together, on the road together.

As the years passed Avril became involved in relationships and eventually had a family of her own. Miss Irie had had a few boyfriends that I remember from back in the day—Nigel *aka* Jumpin Jack Frost, Leroy Bell, and Andy I Ansah—a really good guy I wish she'd have

Sweetie Irie, say he is the man DJ of the future
Well, I, a Miss Irie, woman DJ of the future
The other day, I just mash up Jamaica
What a heat, when I go America
Pure agony, when I go a-Canada
Everywhere mi a go, pure masses, call out fi
murder
Look at mi flavour. How, mi nice and cute, mi
breasts, dem slender
Mi a one woman, who have feminine gender
I spa with the one big batty Brenda
Respect to all the young gal entertainers
Lady G from down a-Jamaica
Hold tight, Shelly Thunder from up America
Every time I come, place catch a-fire
Pure worries and problems
Nothing but niceness when mi a-come round
here
You wanna know why Miss Irie is the best?
'Cause I thinking ahead of the rest
When I come, pure agony and stress
Have fi confess. Well, all gal MC, have fi
confess
Mi run tings round here. If you don't like it,
go hold, your corner
North, south, east and west
My time to shine, this time
Look how mi a-nice, mi, a-fine
Have fi confess, Miss Irie, God bless
The Father, up above bless me, made mi
different, from the rest.

Miss Irie, 'DJ of the Future'
from 12' single(GT's Records, 1989)

married, successful to this day. Her first stable boyfriend was Neveah; in my opinion they made a great couple, and Avril had her first child, Ashanti, with him. What a bundle of joy her daughter was. In the nineties, when jungle was all the rage, there was no one better than Avril's first daughter at dancing to it; she would have the family in stiches, entertaining us with her moves. I know she got that from her mum. Her son, who she had with Mark Dudley *aka* Ripper, was a lovely kid. The only bad thing about my nephew was that he grew up to become a Manchester United supporter.

Some of my sister's past partners would either encourage her musical talents or discourage her. She began drifting from her musical career path. Avril would still come and perform as Miss Irie at Saxon dances, but only occasionally. My sister would still rave and go dancing, but the places she was frequenting for fun were different than the places I would go to have good times. She also began moving in Yardie-style company, frequenting more hardcore Jamaican dancehall venues such as Lord Gellys, Stone Love, Asha World Movements, and Vinyl Star with her good friend Gappy Crucial. Those dances were not really for me as an MC. I loved the vibes of the music, but the people who gathered at the dances were not my cup of tea. There was a huge influx of Jamaicans coming into the country at the during the nighties and this was not a bad thing—but in truth some did not come with the intention of doing a hard day's work. Several earned their cash from crime, such as selling Class-A drugs, or armed robbery, which they used to call a 'sting', as in, 'Hey, Tippa, we just sting somebody'—meaning a person had just got robbed.

Personally, I maintained my presence in my faithful Saxon London vibes. There was a difference. I felt more at ease, and relaxed. Our crowd was not hostile, and there was not a lot of tension in the air. You have to remember that there were people coming from Kingston districts such as Tivoli Gardens and Jungle. Opposing gangs met and feuded; battles were fought out in the dances, and people would, at times, lose their lives. At our dances, no one carried guns, but in the Jamaican dancehalls there would be a good chance a punter could have a firearm.

In front of my eyes, I saw my sister start to move with company that as her older brother, I disapproved of. Our mum would also send out warnings: 'Be careful of the company you keep!' Rumours soon spread in our community. Whispers told me that Avril was not moving in good circles; my little sis was smoking more than weed, hustling in things that she should not be into. In a split second, I jumped in my car and went to Avril's home in Tulse Hill.

On arrival she looked fine, the same bubbly Avril. There was nothing obvious that I could see to make me concerned. Before leaving, I spoke to my sister once again, offering guidance about the people she was surrounding herself with, the hangers-on. At this time, in fact, she was engaged to a Jamaican guy I had barely met... you could hear the alarms bells ringing in my head. 'No, no,' I said to myself, 'really!' But you can't tell a grown woman who she should be dating. Together they had a baby daughter known as Wingy—she will always be my 'little Wingy'—and her tomboy self-reminds me so much of her mother when she was growing up. I thought back on how my sister used to date some nice, sensible guys, back in the day. In silence at her home that day, I wished she had chosen one of them.

In life, all we can do is to offer love and words of guidance. The next part of the process is up to the person to take it or leave it. Each of us has a God-given choice; you can't force another. We all have our own eyes to see; we can't see through another's, we all make our own choices in the end. I had to use rationale and balanced the only reasoning that I could use to settle my mind. Otherwise, I would have been gripped by fear, forever worrying about my little sister and the well-being of her children.

On Thursday, June 25, 1998, I was resting in my bed at home with my girlfriend, my first night after returning back from a tour when the

Man have mercy
Men who give mi trouble
Trouble on the double
Say we a-give them stress and botheration
They say we are miserable
But they are miserable, too. They big up them
chest
but mi and Miss Irie could not care less
Mi cook, mi clean. House fresh and pristine
You, boy, you come, give mi a bun
and mi a-give you none
You still give mi a botheration
This is why: this Miss Irie is a rebel woman.

Paulette Tajah and Miss Irie, 'Vex/Miserable
Woman' from the 12' single (Groove & A
                                    Quarter, 1993)

phone rang. It was 1 AM. A family member, Donnette, was telling me to come now to Avril's home. Something bad had happened. I kissed my teeth, yet moved quickly. I was hoping and praying that maybe my sister was just slightly injured, maybe there had just been a little accident. And I hate to say it. I was tired, and I was in no mood for any drama.

Even though it was a matter of minutes, the journey from my home in Streatham to Avril's home in Tulse Hill seemed like it happened in slow motion. I pulled up in front of the estate and saw that the police had cordoned off the area, a crime scene. As I got out of my car, a police officer stopped me and asked who I was. I got out my driving licence and informed the officer that it was my sister's home. I was told I could not enter the family home, and advised to make my way to King's College Hospital in Camberwell Green. As I was returning to the car, the officer added: 'It's not good.' My heart was beating fast, and now I was wondering about what state I would find my sister.

I rushed to the hospital at high speed and screeched up outside. I ran up flights of stairs and searched desperately for my sister. On entering her ward, I was again stopped by the police and had to show my ID. Next, I came face to face with my little sister lying on a hospital bed. Moving towards her, I saw that her eyes had rolled back.

She had been shot at close range. My legs turned to jelly as I stood by Avril's side. I knew in my bones that I would have to face facts: there would be no coming back from this incident. It was a deep head wound, and the chances of survival were basically zero. To say I was in shock is an understatement. *What had happened? What had she done to deserve this?* This was something completely out of my normal experience, difficult for me to comprehend.

Later, the police informed me of the details. On Thursday, June 25, 1998, at 10:30 PM, my sister's husband had opened the front door of their home on the Tulse Hill Estate. He was rushed at the entrance by four men, who stabbed him in a scuffle as they proceeded to enter by force. My sister and her husband were held hostage. The intruders bound them to chairs using plastic flex. My nieces, aged seven and two, were snatched and put under a mattress in the bedroom. The armed invaders then raided the family home, ransacking the house as they looked for cash, jewellery, and drugs. On leaving the building, these evil gunmen shot my sister in the head at close range. The gunmen also fired a bullet at her husband, but instead of killing him, it grazed his neck. He told the investigating officers that he had lain still, not moving, pretending to be dead until the gunmen left. My nieces remained traumatised but thankfully had not been harmed.

My little sister remained in intensive care, on life support. Her baby girls and her son were all safe. On the other side of the hospital room was my sister's husband. I could see that he had only minor injuries. I thought to myself: 'He was present in the family home alongside my sister and the children. How come the gunmen did not kill him? And why were they so brutal towards my sister?' Through my tears, my mind was spinning. 'Why did these wicked men do this to my sister and not her husband?' That unanswered question has haunted me from that day. I was devastated, completely shattered, heartbroken. I would fall asleep and wake up, asking myself, 'Why? Why?'

The following morning, as soon I arrived at the hospital, I saw Avril's husband in the corridor talking with two of his friends. On seeing me, they immediately stopped talking. I trusted no one around me; I wanted all present to leave me alone, to keep well away from me. My spirit was vexed, and I was raging deep inside. All involved with me had a distrust of my sister's husband and his circle of friends. The same question rose again: why was Avril so savagely gunned down in front of her two baby girls, with a bullet in her head? And how did Avril's husband only receive a graze and some cuts? I was full to the brim with suspicion, and the very idea of revenge comforted me. How good it would feel to avenge my sister's senseless death.

My family and friends gathered around as word of what had

happened spread throughout our community. My sister's flamboyant character meant that Miss Irie had a big presence in Brixton. She was never a woman who could be ignored or easily forgotten. Everyone around was shedding tears of mourning.

We all met at my Uncle Liebert's family home. He was one of the key elders and wise men who had helped guide me in life. Mr Mac was another nickname for Uncle Liebert, my mother's brother. In the front room around 30 men congregated. My cousins who were also sound system people, the Whitley family, were also there. The Acre Lane Brixton posse and the Seaverights said, 'Something needs to be done.' I had two cousins, twins, who were infamous local characters, south London's answer to the Krays. They were a pair of badmen who informed me that they were going to put the word out on the street to identify the murderers.

We had no idea who was responsible at the time. There was plenty of male aggression mixed with sorrow in the room. As Avril's older brother, I felt responsible—like I had to act, to take revenge in her name. Two paths appeared inside me. One: the revenge posse, advocating for retribution. The other: wisdom and reason, calling me to my senses. As I was the famous Tippa Irie, any retribution would easily put me on the police radar.

My friends Slater and Tony Macpherson, alongside my cousin Gary Whitley, reasoned with me. They told me in no uncertain terms that I was heading for positive places, with so much life in front of me. I could not afford to throw away my opportunities, getting banged up in prison for life over a revenge killing.

I chose to succumb to the voice of reason. Believe me, it was difficult, with many others around urging me to take the other direction. I also had three kids to think about. But this did not stop me from putting out the sound to find out who was responsible. I was forced to sit silently in my sorrow, though I felt ripped apart. I held on through the storm. I refused to go down with this horrific tragedy.

Word went out through the underworld. Throughout my life, I never wanted to associate with the underworld, even though it was always only a stone's throw away. That said, I knew everyone there and everyone knew me. The local badmen would never trouble me, because they knew Tippa Irie never troubled anyone in his turn. I was a good man; I prided myself on being a gentleman. The badman life-style was not for me. Being a famous face in Brixton, badmen would respect me. Many local SW9 gangsters were good to me—though many were not people you would want to cross.

I'd see vehicles outside my house in Streatham, and realise that my friends and family were keeping a watchful eye on me throughout the nights, ensuring that my girlfriend and I stayed safe. My friends protected us from any possible attackers or further repercussions. After two weeks, names started filtering through. The word was that a Yardman had been involved in my sister's murder. Local community members and people in my family had done well for me in my sister's name, and my choice of revenge was having these wicked murderers locked up for life. It hurt me so much to witness my mother carrying such pain. Her youngest daughter had been stolen from her, only in her twenties, with so much ahead of her. My elder sister Jackie and my mum have done a wonderful job looking after Avril's children. They were so young; it was difficult to know what to say. All we could do was comfort them. From the day of Avril's death, Jackie Henry became their new mother. It was heart-breaking to feel my nieces' and nephew's loss and suffering. I watched them face so much hurt, so young. I would give all that I could to help and support those little ones, emotionally and financially, or just by being present whenever they needed their Uncle Tony.

There was a twisted political background to my sister's brutal murder. At the time, the Metropolitan Police, in partnership with Scotland Yard, had started cultivating Jamaican-born gangsters, employing them on the police payroll as informants. The way this system worked during the nineties was that gunmen and gang members were provided with a free travel pass to leave Jamaica. This was sanctioned by the UK's Home Office and immigration officials—even though, in many cases, the men were wanted by Jamaican authorities in connection with unsolved crimes.

One such story involved Delroy Denton. Denton was a Kingston-born member of the notorious Rapid Posse gang. He had already received a prison sentence in Jamaica for firearms offences and violent robberies when he applied to immigrate to the UK. He was refused, being, at the time, a criminal suspect in the ice-pick murders of seven women on the island. In 1994, Denton managed to arrive in the UK. He stayed in south London but was soon arrested during a police raid on the Atlantic pub in Brixton. He was charged with possession and distribution of firearms but was offered a plea deal by police. He gladly accepted rather than face a heavy prison sentence and became an informant.[1]

Operation Trident was an anti-gun and homicide unit of the Metropolitan Police. It was formed in 1998 in relation to the rise of gun crime and murder within the African-Caribbean community. This unit began working on Avril's case; as soon I double-checked names coming up through the streets, I would contact the assigned Trident officer and pass the information on. The police acted on the information, and DS Gary Richardson, DCI Steve Kupis, and DCI Reg Field were assigned to the investigation.[2]

Days after the shooting, the renowned Jamaican reggae singer Junior Delgado visited me out of the blue. He talked about my sister's murder. Then the conversation took a very strange turn. I felt as if he was trying to get me off my search for the killers, as if he was attempting to distract me, trying to put me off the scent. Something did not rest well with me. Later, one of the inspectors assigned to the case confided in me that Kingston-born Oscar Hibbert (*aka* Junior Delgado) had, in fact, been identified as the person responsible for inviting the two lead suspects to the UK from Jamaica. I never heard anything further about his involvement, but can you believe the front of these brothers?

Weeks later, I walked into a studio where Delgado was rehearsing for a show, and he jumped as if he had seen a ghost—he probably thought I was going to attack him. His guilty reaction told me all I needed to know. I looked at him and walked out, though I was tempted to rush him on account of what the officers told me; but, as my dad would always say, 'leave it to God.' Later, I received a message that Delgado had died.

Below, Jumpin' Jack Frost, who remained a close friend to my sister, shares his feelings:

> Me and Avril were so close. I was drawn to her style, always smart and matching. She was so sexy and beautiful. Miss Irie had the greatest, wickedest sense of humour. She was fun to be with, nonstop excitement. All were drawn to her big and bold spirit as a great female MC and entertainer tearing up the crowds on the mic. Avril was part of the faithful Saxon crew. I would stay at the family house, and we all mucked in together. After late-night/early-morning Saxon dances, I would follow Tippa and Avril back to the warmth of the Irie home. Avril had red hair, blue, all colours. Her character was as bright and colourful as her clothes. Avril was our own Brixton female superstar. I loved her… my babes.
>
> I was touring Germany as a drum and bass selector, as part of a big European Jumpin Jack tour, when I received the message that Avril had been murdered. I lay there for hours, tears rolling down my cheeks. My baby, Avril, gone. The news was unbearable. I just could not believe it. I was expected to perform on the decks in front of thousands,

but I was completeely numb. I pushed on through, but just wanted to go back to my hotel room. Lying on the bed, still, silent and alone, I pieced together all the wonderful memories. That was the only time in my music career that I did not want to perform.

Avril was Brixton royalty, my real-life queen. The whole of our Brixton community was devastated by the news of Miss Irie's so sudden, tragic death. May she rest in peace, forever.

The people at Greensleeves and so many performers asked themselves, 'How come this has happened to Tippa Irie? Such a nice guy, but what has his family got caught up with?' My sister's murder featured in the headlines, and on the TV news. So many newspapers printed the details of Miss Irie's murder. *The Voice*, *The Sun*, *The Daily Mirror*, *The Evening Standard*, and *The south London Press* all reported on the crime. I kept asking myself why this had happened, what had my sister done to deserve this. I knew her slaying had to be connected to something— money, drugs, revenge. I knew those around her were not 100 percent clean, and were stinging other people.

My view has always been that if you are in an environment selling and buying from wolves, the wolves will come for you. This was the reality behind this evil killing of a young mother, of my dear sister. In life, you must be wise. There are people you can never trust in your company, the type who smile in your face but will sell you straight down the river.

The police investigation resulted in the arrests of three men: the two gunmen, and an accomplice driver. Hyrone Hart, 25 years old, lived in Handsworth, Birmingham; Kurt Roberts, street name 'Pepe', 19, lived on Clapham's Notre Dame estate. The driver, Adrian Francis, street name 'Prento', 22, was from Balham. The two Jamaican-born gunmen had flown in from Kingston and arrived at Gatwick using false

UK passports and fraudulent personal identification. The driver was a wheelchair user who was spotted driving a specially adapted white Renault Cleo. Francis had become paralysed from the waist down after receiving gunshot wounds in a previous gun battle in Notting Hill.

On the night the police raided the assailants' homes, my sister's mobile phone and her gold jewellery were recovered. Police evidence showed that Avril's mobile phone had made numerous calls to the US and Jamaica days after the gunmen had fled. The accomplices were connected to a list of crimes: an armed robbery in Tottenham; my sister's murder and robbery; the murder, rape, and robbery of another woman, Michelle Carby; and the slaying of a man, Peter Ferguson.

In December 1999, the trial began at Camberwell Green Magistrates' Court. My long-time brethren, Peter Hunnigale, supported and accompanied me there every day. In court, I was literally three feet away from the murderers in the dock. Avril had gone. Her children's mother, my mother's daughter, was snatched. As memories of my little sister ran through my mind, anger boiled up inside me seeing the guilty faces of the murderers. The culprits were later transferred to the Old Bailey for sentencing: Hart and Roberts were sentenced to life imprisonment, while Francis was sentenced to 18 months. Judge Neil Denison, in his summary, said to the defendants: 'I will not waste my words with you. Suffice as to say, your conduct is an affront to civilised society.'[3]

At the sentencing, Hart had a sick smirk on his face as he was leaving to be sent down. 'How could people slay a woman in front of her children for money,' I kept thinking. The human stupidity mixed with an uneducated ghetto mentality sickened me to the bottom of my stomach. But I was relieved and thankful that the court case was over, and that justice had been served. I believe there are still men who were involved in my sister's murder walking around with their freedom intact, people who were part of a wider circle of drug dealers and gangsters.

I know full well the differences between the poverty-ridden ghettos of Jamaica and being born Black British. Back in the day, you would never witness such killings here –murders, rapes in front of small children. Wherever you come from, there never can be any rationale for such vile, demonic behaviour. I don't believe the worst UK gangsters would engage in such inhumane brutality; even the Krays would not have gone that low during their gangster reign. Even British criminals had some principles.

Whatever my sister might have got caught up in, I would have sorted it for her. If it was money she owed, I would have paid it. All she had to do was ask. I had just come back from a tour—I had cash. Avril, so talented, caring, and compassionate, the face and voice of our family and community. Avril was a shining star and did not deserve to die because of money. It was nothing but a waste of a beautiful life.

Peter, who I thank so much for his support, gives his version of events below:

> We were on the way to play California. We were supposed to be playing on a bill alongside Nadine Sutherland and Freddie McGregor. The promoter did not give us our money and we were all messed around, so all the artists went our separate ways; Freddie went back to Florida and I returned home. There I received a call from Tippa. I heard what I thought was excitement in his voice, like how it was speaking together when we were building tracks, but this time the sound was different—in his words, it was distress. Then Tippa let me know that Avril had been shot. I immediately rushed in a cab to meet him at King's College Hospital. On the ward, I saw Miss Irie, with major trauma to her head. Tippa was in a terrible state, and the gravity of what had happened was embedding itself into us. Tippa kept wanting to talk, but I saw that around Avril

were people we did not know—so I warned him to calm down and not say a word in the presence of these strangers. News got out around the street. Tippa managed to be by Avril's bedside before she sadly passed from the shooting. It was another chapter in our lives. I knew I would be there for him, always. The police went on to catch the murderers. It was gang-related, drug business. Avril and two other victims got caught up in these arguments. Presenter Mary Nightingale invited us to feature on ITV, and Tippa and I sang a tribute to Avril and to highlight the crime. I supported Tippa every day. I would pick him up and bring him to the court, offering moral support. The murderers, who were from Jamaica, were sentenced to life, but I think they should have been sentenced to life times three for each one of their victims. The trial was a long and painful experience. But the next painful experience was when we laid Avril to rest. I helped carry the coffin and just could not stop crying. The skies were also crying too, as it rained all day. So sad.

The last flight Avril and I took together was in 1989, to bury our daddy in Jamaica. We laid him to rest in Trelawny. I would never have thought, in a million years, that six months later I would be burying my little sister, too. The pain was unbearable. I could not take it all on. The stress alone would have quite easily taken me down to rock bottom. But I had lost my soul mate, and I felt so empty without her.

Everyone who knew my sister's good heart and spirit would truly miss Irie. Papa San, who was good friends with her, phoned from Jamaica to offer prayers and sincere condolences. I used music once again as my comforter, as I had throughout my life. It was an expression and an outlet for my true self. Music has been my therapy in times of need.

In 1991, I released a song I recorded and dedicated to my beautiful sister; the lyrics are on the next page.

Here is Claudette Cummings, Avril's best friend, describing my sister:

I met Avril in 1982, she came to my school Kingsdale Secondary, a new girl in the class and I asked her, 'what is your name?' And she replied, 'Avril.' I said with my big mouth, 'say it again because I had never heard that name before.' She was very quiet not like me, from that day Avril and I strung along, we were tight, thick as thieves, we immediately just clicked. Avril was very quiet and humble, she would not be in your face, watching people and listening, observing more than talking. We would jump school and go to Brixton in Coxsone shop, Pressures, playing Space Invaders when we should have been studying lessons. Academically, Avril was well-behaved and focussed, a very intelligent girl, first class at mathematics and she loved PE. One afternoon Avril let off a stink bomb and held the door with teacher and pupils inside. The terrible smell of off eggs closed the class down and tears were rolling down her face due the disruption caused by her stink bomb planting. As a teenager after school my good friend Avril would be on Stockwell estate, south London, moving up and down with young guys on the block, the Wacka's posse.

Avril was a unique dresser, she wore what she wanted and did not care what others thought. She was a fashion goddess, she run fashion, fashion no run her. Big self-esteem, colourful and differently styled hair, she would dress and wear what she wanted, if you did not like it, it was your problem. One evening she asked me to link her to go to a dance and I had never been before, it was all new

This is a tribute to Avril Elaine Henry aka young Miss Irie
On the 9th December she was born; me still can't believe that she gone.
(chorus)
Tippa, I miss Ms Irie, I miss my sis, it go so then and
Tippa, I miss Ms Irie, I miss my sis
Well, Avril Elaine Henry aka Miss Irie
She a-the youngest in all de family
And now she gone left me and Jackie
Well, me really feel it fi Shane, Ashanti and Zhane
Lose them mummy
Mummy lose a daughter
Me lose a sister
But Avril, we will remember
The wicked took your life away, girl
We're sad that you are gone
There's nothing left for us to say
For you we will be strong
It's like this
Well Dulwich Hospital at wey she born
Ninth of December in at the early morn
I can remember like it was yesterday
And now she gone Daddy Tip feel away
Well, me glad brother Manny him nu deh yah
Well, fe see wah dem do to his daughter
Black people: we too out of order
Why we won't stop kill one another
Well, some of dem come to England
All of a sudden dem turn badman
When dem deh a yard
Them used to dig yam
Come a England now them want to turn Don
Well, me no know which part of a-Jungle you from
Could be from Seaview or the Waltham
Please make sure when you come a-London
You behave like say you is a human
Because we no kill baby mother over here
You might do those things over there
But this one thing we have to make clear
De dog-heart business
We no want it over here

I Miss, 2000, Tippa Irie, Lockdown Productions also release 7-inch on Greensleeves Records and Jahmin Records (France) to me. She said we were going to meet up at King Tubby's on Vassal Road, Brixton and my mouth jumped out as I witnessed my good friend Avril taking up the mic. I did not even know she was a performer, she had stayed quiet about that part of her life. On the sound she completely changed and all quietness disappeared as she DJ on King Tubby's sound system. Tippa, her brother was present rocking the crowd with MC General Slater.

On several occasions the MC Billy Boyo would come to Avril's home and listen to her practising. One Sunday night we were both listening to David Rodigan's show. Rodigan was featuring Billy Boyo and during the session he had stolen and tiffed her lyrics. I am telling you, if she would have caught him, she would have 'bruk im up'.

Tippa would always take his sister with him to perform at live shows, Tottenham, Brixton the Ace club, Stonebridge Park, Hackney Downs, Deptford and Notting Hill carnival, performing at the 'Cage', under the Westway, she would DJ and bust the place. Tippa took his sister everywhere with him, north, east, south and west. Avril began first chatting with her brother on Tubbys sound and then later with Saxon sound system. Avril and Tippa went tour Jamaica with Saxon and Avril sparred and become good friends with Lady Saw, and Papa San within the world of reggae music.

Avril and I were best friends and I have never moved with anyone else like Avril. The jokes we shared, I moved in the same house with her, shared the same bathing water, slept in the same bed and we wore each other's clothes. She had the biggest heart, if she had anything, you would get half. We could never leave each other's side. Avril later in life became a mother and her main goal for her children was for them, to be independent, a very loving mum, she had left the sound systems world, got married and even started to attend church.

One night I was at Avril's house and I was going to see her the next day but I thought I would give it a miss as we had been together for days on end when my phone rung and I was told that I had to reach hospital. I went King's College Hospital to the emergency intensive care, waiting room, where I saw Avril's mum, Aunty Madge she broke down and held me, I remember my body was shaking and I went into complete shock. I stayed with Avril at her hospital bed and never left her side. I remember her head was swollen and she was not responding, all that was happening was she was passing urine through the tubes; I recall all the noise of the machines and the nurses and doctors doing all they could but the doctors informed us that she won't make it, as the gun wound had ricochet into her brain.

I went into shock and I never have truly recovered, every day I think of her, I wonder to myself what would Avril been like in her fifties today. I can never believe it happened, I knew them things happened but we never thought it would come knocking at our door, Avril loved her brother Tippa and protected him always, she was the glue of the family and went she left us, nothing was ever the same. God bless her soul, my bestie, love you eternally.'

On the day of the funeral, I admit I did not want to get out of bed— but I have been taught by both my mother and father to meet things head-on. I had no other choice. Believe it or not, the lady I later married did not even want to attend or pay respects to my sister. There were quite a few red flags with this woman, and this was another. My mum and Jackie were in pieces, broken but still strong. My mum took care of everything, as she always did. People attended in the hundreds, from all over England, family members alongside celebrities, as Avril was such a popular person.

Today Avril would be so proud of her children. They have achieved so much, and each one is special in their own way. Against the odds, her eldest daughter graduated from university and currently manages her own business. My sister's son is doing well in retail, and the youngest daughter, Wingy, alongside her day job, has her own business as well.

It still pains me when I drive past my sister's family home in Tulse Hill, where the murder took place. None of this nightmare will ever make any sense to me. I've never got over the pain of losing Avril, but with time it gets a little easier.

Chapter Nine
Doing It Myself

I FELT BITTER WITH REGARDS TO GREENSLEEVES AND how it all came to an end. I had little control, of what aspects of my material Greensleeves put out on their label. So, when the management decided the marketing plan and it did not work out, in truth it made me feel blamed and unfairly treated. We'd had hits and 'Hello Darling' was the biggest tune reaching the UK charts. In reality we were young people, who were just getting accustomed to making records and we were just blindly following wherever the labels lead. We were naïve and inexperienced at dealing with music industry and record label politics. As a performer I reverted to my old sound system mentality but this time, instead of going out playing from sound to sound, I worked instead with multiple independent reggae labels. Together we shared the knowledge between the young musicians and producers, building us up to be independent. We built our music knowledge on shared skills, disappointments and experiences. I still had some income coming in from sales and PA shows arising from my single 'Hello Darling' and, fortunately, due to its chart success, this exposure led to me gaining even higher public exposure, so that several reggae independent record labels were eager to start working with me.

After leaving Greensleeves, I had no choice but to trod my own road, I had to throw myself into the deep end, with an all-or-nothing attitude and a concrete commitment to my music. I knew it would be a challenge: I had no financial backing, or free studio time, or marketing support, all of which you get from being with a major record company. I moved to GT's Records, run by my manager Grantley Haynes. Grantley had the foresight, wisdom, and the legal knowledge of the music business; he was well schooled and knew what he was doing. The label was an independent registered company, and GT's Records would licence our music, having its own distribution deal as a label. In those days we had a deal with Jet Star Records, and in America I was with IRS and managed by Miles Copeland, the brother of Stewart Copeland of The Police.

Partnership and teamwork within the independent world was just like a smaller version of the major labels. The partnership was we, as artists and performers, supplied the creative energy, while those alongside us possessed the administration, management, and the legal know how. Thankfully in the eighties there was a lot of independent grass roots labels popping up in London such as Fashion Records situated in a rental premises in Forest Hill, south London. LGR records, Stingray records and Ariwa in Croydon. Clarkie and Blackie records. Groove and Quarter records from Harlesden. Steve Clarke from Goldmine records based in Birmingham. Independent labels back in the day could not afford offices so it was generally based in people's houses like Mafia and Fluxy in Tottenham near the football ground. All studio equipment would be set up as a permanent feature in people's homes, once again to show you the commitment to the music. The money would always come in slowly in dribs and drabs so you had to be committed and loyal to this journey of recording DIY. The disadvantage crossing from being employed by a major record label and transferring to being independent was energy and output. I have had to work with a lot of smaller record labels and working with so many independents takes a great deal of energy. If I had been fully acknowledged as an artist the way I deserved to be, I would not have had to do this. Unfortunately, I was also to find out that, even independent

259

businesses can still sometimes operate shadily with backroom deals, just like some of the major record labels.

Grantley, my first manager, really supported me when I went my own way, he taught me and also Pato Banton about how to manage publishing deals and contracts. They were good days, me and Pato would spend all 24 hours locked in the studio writing lyrics. We were both fiercely competitive and dedicated to succeeding within the music business. You need someone with legal eyes and inside knowledge. This was the reason why throughout the history of music, young people with no legal knowledge have been ripped off, gaining a meagre percentage and having no copyright or rights to royalties. The annals of music history is littered with such sad stories of the main artist losing out. I came out of school without one qualification, so I did not know what to expect and what I was really entitled to from my recording releases.

Despite these challenges, throughout my career I have been fortunate to have many great role models within the world of reggae. I learnt from the likes of Saxon's management Dennis Rowe, he showed me how to network with people and about the need to promote your talents, making the audience gravitate to what you are doing. I benefitted from working alongside Aswad's late Drummie Zeb, the first big producer and multi-talented musician that I worked with in the studio. I was only 17 and I admired his professionalism. Drummie showed me the standard that was required to be successful in the music industry. In the studio I learned with Mafia and Fluxy both amazing musicians and producers. John MacGillivray and Chris Lane from Dub Vendor records taught me how to operate good business. All members of the Fashion crew had straight up honesty and they were realistic about the ins, outs and pitfalls of reggae music. Mr Palmer who managed Jet Star records became one of the biggest reggae distributors in the world. Mr Palmer and his brothers who managed the successful Apollo night club in Willesden, inspired me through their entrepreneurship, they had the confidence as a functioning unit to build an empire. I was also impressed with Erskine Thompson Management and the heights he took my friend Maxi Priest to in the music business.

Working independently in the studio was a joy for me. I got a real buzz out of working with so many different talented people. Two of the top musicians I loved to work alongside was Mafia and Fluxy, and they were two of the nicest people in the game. I also collaborated with another partnership, with two of the most talented drum and bass musicians in reggae history, the legendary Sly and Robbie. Mafia and Fluxy had their studio in Tottenham, north London, not too far from the football ground. I remember heading over there and thinking this is the other side of the world, as it was such a long haul to reach them from my ends down south. But I did not care because I was looking forward to working with them. They were part of a foundation British roots reggae band called the Instigators and I really liked their stuff.

When I reached Tottenham for the studio session, I knocked on the door and before they let me in, in jest they asked me, 'what's you name again?' The banter continued back and forth, then we went upstairs to the studio where Mafia was listening to this beat that he had just built. He asked of me, 'What happen Daddy Tip? You have something for this tune of mine?' This Mafia asked with a smile on his face because he knew I did. I had three different songs I could have chosen. I was always ready when I went to the studio and I did not hold back. It was another chance for me to shine so I took it. I was really happy with my work and so were they. The tune was called 'Badda Badda' from my *Talk the Truth* album. It was mixed by the great Gussie P from A Class Studio. Before Mafia and Fluxy had their studio in north London, they used to do most of their work at A Class Studio in Forest Hill. I did a lot of my work there in the eighties for their label, tunes call 'Hip Hip' and 'Gal Yu Too Bright'. I did my album with Papa San there; 'JA vs UK' clash, and my hit lovers' rock tune 'Superwoman' with Winsome. I linked up with Janet Lee Davis and recorded 'Baby I Been Missing You' there as well.

The talented Chris Lane from Fashion Records was another engineer I worked there with. We called him Mr Cheerful as he could be a bit miserable, as if carrying the weight of the British reggae industry on his shoulders. I liked Chris, he was always cool with me. Straight up he said what he thought and was always honest with you. As an artist if what you did was not happening Chris would tell you.

At the end of the day, as engineers managing their own independent record label, it was their financial investments and incomes at stake. Chris and his business partner John MacGillivray taught me a lot. Being an Arsenal supporter myself, the only thing I totally disliked about John was that he was a Manchester United supporter. I admired the way they ran their Dub Vendor record shops in south London's Clapham Junction and over in north-west London at Ladbroke Grove. If John sold your records, your money was there on time. He was 100 percent trustworthy. Without fail, you got your statement on time, and if anything was out of sync you called John and immediately he would sort it and put it right. He always addressed me as Mr Henry. I had a lot of respect for John, he knew how to deal with people and was always respectful. I thank them both for believing in my talent.

Personally, the central motivating factor for me in being an independent artist, is that you still have your own creative freedom. You could do your own thing without a gatekeeper, without someone else governing your ideas. You have total power of what, when, and how you put out your own material. Everything works at your own pace, including touring and recording. I could make the music I wanted to make. On another level I believe that being independent has provided me with a better relationship with the audience and my fans. Everybody that sees me perform knows that I am doing what I do because I faithfully believe in the power of music. I believe in what I do and the unity and togetherness. I bear witness to the collective strength and energy that music gives people. The memories connected to going to your favourite gig, festival, or hearing your all-time greatest song; these can all be life changing events.

Being a do-it-yourself artist, I can create the picture on my own canvas and if all goes wrong, I only have myself to blame. Over the length of time I have been working within the music business, I have made plenty mistakes and wrong moves. All you can do is learn from the error of your ways, brush yourself off and start again. One factor that appears again and again in my history is the sad and obvious truth that this country never recognises and appreciates its own. As a British reggae artist, you can't get radio play on major British stations and big record companies have their own agenda, who they want and who they don't want. This place does not value its own home-grown talent.

The most significant change I have witnessed take place within our world as musicians, entertainers and performers is the transition from the public purchasing vinyl records and CDs at the record store with hard-earned cash. Back then we got paid for our studio recordings and releases, sold and distributed through the record labels. You would make direct links with manufacturers of your product and collect from the pressing plant. Go personally and visit all record outlets across London, delivering by hand, the new release, on a deal with the record shop for sale or return. Our social media back then were sound systems, dances, distributing flyers and leaflets or using pirate radio stations. These were our only outlets within our Black community. The birth of the internet and social media made us broke. Downloading our tracks short-changed us as our talent was once again exploited by the multinationals and corporate world. If you have your tune uploaded onto social media, you'll only receive a small payment from Spotify and other music streaming platforms. As an artist, you'll only earn a few pence per track so it's only really any good for use as a form of marketing, advertising and publicity. Straight up, you don't make as much money from your music from social media and the internet.

As an artist, in reality, you can only make money and an income from live shows and touring. The Performance Rights Society (PRS) will help you collect what is entitled to you if your song has airplay through royalties such as PPL and MCPS radio.

In terms of business and marketing your own product, I had to research avenues that I could afford, or look for where I could market myself for free. Look towards partnering with local or national newspapers for free press and advertising. Use social media and internet? In my generation to post something meant that armed with a pot of wallpaper paste and a brush you would post up on bus stops and the walls of empty buildings, the flyer for your next dance or record release. It was painstaking, physically taxing and often illegal. Nowadays, on social media, you can post to thousands of people across the world with one click of a button.

Working with major record companies, they plan, stage, and market, developing your image through fashion and photo shoots. As an individual and independent artist I have realized that ego, flashy dressing and glitzy photo shoots, it's not my thing, not in my personality or character. In terms of image I just like to let my music do the talking. I have always liked to dress in what makes me feel nice and comfortable, I have never really been part of the 'dress to impress' brigade; simply just not me.

There is in truth, excitement connected to the signing to a major record deal, having a reliable weekly income, a secure financial backing and marketing. I have experienced that kind of top company's marketing exposure. I released two LPs for Island Records. Chris Blackwell was coming out of his office when he saw a new display on the marketing billboard, advertising a photo of me and Peter Hunnigale dressed in traditional African clothes. He smiled and affirmed to us that he liked our shoot and we were signed. Things were going well, but instead, after a while, Island concentrated on investing in they saw as the latest flavour, and eventually we were dropped. As young artists, we had not been given investment advice or guidance.

Life is always about who you know. My advice to any up-and-coming artists today, even with the internet and social media playing such a big part, is that the tried-and-true methods of doing your homework, networking, and working out upfront outgoing costs, still provide the best path to stability and success in the music business. Organize, create a work list establishing actions with targeted timescales. Start ticking goals off your to-do list, establish what will be the most beneficial and cost-effective outcome for the release of product. Rub shoulders, get out there and speak to other musicians. Use word-of-mouth, the grapevine, to hire people to work with based on trusted recommendations. When it comes to the central aspects of a performer's career, employ a music lawyer and seek advice and guidance from the Musicians Union in relation to contracts, music management, royalties and owning your own publishing. Owning your own publishing is the best, most fruitful, way forward for entertainers.

The next stage of my journey in music was to establish my own studio. I was reaching another level of independence, no longer having to rely on hiring anyone's studio and paying hourly for an engineer's time. I picked up second-hand, discount equipment here and there, learning the craft. The freedom I possessed enabled me to lay down tracks at my leisure, and at my own pace. For the very first time, I felt truly in control of my art and destiny. I put my earnings straight back into my own music, managing my own marketing and promotion, organising studio time with different clients and working with up-and-coming young talent and old-school talent as well. I was paying from my own pocket for photo and video shoots, as they, too, had to be done.

Going independent means, basically, learning to become

dependent on yourself. When people let me down this made me learn the programmes myself and while it was a challenge it meant I gained serious important knowledge about another aspect of my craft. It also meant I was saving on the cost of employing a producer or engineer. When I got payment from my The Black Eyed Peas work, I invested that income into my own studio. Over the years developing my studio knowledge, I picked up ideas and skills of some great engineers including Chris Lane, Lindel Lewis, Mad Professor (Ariwa), Peter Hunigale, Flowers and Fitzroy Blake (Groove and Quarter records). These were all friends and colleagues in the industry I knew I could call on to assist and support my new-found knowledge. I would learn the pre-set, how to EQ my own vocals, and establish my own sound levels, quality and power of the sound. My ear became familiar with what sounded good or not. I can now lay down the track and mix. Reggae music is about having two things an ear and a feeling for the music, catching a vibe on the tune.

My first studio was situated at the other end of the Rotherhithe Tunnel in Cable Street, east London—a shithole truthfully, but you have to start somewhere. The building was owned and managed by an old Jewish geezer who did not believe in refurbishment. John Mitchell, G Vibes, Dominic Walch (then managing me) and I put in a lot of work to build a great studio in the space that we had, so the inside was very nice (it was embarrassing when clients went to use the toilet, though). We set up our own independent record company, Lockdown Productions. The building was a unique environment, with all walks of life and strange characters on the site. Also, we witnessed all kind of happenings—people making love in the passageway, whether gay or straight, but we just got on with it. As my mum would say, 'See and blind, hear and deaf, we no trouble them and they no trouble we.'

One thing I loved about the place was that we were working next door to the grime crew Roll Deep, so every other day I would see Wiley, Danny Weed, and DJ Target. I would also see Chipmunk when he was just starting out and just wanted to get on one of Wiley's productions. They were all very respectful and looked up to me as an elder in the business. They all knew of my son, Messy, who was a big part of that scene in south London as a member of a group called South Soldiers. Also located in the building was the famous reggae studio Easy Street Studios, with EddyMan, the owner. I remember Easy Street from my early days recording there with the likes of Dennis Brown, Gregory Isaacs, and Carroll Thompson; they made some big tunes in that studio.

I really liked the vibes in Cable Street, but later relocated to Croydon, where I lived. I rented a new location inside an industrial unit; it was the same kind of setup as in east London, but scaled down—and thankfully, the toilets and kitchen area were nice and clean. The building manager was a bit of a jobsworth, but most of the businesses were very welcoming. There were quite a few other music studios within the unit: Andy Peters, who produced house and dance music at his Online Studio. A brother next door to me had a state-of-the-art studio he invested thousands into. At my own studio, I recorded and produced various LPs—for example, an international showcase album called *UK Flu* (two volumes) and a compilation LP called *Free*, which was influenced by me leaving my now-ex-wife, free as a bird.

I also produced the 'Driver', 'Conversation', and 'Sweet Flavour' rhythms; and recorded most of the vocals on my *Stick to My Roots* LP. So many more of my works were created in Croydon. It was really great having that studio—but it was not paying for itself. We would get clients, but not enough. So, next came the best move I've made: to relocate again. This time I moved the studio into my home in south London, with no overheads.

Even at this point in my career, I am still learning new ways of working in the studio. I have always had a strict work ethic—that's how my parents raised me. So, if I get a request to voice a track or dubplate at midnight, I can do it straight away, and lay it down and move on: job done.

To me, independence is about working with my own creativity, moving positively with my own energy, building on my talents without anyone holding me back along the process. To be a successful artist you have to focus on the production of your own art, and maintaining a strong belief in yourself. I knew that major record companies were willing to work with me, so I knew I had a talent that was worth investing in. I extended this confidence to my working environment, and established myself independently, making my own 'stamp'.

Part and parcel of this journey of independence was that I began to tour on my own, without any entourage—just me, flying alone, mapping my way around the globe as I organised my tours myself. I would book my shows on social media, contacting promoters and sound systems along the way, depending on which part of the world I wanted to work in. As an artist, you have to network and be approachable—and over the years, I have built up a large international network. If I am going to Thailand, I link up with Gappy from T Bone, or the Reggae Rajahs in India. I link up with the Heavy Hong Kong crew when I perform in that country. And I can't forget Masia One in Singapore, big up the Asia crew—I love that part of the world. Wherever I go, it is the same kinda thing: Europe, America, Russia, Africa, it's the same principle.

I have been to so many destinations and venues, sometimes I take my DJ with me—but if it's a sound system I can trust, I go on my own. I have my own backing band, and on occasion I employ local musicians to work with me, depending on which countries I am touring. On tour, I didn't mind my own company, but at times I liked to party—and I always met people and made friends and acquaintances along the way. On the road, you have to have a balance, knowing when to party and when to rest.

Below, my former manager Grantley Haynes—also known as GT—shares his experiences of working in partnership with me from back in the eighties; GT and I still do some co-productions to this very day.

My family are from the parishes of Saint James and Saint Michael, in Barbados, and I was born and raised in the working-class areas of Birmingham. My first musical exposure was to my dad playing bluebeat, early rock-steady, reggae and, of course, our national dish as Bajans: calypso and soca, our first love, the likes of the Mighty Sparrow. In my youth, a man would come door to door selling imported vinyl. Music drew me in as a youth and I wanted to be involved in some way. I had an uncle who resided in south London, and my main objective was to reach Brixton, the reggae capital. I was hungry for the vibes. I learnt as a teenager from the local Brixton talent. Fester and Prince Jazzbo, moving with the Coxsone crew and Frontline International, famous Brixtonite Blacker Dread and Castro Brown.

I began working with music professionally from the age of 18. The place was Birmingham and my mobile disco, GT-600—where I got my nickname from. I used to make plenty corn, playing the latest white-label, party to party.

This was the first time I took in the Saxon Sound System, at a clash at the Botanical Gardens in my home-town. Saxon were challenging Radics, our local sound system. Impressive vocal talent, with Mr Tippa Irie on the mic. I was fortunate to be two feet in front of Tippa on the night. Explosive: the crowd rocked to and fro, chanting, 'lickwood', 'jack it up', 'tear it up' as Tippa rode the crowd. No one could match his talent in his prime. Every dance was a roadblock, dancehall. He raised the roof.

I began travelling to London, and came down south with my brethren, the great reggae performer Pato Banton. At this time, I had started movements in the direction of reggae management, in tasting the business. It was a ruff old world, especially for UK reggae performers. So much talent, so poorly treated. Underrated and not recognised for their true artistry. I wanted to actively change that. I began studying one book to another, quietly, at my local library, long before internet research days. This was library card-and-membership times, old school. I began reading and taking notes. First general business, then books on the music industry and, finally, literature on legally binding contracts. I knew first-hand about organising a good business. Daytime, I was a skilled chef, and lived well from this. My knowledge grew, and my first client as a manager in the music business was Pato. One time, me, Tippa and Pato were chilling in Brixton. This was an era when some selected reggae artists were earning some corn, having record contract signings—Smiley Culture and Maxi Priest, to name two artists from the Saxon posse. Pato and I had started doing well as a management team, with a good few successful shows and recordings.

Just before Tippa and I left for Jamaica to perform at Reggae Sunsplash, Tippa drove out of a car showroom with his brand-new, white convertible Golf GT Sport. Things were moving in the right direction: when I first met Tippa, he only had a few hundred quid in the bank. He could now start living like Pato, with the luxurious life they deserved for their talent, entertaining crowds, dedicating their lives. One of the first tours Tippa and I went on that took us away from home was performing in France for six months straight.

As Tippa Irie's management, we have travelled all over the world. One of the first times we knew we had smashed and conquered it was touring America, hitting the bright lights of Broadway with a regular slot at the Palace Theatre (Tippa hated this slot, booking him to perform his 45-minute set twice a night at the same venue). But first, it was Sunset Boulevard, live shows at the Whisky a Go Go, Skidos and the Roxy Theatre.

I remember vividly the first night of the Tippa Irie American tour. One promoter, two hours before the show was to begin, invited me to take a spin and look at the city lights. Not 10 minutes down the highway, a set of orange lights were flashing us down. The cops ordered us both out of our vehicle, hands on the roof as they pulled their guns. They were about to harass and arrest the dance promoter, who was driving and was Black American. I thought we were going to miss Tippa's first resident night. One of the cops asked me where I was from, and I replied 'England.' Immediately, they released us and told us to go about our business. Before we pulled away, the taller cop informed me that had I been a Black American too, he would have taken us both down to the station. I got a slight taste of what Black men experience at hands of the American police... shameful.

Tippa Irie, live. A natural-born entertainer. No matter the size of the audience, from dancehall to stadium or festival, with the confidence and ability to slow down or mad up the crowd. I have personally witnessed his MC style mashing up venue after venue, country after country, all four corners of the world. I have had the pleasure to be alongside Tippa as his manager and friend.

He is the winner for melodic flow, built in with perfect

timing and perfect delivery. The audiences feel his energy positively. Tippa Irie and his authentic reggae sound is transferred to the people. Whether sound system or live show, he has the crowd eating from his hands. Tippa works hard—very hard. He's a perfectionist who works on the premise that practise makes perfect.

Music means more to me than any treasure
I love it more than gold, platinum and silver
So, dancehall fans in every area
I am a lyric maker from England and not
Jamaica
My name is Daddy Tippa.

Tippa Irie, 'Lyric Maker'
from the LP *Is It Really Happening to Me* (UK
Bubblers (Greensleeves Records), 1986)

Chapter Ten
Conclusion

I WANT TO BEGIN THIS FINAL CHAPTER OF MY autobiography by answering a question so many people all over the world have asked me: 'How have you lasted so long in the music industry?'

The ingredients that have enabled me to maintain my longevity include a combination of a strong, determined character, talent, and personality. You require natural skill, but also an awareness of your calling, or with what my elders would call your 'God-given talent'. If you know you are blessed with talent, you feel it in your bones; you have flair about you. Then the people around you will provide you with positive feedback, acknowledging that they are enjoying and benefiting from your gift. My journey as a reggae dancehall MC started when I knew, myself, that I had a unique talent. I *knew* that chatting lyrics on the mic, sending an uplifting vibration, was my calling. The connection was so strong that I could not be drawn to anything else but music and its potent energy. It has maintained me through life's twists and turns. Music has been my life, my friend through good times and bad, an escape during both the ups and the downs. Its power changed me from a working-class boy coming from the Brixton sound systems to an internationally recognised artist and performer, flying across the globe. Music has granted me food on the table, and it has provided for both me and my family.

Once I recognised I had personal and creative talent, I dedicated and committed myself to building my own foundation, nurturing my craft along the way with the sole objective of becoming successful. I was taught the old way: nothing comes straightaway, it's practise that makes perfect. Putting in the training and time, investing in your talents, aiming at the top of your game, reaching for the highest. Ask yourself the important questions of self-refection. *Are you going to live and eat from your craft? Is your music truly good enough for the competition ahead? Can your creativity bring in revenue?*

On my career path as a musician, many people have doubted me or put obstacles in front of me. So don't let anyone hold you back with their negativity, placing doubt in your mind. To keep ahead of the game as an MC, I had to be dedicated and focused. Working within the cut-throat music industry also requires that you have a strong backbone.

I learnt very early in life that you need to have personal and professional goals, to know where you want to reach in this precious life, alongside a plan of how you're gonna get there. Do research, empower yourself. Read and acquire knowledge of music contracts. Don't walk into business situations where you are blindly led by record industry bosses. Educate yourself on how the music business actually works.

My character and personality have been formed by simple concepts:

Treat others as you wish to be treated yourself.

I have always lived by this old-fashioned line; it's been my guiding principle.

No matter what happens in this life, you have to *try and let go of your worries and troubles*. Carrying old fears and stored-up emotional baggage only holds you back, like keeping grudges against people. If you keep such thoughts close to you, in the end they will only harm you.

Respect is one of the central keys for good human relations. If you

Well, I have had hits in the 80s
hits in the 90s
and in now 2000, me a-still going strong
Mr Irie, I am the man
down live with Lockdown Production.

Tippa Irie, 'Pick Up My People'
from the 7' single
(Lockdown Productions, 2005)

maintain a humble and kind spirit, people will be drawn to you, and warm to you. Show me those around you, and I shall know who you are. What legacy will you leave behind? What do people say of you? This is the testimony to your true character and spirit.

My legacy has been carved out of reggae music, going on tour, performing live, being away from home for extended periods of time, maintaining recording contracts, being ever-present, motivated, and available for social media and press coverage. My private life changed hands, became cancelled and I became public business. If you are a lazy person and like to sleep on the job, the music business is not for you. It may look to those on the outside like fame is just a glory road, but in reality, entertaining the public is hard, nonstop graft, requiring 100 percent dedication. It is a lifestyle that requires you to put your own personal needs on the back burner.

Being a professional musician requires a balanced mind and I wanted to be known as a performer that you can trust: what you see is what you get. So, I stay grounded and down to earth, with no big, flashy ego or plastic personality or pretence. Most importantly, as an artist, if your music is to be kept alive and you want to remain in the game, you will need to be welcomed and *invited back again*. So, alongside my artistic and creative abilities, my character goes before me. Others speak well of me. Promoters don't want to work with moody and un-reliable characters.

I still maintain friendships with people I grew up with from primary school. I am presently working in partnership with countless musi-cians, record producers, and studio engineers I had originally worked with during the eighties. I have successfully maintained good, trusting relationships in the music industry for over 40 years. Trust me—*burning your bridges just does not work*. The music industry and the national press represent a very small, interlinked, tight-knit community. If you are known as unreliable and unprofessional, that reputation can stick like glue, and no one will want to invest in you or your product.

To succeed in the music industry, I built an inner determination combined with a strong self-belief. I have always been blessed with boldness, armoured with single-mindedness and purpose. Others around me might have been experimenting with music as a hobby— but I knew it was going to be my life, so I had to be focused. I made the decision in my teenage years that I was going to live from my music. Music has no time limits. It's like a clock with no hands, a mystical, creative energy you just get lost in. Being a professional in music industry is a full-time business, requiring every part of you. Touring from country to country, I would get used to being away from home, separated from my community, my family and loved ones. In the eighties, I was performing live in France every weekend for twelve months straight.

Another big sacrifice to me pursuing music was being an absent father. I had to face up to the truth that I could not physically be around for my children as they grew up. None of us who chose the music business as a career were there for our sons and daughters. It was a difficult juggling act to perform, maintaining both family and fame. These lifestyles are in total opposition to each other. I was out at night, and asleep in the daytime. Musicians are all absent parents. I regret missing out on quality family time, in truth, not being around for my children's achievements as they grew up, not being in their memories. My life as a performer has taken all of me to make my craft manifest, and sadly my loved ones paid the price. Now I am trying to catch up on the time lost, giving more love to my children now.

As Black artists, we had to work twice as hard as our white counterparts, especially living in the UK. If we had had more opportunities, such as having our music played on mainstream radio stations and TV or covered in national newspapers and magazines, I would have had more revenue, greater ability to pick and choose the work I wanted to do, more quality time for kids and family.

A message to new entertainers coming forward: is it the love of music that drives and motivates you? Why limit yourself to the same old style? Challenge yourself and try something new, allow your ears to be open to new sounds and vibrations. This is one of the keys of my musical longevity. I opened myself up as an artist to different challenges and experiences. This allowed me to produce roots, dancehall reggae, dub, lovers' rock, ska, pop, bhangra, dance music, hip-hop, jungle. Adapting to multiple musical styles has offered me varied platforms of exposure, in turn it opened more doors and opportunities.

Over the years I have stretched creatively, kept on moving, never stopped working as an MC. I resisted getting pigeonholed, stuck in a box, limited. My wish was to expand on my talent, staying versatile, flexible, and stretching myself to see how far I could go with my craft. I have always been drawn to a personal challenge—I guess that's the sound system culture at work in me. The dancehall sound clash, the competition—this is the creative drive from back in the day that put fire in my belly. It was a perfect training ground; if you didn't have the stamina, you'd be left out of the race. As they say, the race is not for the swift, but for those who can endure. The same applies to maintaining longevity in the music industry.

In 1985, Tippa Irie was a strictly grassroots, dancehall, sound system reggae artist. On first hearing the mix of 'Hello Darling', the jazzy, swing-type beat struck me. It had a very different sound. My 'authentic' reggae ears were not used to it. The lesson here was about versatility. Because I was open to different, styles, 'Hello Darling' became my greatest hit, making me a world-famous performer. It sold over 80,000 copies—and in the eighties, that was a hell of a lot of records.

One of the roads to maintaining longevity in the music business, whether you sign to a major label or an independent, you need to put together a good, experienced, and trustworthy team around you—genuine, knowledgeable fellow professionals who will guide you in the right direction. Social media managers, tour promoters, artists, film crews, marketing teams, engineers. It's essential you have an organized, skilful, loyal, and dedicated team if you are to succeed.

Let us now crack an egg and put racism, culture, and prejudice into the frying pan. Being a Black male born on British soil has both its blessings and trials. The journey of Black people in the UK is different from that of any other Black culture. You would only understand if you stood in our shoes. At times, on our own turf, we can feel rejected and unwanted, like outsiders, not feeling truly a part of mainstream British society, unrecognised and un-valued even after all we have contributed, still, today, to British society.

Recently I listened to an interview on AFTV (a YouTube channel for Arsenal fans) with a guy named Troopz, who echoed the same words. He was facing the same problems through YouTube culture that I had once faced. Troopz said he does not get invited to all the industry events because he is Black and from the streets—his face did not fit the mould. They might have his voice in a FIFA game, but he is kept out of the FIFA party—not invited.

To describe the experience of being prevented from progressing as a performer in the music industry is like an invisible hand clinging to your shirt collar. Our brother Malcolm X stated, *'We didn't land on Plymouth Rock, Plymouth Rock landed on us.'*

This was the Black British experience back in the eighties. I listened to close friends describe how, in London prisons, Black prisoners were labelled *nigger* and *sambo*. This crude racism was even spouted proudly from the lips of prison officers and fellow working-class white inmates, in notorious racist lock-ups such as south London's Wandsworth Prison.

West Indian soldiers fought battles during the First and Second World Wars and were willing to sacrifice their lives to protect the Crown and country. In 2017, the African and Caribbean War Memorial designed by architect David Adjaye was unveiled in Windrush Square,

Oneness, oh yes, it's a oneness
when I see my brethren it's a oneness
When mi see mi sistren, it's a oneness
Mi ever blessed, mi a-deal with righteousness
Mi sing it's a oneness
When I see mi brethren it's a oneness
When mi see sistren, it's a oneness
Mi ever blessed, mi a-deal with righteousness
Well, love and unity a-we bring,
anytime the youth hold the mic and sing
When the DJ settle down pon the rhythm
have to give thanks for the father's blessing
It's not about colour, it's not about skin,
Yes, everybody gets the same feeling
The feeling of joy in a music ting,
when stage show a-gwaan, what a gathering
I know it's an old cliché but Mr Irie
have to say it every day
Unity, is it is strength, so me don't know
why they move certain way
When the sweet music a-play, everybody
shout
'Hip, hip hooray' and every day it's like Tippa
birthday,
when people gather and I mi a DJ.

Tippa Irie, 'Oneness'
form the 7' single (Oneness Records, 2008)

I am dreaming of a brand-new England
a place where white love black and all who
believe in love
betta know that we want racism to stop
It's a serious matter and it won't go away
and after four hundred years, it is still here
to stay
still here to stay down in the UK
but I know it must get better one shining day
I say, hip, hip hooray, is what I would say
if all of the racists gone fade away.
They gwaan, like we asked to be taken away
from the land, that our I father wanted us to
stay
Dem take us from Africa to the UK
We help them bill up their place
Now, they want us to go away
It no go, so, sorry, no way
and Tippa na business, who feel, away
I know, it's very serious Mi, no joke, mi, na
play
So much racist attack, gwaan every day
Rolan Adams, Stephen Lawrence,
just two of the youths who have passed
Now six feet under the ground, dem a-lay
'cause
them skin black, them skin never grey
Whoever done the crime them think they got
away
but I know one day, dem get their pay.

Tippa Irie, 'Dreaming of a Brand-
New England' from the LP
Rebel on the Roots Corner
(Ariwa Records, 1994)

Brixton, which recognised and acknowledged this significant contribution. But then our African-Caribbean elders, after 60 years of making Britain their home and working as foundational staff in the NHS as nurses, or as transport workers, or independent business owners, or factory labourers, received the message beginning in 2012 from the Home Office under Prime Minister Theresa May and her hostile environment ideology: *go back where you came from*. Our own Windrush Generation elders, hard-working, God-fearing, after giving so much, now had to campaign in order to resist deportation. There have been so many signs in front of our eyes, reminding us that *we don't really fit in*.

When I travel to Jamaica even though it is the country of my heritage, I am still identified as a foreigner by my own people. Calling you out in the streets of Kingston, 'Hey you, English bwoy!' Yet another psychological layer of rejection gets put over us, preventing us from being truly part of our wider Jamaican family. Being born Black British gives you a difference set of eyes, looking out from a different narrative. Jamaicans naïvely, arrogantly, and mistakenly reject their own African ancestry. This is why education and knowledge of self is the path to our destiny. This is why I was proud, and I pushed my own unique Black British culture to the forefront of my identity and to compliment my style of dancehall music. Saxon Sound System were so different and successful because they chose not to copy anyone. We were all fellow south Londoners, proud, bold, and comfortable in our own skins, no worries.

Saxon was a Black community business and collective, that was independent and self-managed. This factor of celebrating uniqueness is what made Saxon carve its name into reggae history, recognised worldwide. The legendary Saxon! Nothing had ever been witnessed before like them, and nothing like it has been witnessed since. So many British reggae artists launched into major record deals and fame through their involvement with the mighty Saxon Sound System. Saxon, therefore, is an example of a winning Black British independent business; the fame came from all of us being proud of our own identity.

The worst form of direct racism I ever experienced as an entertainer was in 2006 when I was performing live in Sydney, Australia. The vibes were great, everyone in the audience was dancing and having fun. It was a concert I will always remember, because I got to meet the West Indian cricket team there, and then-captain Courtney Walsh; they were on tour at the time. They came up to me after the show and said, 'Wow, you have a lot of energy!' I don't think anyone on the team had heard of me before, but they sure remembered me after the show. That's when I was invited by two lovely ladies to another bar for a drink. We arrived, and all around, I was getting hard, cold stares and frowns. I was thinking to myself, 'What is going on here?' This place was a completely different vibe from my sold-out show. At the bar, it took me forever to get a drink; I was sure that the barmaid was ignoring me. She was serving everybody else but treated me as if I was invisible. I raised my voice to get her attention, and she still behaved like I was not there. I said to myself, 'sod this' and went to build a spliff. The two ladies who had invited me went to get our drinks instead—because I knew that *they* would be served. Otherwise, I would have been standing there all night.

As I was smoking something illegal, I took time to stroll down the road away from the bar, but would you believe it—the same bloody barmaid came following me, checking on what I was doing. She knew I had to return, as my friends were back there, and she asked me what I had been smoking. I replied, 'What has it got to do with you? Are you the police?' She said, 'If you don't tell me, you won't be allowed back in.' I lied just to get back in and said I had been smoking a roll-up. Then I told the girls, 'Look, I'm out of here—don't like the vibes. The people in this place think I'm the wrong shade. Sorry, but let's leave before I get myself in trouble.' I think that woman was the manager, and certainly racist.

Back home, I had a lot to be proud of within the Black community: Rastafarian Poet Benjamin Zephaniah had been selected by the Tony Blair government for appointment to the Order of the British Empire, but he rejected it on account of Britain's invasion of Iraq, as well as the OBE's association with slavery and the barbaric treatment of Black people in the name of the British Empire. On the other side of the spectrum, now-Baroness Doreen Lawrence was awarded an OBE in 2013, in recognition of her struggle for equality and justice, after many years of tireless campaigning in relation to the racist murder of her son, Stephen, in Eltham in 1993. The campaign led to the Met Police being once again exposed for institutional racism just as back in the eighties on my doorstep in Brixton.

There were many cases that showed the Met Police for the corrupt and racist organization it was and still is, as more cases are still coming to light today. For me there were two that hit me particularly close to home. The first was Smiley Culture. The sadness I felt with the loss of my good friend Smiley Culture was overwhelming, he was a real character, always making me laugh. I have so many good memories with Smiley. He was a great lyricist, so creative and original, but could also be a very serious, focused dude—and would do what it took to get him by. He was not afraid to go into record companies and stick them up, demanding his money. On one occasion, he did this to Polydor Records and he got the money that was due to him, which they were trying not to pay. A lot of people did not like Smiley; they thought he was boasie and cocky. But I think you need a bit of that self-confidence to survive in the music industry and he was full of it.

One afternoon in 2011, I received a phone call informing me of the devastating news that Smiley had taken his own life during a police raid on his house. Immediately, alarm bells starting ringing. This did *not* sound like the Smiley I knew. All I knew was that whoever went into his house wanted to shut him up, for whatever reason. Many questions remain unanswered to this day.

In 2011, Dorothy 'Cherry' Groce, who had been attacked by police during the home raid that kicked off the Brixton riots of 1985, sadly passed away after spending 26 years paralysed from the waist down. It had been proven in court that the Brixton police were guilty—responsible for a total of eight failings that led to the raid and the gunning down of Mrs Groce. The Met Police commissioner delivered an unreserved apology to the Groce family when it was proven that the bullet wounds inflicted upon Mrs Groce had contributed to her constant pain and eventual death. In 2012, a monument and a blue plaque were erected in Windrush Square in memory of this community elder, who was the mother of my long-time sistren MC Lorna Gee.

There have been many new cases where the Met Police has been exposed as having crossed the line, from the phone-hacking scandal, to criminal police officers found guilty of serious crimes. The time for real change is now.

Throughout my life, I have possessed an inbuilt, better-must-come outlook, alongside a rock-solid survival instinct. I learned my life lessons from Jamaican elders: they made their way with strong backbones and broad shoulders, carrying their heavy loads with a smile, staying positive and pushing on until they reached a better place. As a Black British child, part of the second generation, these values were passed down to me. I got my foundation in life directly from my mum and dad, also taking in guidance from my wise Uncle Liebert and Auntie Gee. The teachings that came from them were like Biblical proverbs, coming from an era in which laziness was frowned upon. I was raised to be a doer, an achiever: 'Go on, Tony, let your light shine.' I was directed to make good out of something, make myself better. The elders in our families and communities went through a whole heap, but rarely would you hear them chat negativity. They never outwardly groaned and moaned about their trials and tribulations. My parents were no exception: they were both very private people, reserved about their emotions. Being parented by Jamaicans instilled in me a strong will: push on through, no matter the weather. As Bob Marley, the King of Reggae, told us: 'Get Up, Stand Up'.

Music, aside from being a lifelong career, has equally provided me some serious healing. This is why my bond with music has been so strong, I made it my therapy. Following the evil murder of my beloved sister, I took solace in leaning deeply into music, listening to all the old tunes, taking in lyrics that provided both hope and upliftment. Like a bridge over my troubled waters, music has always been my comforter. When, truly, I could not face tomorrow, trapped in total darkness and feeling heartbroken, I managed to draw myself up and rise from the ashes. For these reasons and more, I owe music my life. When I got divorced from my wife, I once again turned to music to get me through the difficult times of separation. Music enables me to move the negativity out of me, to keep afloat and maintain my inner strength.

Many times in life, like we all do, I have reached challenging crossroads. *Shall I turn this way, or that way?* Life's journey has taught me that you have to remain open to change. No matter how hard or good, you will receive a lesson from change, and learn something about yourself, like you're looking into a mirror. I have learnt to remain flexible and adapt. I have ridden the rhythm of life, and I don't let its stresses consume me. Going down or under has never been part of my upbring and my focused positive thinking. In the trials I have experienced firsthand, I have learned the importance of surrounding yourself with family and friends. Having a sociable spirit gives you another sense of healing, being part of and surrounded by genuine people. It helps good energy to flow—and it lets the good times roll. Music being my comforter, dancing joyfully to favourite tunes; going down Memory

Lane with Buju Banton or Shabba Ranks; recalling all the ladies in the club singing to Janet Kay's 'Silly Games'... music has the power to bring back the love.

I will never forget the originators of reggae, the messages that they taught me; I owe it to the reggae greats that have gone before and the artists carrying the torch for the music in today's generations. The elders who built this foundation provided a much-needed dosage of positivity, One Love. One Heart. One God. One Aim. One Destiny. Reggae and its rich traditions can never be forgotten. My objective in this book has been to scribe, to leave a personal testament to our legacy. Today, dancehall music features messages and elements I do not personally associate with the foundations of reggae. Back in the day, I would at times perform tongue-in-cheek songs about women, adding an element of humour, a bit of slap-and-tickle—but currently, dancehall slackness tunes contain lyrics cussing aggressively, containing derogatory and harmful words directed towards women alongside lyrics about guns. These are our mothers, aunts, sisters, daughters, our Black African queens, not the *bitches* and *hoes* found in dancehall lyrics. Performers who do this are not, in my eyes, true and authentic reggae artists. They do not represent the foundation of reggae; this is not sticking to our roots. I think of Yellowman and General Echo: even though they chatted slack lyrics, their songs were humorous and tasteful, not raw, offensive, and degrading to females. My roots are connected to peace and love, unity and togetherness. Lyrics about guns and gangs promote violence and hating over loving, which destroys our communities. If it is not of love, it is of hate and division. Reggae and its origins come from an energy that drives towards the unity of the human race.

As I have said, reflecting on my experiences of moving in famous circles, the egos and large personalities alongside the hedonistic drug culture and high life, neither drew me in. I would remain an outsider,

Just me and this mic, all day, all night
Just me and this mic, all day, all night
A-just me and this microphone, well mi na leave
it alone
It's part of my skin, flesh and bone
It's an essential part of my home
Any time the Tipp hold mic in my hand,
well, it's the ultimate satisfaction
Yes, Mr Irie now the living legend
and this you fi have to understand
Yes, me and this mic all day, all night
yes, it a-mi shining light
Just me and this mic, all day, all night
still a-make me future look bright.
The mic make me go a Jam One, do Sunsplash
The mic make me go up a-Japan and earn cash
The mic make me go a-Australia and back
A matter of fact it take me all round the map
That's why this thing ya, mi just can't stop
'Cause everywhere we go, mi cause roadblock
My lyrics mi no lack, my style dem hot
and I'm gonna keep on giving what I got.
Well, this microphone, you know we must stick
together
must stick together through all kind of weather
Well, the microphone is coming like my brother
'Cause we always seem to be together
We must stick together, like a-bird of a feather
See, the microphone, I will leave it never
Forever and ever, it give me nuff pleasure
because the microphone it a mi favourite treasure
If I'm at work or at leisure
my love for the mic, you know you just can't
measure
My bread and butter, it took mi out the gutter
where me and my mother did a-suffer.

Tippa Irie and the Far
East Band, 'Mi and this
Mic' from the LP *Stick
to My Roots* (Lockdown
Productions, 2010)

never invited into the inner circles. To me fame was a path full of many people I could not relate to, with many wonderful, talented performers becoming addicts, losing their creativity to and for drugs. Being on the road with musicians who can't get their fix, it's a frigging nightmare. I saw the true sides of performers when living amongst them daily with their multiple addictions and bad habits.

Fame never really turned me on because I have a love for and connection with the common people, that's where life is for me and reggae is the people's music. I still live in and love my community, the family and friends who have supported me from my early sound system days to my *Top of the Pops* appearances; I've never left their side. Staying focused and genuine, being grounded, has enabled me to maintain my musical legacy. I beat my own drum, staying independent, just being myself.

I understand that music gives us an international unified voice. People from Jamaica to Japan, everybody feels the power of dancehall music. My performances around the world always keep people connected to peace, love, and happiness. It's only when we are divided and separated that we fall. As an MC, I know I have been blessed with the ability to connect to the crowds. Tippa Irie is a conductor of happiness, removing the frowns and turning them into happy, smiling faces. Money can't buy that feeling, of possessing the energy to make a difference, to brighten people's worlds for a while. I still have a duty to educate my people and keep them awake to all the political and social issues that we need to be aware of in the twists and turns of today's world.

It makes me very proud knowing that Jamaica has produced a global music, a genre of music that has shook the world. I will always be thankful that I am part of the continuation of reggae's legacy. Life has taught me that culture is the thread that knits people together. In Japan, I witnessed the Japanese reggae community connecting to my own cultural heritage; they embrace dancehall music and are drawn to the Jamaican way of life.

It is a blessing when people acknowledge that they enjoy my work, when I am out on the street and strangers—both Black and white—approach me with respect. The essence of fame for me is to know my music has touched the lives of people in some way. My music being popular and making impact on the public for so many years, this is truly a special gift for me. I write lyrics that people can relate to; I share words that express what ordinary people are going through, forming a connection and a relationship that's what creates human electricity.

Today I could be offered ten grand for performing and recording a song. That same tune may go on to make millions. The question you have to ask yourself is, *Do I or don't I accept the deal? Do I take the ten thousand or hold out?* Okay, it would have come in handy, but I refused on principle—it was a bad deal, I would have been sold short when the company would have been raking it in. Thankfully, I was in a position in my life to be able to turn it down. This is why I have always been a paid member of the musicians' union, which provides expert advice and works to protect artists' and performers' financial well-being. The union will even read contracts for musicians before they sign. Negligent artists walk blindly into deals without knowing what they are actually signing. It's essential to join organisations that support performers. If you don't need the money immediately, my advice is to try to hold out, as getting a decent percentage of royalties and publishing will benefit you more in the long run. It is important to listen and learn from the testimonies of performers who have gone before, musicians who have already trod the path so you don't suffer the same errors and pitfalls. I compare it to learning from our elders. In the history of reggae, we have always had to be independent, because we were held back.

In the eighties, when 'Hello Darling' was a big hit, I was getting live bookings everywhere. After performing one evening at Stringfellows in the West End, straight after drinking champagne with the *EastEnders* cast, I returned to my home turf to perform on the mic with Saxon and be surrounded by my people. Back to my roots. The famous people

I was rubbing shoulders with hadn't grown up with me; they didn't know where I was coming from as a Black British reggae artist, born and bred in Brixton. Strangely, something I learnt about the entertainment industry—apart from its plastic personalities—is that so many famous mainstream entertainers aren't even that talented, after all: most of that is media hype. In the area I grew up in, there was *genuine*, unique homegrown talent everywhere.

From the beginning, I wanted to be known as a UK reggae artist, flying the British flag proudly around the world. Thankfully, I have achieved this goal. And I feel very proud to be recognised for sticking to my roots, nourishing and carrying the music of my heritage. But my generation is dying out. So, who is going to carry on the flame, when the new generation is drawn to other genres such as Afrobeat, grime, drill, hip-hop, and others? There are still a few reggae artists left in the UK, though, such as Elisha Scott, Christopher Ellis, and Claire Angel, and in Jamaica, Lila Iké, Chronixx, and Jesse Royal. It is our duty as performers to keep our culture of reggae music flowing across the globe, for generations to come and share the vibe.

As a pioneer of dancehall music, I know the original reggae foundation will never change. Even though there may be many different styles, the musical ingredients are central: snare, rim shot, percussion, and Nyabinghi drums, the floating acoustic electric guitar and rolling bass, accompanied by the grand piano or Yamaha organ and, finally, horns and brass to make that authentic reggae sound. Whether conscious roots, dancehall, dub or lovers' rock, the reggae background remains the same. It is the energy bred within reggae that makes people jump to their feet and joyfully dance their troubles away. This is the magic that has survived, against all the odds the history the developed reggae in the small, sweet island of Jamaica, my second home. It's June, my birthday, month the year 2022, and once again I have to pinch myself because I am in Kingston sitting with my brethren Mark Wallis, the co-author of this book, and fellow MC Jack Reuben.

The famous King Jammies, is one of the most forefront and respected engineers and producers across the island. We recorded a Jamaican anthem together in Jammies studio. Blue skies, scorching hot sun and a cool super malt, life can't get any better.

I hope my life story has given you the strength to have faith in yourself. I envisioned a dream; a seed was planted, and it grew into my reality and, I stuck to my roots.

Love, peace, and understanding, until we ride again.

Tippa Irie

Acknowledgements

I would like to take this opportunity to thank my family and friends who have been a significant part of my life story, and the many people who have contributed to making this book a reality:

My Father : Steven Alexander Henry
My Mother: Celeste Henry
My Sister : Avril Elaine Henry
My Sister: Jackie Henry
Micah Newell
Kash Powell
Raphael Henry
Rochelle Henry Redway
Lynn Rossetto
Mark Wallis
Grantley Haynes
Maxi Priest
Ali Campbell from UB40
Jumpin' Jack Frost
Rude Bwoy Monty
Janet Kay
General Slater
Sir Lloyd

Raymond Roberts aka Daddy Rusty
Little Jackie
Claudette Cummings
Peter Huningale
Greensleeves Records
Simon Buckland
John Dub Vendor
Fashion Records
Cecil Rennie aka King Tubby UK
Mikey Rennie RIP
Tony Murrey
Neil Sarisom
Trevor Sax
Oneko Arika
Patrick Donegan
Saxon Sound
Pato Banton
Sweetie Irie
Ragga Twins
Tony Williams
Ranking Miss P
Drummie Zeb
Roberto Angotti
Sandra Izsadore
Dennis Seaton

Thank you to the entire team at Jacaranda Books for literally bringing this book to life.

And last but not least, thank you to my fans. I will never be able to express my gratitude for your support these past four decades. You inspire me to keep making music.

About the Author

Tippa Irie, otherwise known as Anthony Henry, is a British Jamaican singer, songwriter, MC and DJ. Hailing from Brixton, south London, he first came to prominence in the early 1980s as an MC in the original Saxon Sound International. Tippa first achieved international exposure in the mid-1980s with the hit singles 'It's Good to Have the Feeling You're the Best' and 'Complain Neighbour' before hitting the UK Top 40 with 'Hello Darling'.

Tippa released his first solo album *Is It Really Happening to Me* in 1986. He has had several #1 hits in the UK and around the world including 'Hello Darling', 'Raggamuffin Girl' featuring Peter Huningale, and 'Superwoman' featuring Winsome. In 2005, Tippa was nominated for a GRAMMY® for Best Rap Song for a tune he wrote with will.i.am of The Black Eyed Peas called 'Hey Mama' appearing on the BEP album

Elephunk. Tippa has toured the world extensively and continues to headline festivals and perform for capacity crowds on every continent.

In 2022, Tippa released his 18th career studio album, *I'm An African*, receiving critically acclaimed reviews from publications and fans around the world. The 16-track album features several well-known artists and draws inspiration from his family's roots in Africa and Jamaica. Arguably his best work to date, this album reflects a wide range of genres and moves effortlessly between the dancehall and thought-provoking discussion about the state of the world. This work truly exhibits why Tippa is referred to as Mr. Versatile.

Tippa Irie continues to be one of the most consistent artists' on the scene and is not afraid to repeatedly reinvent himself and venture into different genres to keep his music
fresh. He continually attracts new fans while still pleasing those who have been listening to his music for decades. Tippa has a long and distinguished list of collaborations and has maintained a constant stream of new releases. He continues to delight fans wherever he performs with his fast-talking style and high energy shows.

To learn more about Tippa Irie, or inquire about an appearance, check out www.tippairie.com

Endnotes

1   Graeme McLagan, *Guns and Gangs*, Allison and Busby, 2005

2   Graeme McLagan, *Guns and Gangs*, page 51, Allison and Busby, 2005

3   Graeme McLagan, *Guns and Gangs*, page 54, Allison and Busby, 2005